THE
GOD-SYMBOL

OTHER BOOKS BY THE AUTHOR

Fear and Anguish: Primary Triggers of Survival and Evolution (Hunter House)

Psychological Healing: An Intimate Approach to Curing the Whole Person (Hunter House)

The Psychology of Motivation (Hunter House)

Symbolism in the Bible (Harper & Row)

Symbolism in Greek Mythology (Shambhala)

Psychology of Reeducation (Shambhala)

THE
GOD-SYMBOL

Its History and Its Significance

PAUL DIEL

Translated by Nelly Marans

1817

Harper & Row, Publishers, San Francisco

Cambridge, Hagerstown, New York, Philadelphia, Washington
London, Mexico City, São Paulo, Singapore, Sydney

Originally published in French by Payot, Paris, in 1971, under the title *La Divinité, le symbole et sa signification.*

Library of Congress Cataloging-in-Publication Data

Diel, Paul.
  The God-symbol.

  Translation of: La divinité.
  1. Psychology, Religious. 2. Symbolism. I. Title.
BL53.D513   1986   292.2′1′019   85–51824
ISBN 0-06-254805-0

86 87 88 89 90 HC 10 9 8 7 6 5 4 3 2 1

Contents

Introduction

A. THE OBJECT OF ANALYSIS

History shows that man's effort to find methodical and scientific solutions to the problems of life was often preceded by speculative attempts based on affectivity and imagination. Thus chemistry became a science as a reaction against the speculations of alchemy; in the same way, astronomy followed astrology. In keeping with this very common thought procedure, psychology did not start to become a scientific discipline until it parted from philosophical speculation, be it metaphysical or moral.

By dint of a sustained effort, chemistry managed to purify its terminology from the superstitions that the beliefs of alchemy persisted in keeping alive. It was the cost to be paid for becoming a genuine science. Yet, chemistry found itself compelled to face anew the central problem of alchemy: the transmutation of matter. The difference lies in the approach: chemistry does not speculate, but views the problem methodically, and thus is able to find a genuine solution.

Is psychology confronted with the prospect of a similar return to its origins? It parted from philosophy by using methodical means to scrutinize psychic functioning not only on a conscious but also on an extra-conscious level; is it not faced now with the necessity of tackling the age-old problem of philosophy, namely, the meaning of life? Such a problem stems from life itself, from its intrinsic need to be reflected in thought, to become thought, and this need is the origin of all sciences. Is there any hope that psychology will be as lucky as chemistry in its finding a solution to alchemy's problem and will be able to solve the metaphysical and moral problem? Metaphysics has certainly fallen into disrepute, but is it worse than that with which alchemy was for so long confronted? However, for psychology to go back to the most ancient and fundamental of life's problems could only be justified if it succeeded in proving that this problem—as was the case with chemistry and its return to transmutation—does in the final analysis belong to methodical research, almost against its own intention as it were, and that it must be viewed on another plane and with a new approach.

In order to break away from speculation as radically as possible, psychology first attempted to give up not only the method but also the

1

problems of philosophy which appeared to be too comprehensive. It voluntarily limited itself to the analysis of conscious functions: thought, will, feelings. Such a distinction had in fact been inherited from philosophical speculation based on too hasty an introspection. Indeed it would have been quite difficult, if not impossible, to give up those relics of an introspection which was admittedly inadequate since it dealt only with conscious functions, yet which had the merit—in the absence of anything better—of setting up a classification enabling the definition of the object of research and its functioning. Yet it was hoped that a more objective viewpoint would be achieved by stressing, rather than those intrapsychic functions, their externally observable outcome: actions, behavior. Experiments were set up to produce reactions and obtain statistical measurements through tests.

However, it was quickly realized that behavior is not only determined by conscious functions but also by a preconscious process whose functions are the reflex action, automatism, and instincts. Such preconscious reactions which are predominant in animals remain the substructure of human action. Thus an attempt was made to establish human psychology on the experimental study of animal unconscious behavior. The experimental study of animal reactions can undoubtedly produce—no less than the observation of human actions—significant results. But the danger of the currently popular behaviorism is to jump from conclusions which are valid for animals to conclusions applied to human behavior while neglecting to define at the outset what man and animals have in common and what separates them in evolution, the latter differences being precisely psychic ones. Like the animal, man seeks to fulfill his elementary needs—nutrition and procreation—which are life values since they are indispensable for the survival of the individual and the species. Unlike the animal, though, man has appetences that have become diversified in a multiplicity of frequently contradictory desires; moreover the latter can be imaginatively exalted. This difference is of such importance in all the coming developments that it must be specified. Having become conscious, man must think about the inner life of his desires which, since he values them according to their promise of satisfaction, become motives for further actions. Since the valuating spirit[1] is prone to error—principle of vital dissatisfaction— the destiny of man is to seek satisfaction of the spirit: truth, which is the

1. French "esprit" has been translated either by "mind" or "spirit" according to context. Diel defines it as the organizational aspect of matter. The concept is thus extended to the whole of nature instead of being restricted to man's thought. This definition is fundamental for the understanding of Diel's thought.

In spite of its undesirable spiritual connotation it is preferable to use "spirit" 1) because the word "mind" is too extensive, covering at the same time psyche, spirit and intellect, which are concepts that Diel clearly distinguishes, and 2) because "spirit" links up better with "spiritualize," which as defined by Diel is the fundamental function of the human spirit.

best way to adapt oneself, to show the aptitude to conduct one's life in a meaningful manner. There lies the deep biogenetical root of the ethical problem which was only sketchily studied by philosophy and too radically ignored by all forms of behavior psychology, tests, psychometry, behaviorism, pavlovism, organicism, psychiatry, etc. It is fitting to add that—in the absence of the indispensable biogenetical substructure which should take the place of the ancient metaphysical speculations—the ethical problem is equally misunderstood in the pseudo-philosophical speculations of our time (existentialism, phenomenology, structuralism, etc.).

Thus modern thought—seeking to fill the tremendous gap in the sciences of life—has started to go back to the necessary investigation. In-depth psychology, bent on containing psychic illnesses, attempts to fathom the extra-conscious depths. To do so, it must use some kind of unavowed introspection, hence one which is not sufficiently methodical. When all is said and done, ancient philosophical research was nothing more than a species of excessively interpretative introspection, though it was able to unveil to the inner eye deep truths which escape the pseudo-objectivity of an exclusively behavioral study.

There is a great deal of opposition to such a return of psychology to an interpretative method which is too easily confused with ancient speculation and undoubtedly also too easily prone to the danger of speculation. But does there exist a method devoid of sources of error? The fact is that, due to the psychoanalytic study of the extra-conscious causes of mental illnesses, the essential dilemma of psychology is defined: either one gives up once and for all understanding the complementary aspect of behavior, i.e., the intrapsychic motivating functioning, or one resorts to an introspective form of explanation which—in order not to be speculative—would have to be able to give an account of its methodological foundations. Freudian psychoanalysis, being half introspective and half speculative, remained halfway in its search for a solution to the inescapable dilemma. If mythologies, which are historical documents, contain—as Freud supposed it—an underlying psychological truth, is it not evident that they must be the product of an ancestral introspection endowed with elucidating power? And what are nocturnal dreams if not an introspective state during which the unquiet soul reviews its concerns and its hopes, in the guise—as is the case in mythologies—of fictional characters that symbolize the personal intentions of the dreamer in search of a solution for the conflicts of his daytime life? If collective dreams—myths—and individual dreams know about secret motivations, should we not come to the conclusion that introspection as well as symbolic expressions of the extra-conscious are essential properties of psychic life to the extent that, rooted in ancestral and mythical origins, they still keep company with and even lead human life, in the form of oneirism.

One could argue that neither mythologies nor dreams contain an underlying psychological truth.

The problem is of major importance here since we have to analyze the central symbol of all mythologies, namely, the divinity.

To settle the question, we only have to ascertain the following: does conceptual vocabulary—in its most elementary form (thoughts, feelings, volitions) inherited from time immemorial—contain truths pertaining to intrapsychic functioning? If the answer is negative, it would have to be abandoned and one would have to seek—with the help of introspection—a psychological vocabulary endowed with genuine meaning. If it is positive, would this not be the proof that such a vocabulary was built on an introspection, leading us to think that symbolic and mythical vocabulary could also be of pre-scientific value?

On the strength of such a dilemma—which in fact points to an inescapable necessity—psychoanalysis, though it was only a first attempt, insufficiently purified from the danger of speculation, increasingly managed to impose its method of interpretation. It can be rightly reproached, not for giving up the methods of experimental psychology and behaviorism, but quite to the contrary for falling into the same methodological error shared by experimental psychology and behaviorism; psychoanalysis insists on giving to the subconscious process it studies prevailing importance among all the psychic processes. It shows an unfortunate tendency to explain all aspects of human life through the distorting functioning of the subconscious.

A growing tendency, though still insufficiently carried out, can be noticed, from experimental psychology to behaviorism to psychoanalysis to go back to an explanation of the whole of life and its functions. In the final analysis, the aim is to grasp the meaning of life. Indeed what definitive goal could one assign to psychology, even for that part of the discipline dealing only with behavior, if not the discernment between the various aspects of behavior, normal and abnormal, healthy and unhealthy, for the purpose of finally attaining the healthiest behavior: meaningful behavior? Attempts at psychological explanation differ from philosophical speculation since they are based—or should be—on psychological theories founded on biology. The psychology of human beings is linked to that of the animals, thus to biology, and subconscious distortion is nothing but a morbid attempt at regression from conscious and human functioning to an unconscious and animal one. Psychology must therefore reconstitute the biogenesis of the past. Yet how could it do this without being led to project it onto the future, thus giving to life a direction, a meaning? It is quite evident that such a natural ambition of psychology will not be able to achieve its legitimate satisfaction without first studying all the psychic processes as well as their interactions. To project that past onto the future would be mere speculation if the theoretical ambition did not correspond to a psychic fact, a new process in the making, destined to fulfill the evolutionary future.

Such a new process can be neither conscious (i.e., intellectual) nor unconscious (instinctual) nor subconscious (pathological); it will be *superconscious*, i.e., more-than-conscious. It is characteristic of human beings, and distinguishes them most decisively from the animals. It takes on the evolutionary purpose of the human species. It is at the same time a reality and an ideal. It determines the only ideal based on reality, not on speculation. This superconscious process in evolutionary making is the most important, yet the least studied of all. It shows itself in the tendency to regulate all the psychic functions, to harmonize and render them conformed to the law of psychic life. Directed toward the outer world, it is the impulse[2] toward pure knowledge (not wanting to know the nature of things in order to use them, but to understand the lawfulness of their relationships); directed toward the inner world, it is the will to harmonize desires (as the restraint of reason). This superconscious process shares one factor with consciousness: foresight; but its foresight does not deal with accidental facts as does the intellect's. It concerns lawful relationships and deduces lawfully foreseeable consequences: it is clairvoyant. One trait is shared with the instinctive unconscious of animals: unerringness. But the latter is not automatic; it is intuitive and its evolutionary tendency is to become certainty of the spirit. It also holds something in common with the subconscious process, namely the possibility of pathological distortion. The latter is very strong because of the frailty of a function in the course of evolutionary development that is—for each human being—more a goal to be reached than a stage generally achieved. When distorted, superconsciousness loses its quality of intuitive clairvoyance. The genuineness of the intuitive spirit loses itself in gratuitous speculations, in superstitions, and in all kinds of foolish beliefs. If the superconscious process and its intuitive clairvoyance did not exist, philosophy would only have produced errors while seeking to find a solution to the essential problem of life. It is an authentic vision insofar as it stems from superconscious intuition; its speculative characteristic is due to the frailty of superconscious intuition. When it covers its entire realm—the extra-conscious as well as the conscious aspect of the psychic functioning—psychology is necessarily confronted with the essential problem concerning the meaning of life, the ancient problem of philosophy. It is a mistake to think that psychology must free itself from its philosophical origins by excluding from its research the essential problem regarding the meaning of life, a problem which was indeed wrongly tackled by ancient philosophy in the form of morals based on metaphysics. Quite the contrary, psychology should approach the essential problem methodically shunning any metaphysical speculation. In order to achieve this, it

---

2. "Élan" or "élan vital," a word used by Diel to express the fact that all living beings—and therefore man—are animated by a mysterious force. The translators chose the English "vital impulse" or "impulse" to render the dynamic concept of élan. The term "élan" itself would have led to confusion with Bergson's "élan vital."

should analyze the superconscious process which gave birth to the intuitive and speculative solutions of the philosophical systems, but also created the superconscious dreams containing the real solution to the essential problem: the mythologies whose central symbol is "the divinity."

It is not too early at this stage to introduce some supportive references for these rather surprising findings on which all the conclusions of this present work are based. Among all psychic processes the superconscious has been the most neglected, if not ignored, so that an unbridgeable gap was opened between psychology and the problem of life. The superconscious was not even recognized as a separate process. Since it is so easily distorted, the superconscious process or ethical conscience is rarely to be observed in a pure state. Having something in common with the other processes, it is too easily confused with one or the other among them. From the outset, psychology mistook it for the conscious process, behaviorism for the unconscious one, and psychoanalysis for the subconscious one.

Such frequent confusions give all the more importance to the finding that this clear distinction between the four processes is expressed, quite independently from the present work, in M. Pradines' book *Traité de Psychologie Générale*. After having defined the conscious function, the author deals with a constitutional unconscious (the superconscious) and a dissolutional unconscious (the subconscious). Having made such a distinction, the author adds:

However, one should further distinguish here between a banal and common unconscious, without which no conscious activity would be possible, and an extraordinary and rare unconscious, which is not abnormal or morbid but exists only among very few subjects in the form of *intuition* or *inspiration*, and is in them like a kind of perfecting and adjusting mutation similar to what can be assumed to be the origin of progress in certain species. . . . Reflection lends to its underlying automatism a drive that goes beyond reflection itself. The consequence is then brought to mind before the reasoning which is its logical foundation, the relation is imagined before the justifying and legitimizing perception, and the result of the activity is represented before the intelligent combination of the motions that implement it. What is normally the fruit of labor is provided to the inspired being as if it were a gratuitous gift. Instinct, according to Bergson's profound remark, is penetrated with light if not with conscience. There could be no better proof of the fact that the unconscious is intimately linked to psychic life since, though it is normally meant to sustain it, it can become capable of preceding it. (*Traité de Psychologie Générale*, M. Pradines, 1: 28–29).

This is a clear finding of the existence of a more-than-conscious, superconscious process and of its functioning whose intensity varies with each individual.

As far as the relationship between psychology and philosophy is concerned, it would be useful to quote the following lines from William

James, one of the greatest psychologists, whose endeavors preceded the analysis of extra-conscious processes. James is remarkably frank in lamenting the absence of a methodical foundation in psychology.

Here is what the author writes in the conclusion of his "Psychology: a Briefer Course:"

When we say that psychology is a natural science, we have to be careful not to mean by this that it is founded on solid ground. Quite to the contrary, such a qualification stresses its frailty, the frailty of a science oozing metaphysical criticism from all its pores, a science the hypotheses and the fundamental givens of which, far from having a personal and absolute value, are, on the contrary, connected with theories going beyond them and according to which they have to be rethought and reformulated. In brief, to make a natural science out of psychology is not to exalt it, it is to depreciate its authority. . . . We are even unaware of the terms between which the fundamental laws—which we do not have—should establish a relation. Is this a science? It is barely the hope for one. We only have the matter out of which this science will have to be extracted. . . . Up to now, psychology is still at the stage chemistry was before Lavoisier and the law of mass conservation.

And in affirming that the Lavoisier of psychology will come, the author has the surprising courage to add: "There will come a metaphysicist; the nature of the psychological problem calls for it."

One cannot exclude the possibility that in the future it might be pointed out that Freud, in proving that extra-consciousness could be analyzed, did for psychology what Lavoisier had done for chemistry. The only reproach one could level against him is that he was not enough of "a metaphysicist." To express this in less startling and more psychological terms: he confused the superconscious and the subconscious. The superconscious is the process that created the metaphysical images of the myths, among which the most important is the "divinity" symbol. *In this respect, it is extremely important to know that genuine metaphysics endowed with a psychological bearing has only one purpose, i.e., the criticism of speculative metaphysics whose chief error is to believe that mythological figures, including the divinity, are actual beings.*

The purpose of the present book can be summed up as *criticism of speculative metaphysics* through the analysis of the superconscious process, which necessarily implies an analysis of all the psychic functions.

A preliminary question must be settled: how can the conscious account for the extra-conscious processes?

The psyche is not a spatial object divided into compartments. The phrase "psychic process" means nothing more than *particular mode of functioning*. Each process defines a differentiated form of the psychic functioning; it has no existence outside of its way of functioning, and all the psychic processes interact in fluid dynamics.

The conscious is logical; its tool is conceptual language.

The unconscious is instinctive and automatic. It already exists at the animal level. Its way of expression is, as it were, organic language: the automatic reaction of the body to stimuli. Its "language" is not conceptual and it is not symbolic, but far more direct: it is reflex action, complicated by the evolved reflexes embodied in instincts. The organic functioning of the unconscious cannot be translated into conceptual language, at least when it comes to its deep-seated and directly experienced contents. Here explanation can be no more than description. This means that the unconscious functioning is not accessible to conscious control. (Moreover, were it accessible, such control would only disturb its regulated automatism).

The subconscious is an imaginative and symbolizing function. Its relationship with the superconscious—which is also a symbolic function—calls for a detailed study in order to understand the nature of the functioning of the superconscious.

Subconscious functioning expresses desires which cannot be reconciled with reality (because they are imaginatively exalted) and which, due to this fact, cannot find satisfaction through an organic and automatic response of the unconscious; moreover, the conscious refuses to lend them its ability of logical implementation. These material and sexual desires, being imaginatively exalted, cannot therefore be fulfilled, either through the reflex action of the unconscious, or with the help of conscious reflection, either automatically or logically. They can thus be expressed only in an illogical way. Cut off from the automatic expression of the unconscious and from the conceptual expression of the conscious, these desires are repressed. They are repressed in two ways: their discharge is blocked, and their understanding is *symbolically veiled*. Yet, precisely because the energy of these illogically exalted desires does not cease to manifest itself from the depths of the subconscious, the way found by their repressed energy to express itself, their *symbolism*, can still be translated into conceptual and conscious language. Thanks to this translation—raising the repressed desire to the level of consciousness—the blockage gives way. The continuity of logical understanding being restored, the desires can at last find a way to a real discharge, provided however that conscious control manages finally to dissolve not only the symbolic form but also the energetic distortion caused by imaginative exaltation. This translation is not merely descriptive: it represents a vital intervention; it is not only a theoretical intervention, but a very practical one. It is possible only as an *introspective effort* fighting and dissolving the vain promises of imaginatively exalted desires in order to recover their energy that had previously been escaping conscious control. Spiritualizing introspection, by dissolving affective clouding, makes the previously repressed desire not only accessible but acceptable to consciousness. Through accepting one's error, the repression which had caused unhealthy and pathological functioning is definitively eliminated (at least when it comes to that part of energy taken over by the repressed desire)[3]. Symbolic expression disappears, not only in its formal aspect but also in it energetic aspect which is the psychopathological symptom. The symptom disappears even if its form of expression is organic. This is possible because repression is a regression to the primitive and unconscious process, characterized by automatic and organic "language." The symptom is a disturbance of the conscious as well as of the unconscious. It is a psychically conditioned organic expression: a wrongly motivated one. By eliminating the psychic condition—*the wrong motivation*—the organic and morbid expression of the repressed desire loses the condition for its existence, its *raison d'être*. It collapses. Translating a symbolic symptom into conceptual language does therefore have a therapeutic value. In a previously published book, *Psychologie de la Motivation*, the author proved that at the root of every exalted imagination causing repression there is an unbearable feeling connected with all senseless desires. This painful and unbearable feeling—guiltiness—is not the product of education's interdicts (as psychoanalysis would have it) but the indication of a disturbance of the essential (and superconscious) need of human nature, of the essential desire to harmonize the desires, the condition for durable satisfaction, for joy. A feeling of guiltiness points to a loss of joy and the weakness[4] of the subject who—prey to senseless desires, i.e., desires that cannot be harmonized—cannot attain joy, the meaning of life. Repressing the feeling of one's weakness is the essential guilt of human nature, is vanity (the inability to admit one's own faults). In guilty vanity are concentrated all the multiple forms that wrong motivations can take; guilty vanity is the common and lawful cause of all subconscious distortions. In order to overcome these character flaws (which are not necessarily pathological symptoms but can be mere signs of irritation, overexcitement, nervousness) man must have the courage to see himself as he is, to see what he really is and not to let himself be duped by what he vainly believes himself to be.

---

3. See *Psychologie de la Motivation* (Theory and Therapeutic Application), 3d ed. (P.U.F. and Petite Bibliotheque Payot, 1970).

4. This weakness or *vital guilt* (in French "coulpe vitale") is a key word for Diel which he defines as follows in *Symbolism in the Bible*: "Vital guilt, the insufficiency inherent in all that exists, is a condition of life itself and the evolutionary prime mover is nothing else than the vital necessity to overcome this vital insufficiency which is the cause of suffering."

In man, vital guilt is accompanied by a warning feeling of guiltiness—*essential guiltiness*—(in French, *culpabilité essentielle*) the repression of which leads to *vain guilt* (in French, *coulpe vaniteuse*), the denial of any insufficiency.

But insufficient we are. So this vain denial means that our essential guiltiness (or essential feeling of guiltiness), being repressed, becomes exalted into a *vain guiltiness* (in French, *culpabilité vaniteuse*).

The translation has tried to respect this distinction between "coulpe" and "culpabilité" by reserving the word "guilt" for "coulpe," in spite of its more general meaning in common usage.

This has led to translating "culpabilité" as "guiltiness" or "guilty feelings" (according to context, though a more usual translation would be guilt or guilt feelings.

Now to admit one's own faults and to be able to correct them has always been the only possible definition of moral feeling. The psychology of the extra-conscious thus leads directly to morality, to a moral science which is the opposite of moralism and which is capable of taking the place of philosophy's speculative systems. The latter did not take the time to analyze what one must not do (which is defined by subconscious functioning); they hurried to formulate what must be done. However, "what must be done" (with regard to the meaning of life) is not, from the outset, conscious or easily defined. Yet, this "duty" for the sake of one's own essential good is neither vague nor of a nature strictly opposed to any conscious function. The meaning to be attained, the evolutionary goal is inherent in life; life leads to it; and this goal is inherent in man's psychic life (insofar as it is not psychically beclouded and in the process of regression toward the unconscious) in the form of an essential tension, of an *essential desire*, a guiding pre-sentiment which can best be described by naming it: the superconscious.

The *superconscious*, in its most primitive form, is a vague feeling rather than a knowledge, yet this feeling is more precise and surer than a theoretical knowledge, at least as long as the latter is not based on the knowledge of the functioning of the psychic processes. The superconscious cannot be separated from the subconscious, (they are both functional complications of the conscious psyche and its multiple desires) because its pre-sentiment, at the same time vague and precise—commonly called "conscience"—appears in the form of a guilty feeling (the repression of which defines the subconscious functioning) indicating the disturbance of the superconscious ideal of harmony. This superconscious feeling, *ethical superconscience*, cannot lose its lack of precision, cannot become a conscious and truly precise knowledge unless one fully understands in detail "what one must not do," unless wrong motivation ceases to be a subconscious affect, unless it is consciously known, knowingly understood, translated into conceptual language. From the knowledge of wrong motivation follows necessarily the knowledge of right motivation, which is the exact opposite of the former. Subconscious and superconscious are antithetically linked. Subconscious feelings are the motives which distort, superconscious feelings are the motives which develop psychic functioning. If we are not afraid of a moral terminology, we can say that the former are opposed to the latter as evil is opposed to good. In fact, this moral terminology does not acquire its justifiable meaning if not through the antithetical motivation determining unhealthy distortion and psychic health. What morality calls "Good" is nothing but the opposite of guilty vanity: modest pride, i.e., a quiet self-confidence in one's own value, which is not only imagined but achieved and attested to by actions stemming from superconscious motives, is actual morality.

B. THE METHOD OF ANALYSIS

Insofar as philosophy is concerned, actual morality remains a vague phenomenon whose conditions it tries to find in order to formulate precepts. For the psychology of the extra-conscious, actual morality is a vital experience of development of character which cannot be achieved except through the analysis and formulation of the laws of harmony and disharmony. Experiential development is the result of sublimation; lawful formulation is the result of spiritualization, sublimation and spiritualization being products of the superconscious functioning considered in its energetic and motivating form.

A function can be understood only through the analysis of its products. In order to understand the function of the superconscious process one can analyze either the product of sublimation, i.e., healthy characters, or the product of spiritualization: true theories. Sublime characters are rare phenomena, subjective and bound to the fleeting life of individuals. Theories, which are often contradictory, are frequent phenomena with claims to objectivity, and they have survived through the centuries. Philosophical systems would thus provide the matter for the analysis of the superconscious, were they not so many and contradictory, or—and this amounts to the same thing—were they not so fraught with errors. If these systems were entirely true, they would easily have merged into one sole theory devoid of contradiction because it would itself be the result of a true analysis. But the superconscious function that has been operating since the beginning of the human species has perhaps created other products of spiritualization, more genuine and less fraught with speculative and individual error. Analysis of the superconscious and of its productive force could lead psychology way beyond its remote origin: philosophical speculation. Philosophy did not make up the fundamental problems of life. They have always existed. Religions bequeathed them to philosophy, and the latter is after all nothing but an insufficiently methodical endeavor to translate religious images into conceptual language. Religions and their images are the oldest product of the superconscious vision. Could it be that they contain both the strength and weakness of the superconscious vision, i.e., truth and error? The source of error could only be the tendency to dogmatize shared by all religions. This tendency to dogmatize is applied to the intuitive substructure of all of them which is expressed in the myths. Could one find in the form of these myths the most primitive and truthful product of the superconscious vision, a product whose analysis would be directly revealing as to the nature of the superconscious process?

This is exactly what this book aims to prove.

Long before thought had evolved its conceptual language, enabling individuals to try and formulate speculations about the meaning of life, the superconscious and intuitive function created truthful visions pertaining to life and its meaning. Human beings cannot live or form cultural communities without having such visions. But such pre-conceptual visions made use of an extra-conscious means of expression: symbolic images. In its primitive and collective form, the superconscious is a symbolizing imagination. It produces a superconscious dream about the meaning of life, i.e., myth.

If this is true, myths must contain a meaning which is hidden under the symbolic facade. Just as nocturnal dreams contain a hidden meaning which is the truth concerning the disorderly state of the individual's desires, superconscious and collective dreams—or myths—must contain a hidden meaning which is the truth concerning the desire for harmonization shared by all the members of a species given to disharmonization of the desires, to their imaginative exaltation. In the mythologies of all peoples, the ideal goal of this essential desire, the ideal achievement of harmony, the superconsciously idealized human quality, is expressed by the "divinity" symbol. All things considered, the endeavor to conceptually define the significance of "God," the supreme symbol of myths, is the center of gravity for all philosophical speculation, which is in turn the remote source of psychology's methodical effort.

Thus psychology remains, through philosophy, inseparably linked to the "God" symbol. Such a bond does not impose on it the old beliefs, but the need to understand the meaning of the symbol.

However, the significance of this symbol—supreme product of the superconscious—can only be understood in relation to the totality of mythical symbolization. If it is true that the product of the superconscious in its *sublime* form is right motivation or morality, and that the most genuine *spiritual* product of the superconscious is the myths, the conclusion is that *the hidden significance of mythical images has to be the right motivation, i.e., the foundation of ethics.* Myths have to be the enigmatic expression of a morality which was not established through speculation, but based on the very nature of human beings. Since the contents of the superconscious, right motivation and its theoretical formulation—be it only in images—become psychologically definable through the analysis of the contents of the subconscious and its wrong motivation, the study of motivations has to be the key to the translation of mythical symbols. Such a possibility has already been demonstrated in previous works such as *Le Symbolisme dans la Mythologie Grecque* (or Symbolism in Greek Mythology) and exemplified in the translation of many myths.

The present work will analyze the superconscious process and its functioning through the study of its most authentic product: the Divinity. But since a complete analysis of this symbol contained in all the myths goes far beyond the scope of a single book, we will have to limit ourselves to analyzing the symbol which is the acme of all mythical symbolization and the symbolic expression of morality: the "Only God" symbol.

All cultural eras, since the beginning of time, have been centered around the "Divinity" symbol.

Moral values have always been conceived in relation to this symbol. Cultural decline, i.e., the depreciation of moral values, has always had the same cause: the dogmatizing tendency to eliminate the symbolic depth of the mythical image by turning it into a simple reality, which led to ambivalence between belief and doubt.

In ancient cultures, symbolism dealt with multiple deities. Nowadays, our culture is based upon the Christian myth in which the "God" symbol consists of three symbols: God-the-Father, God-the-Spirit, and God-the-Son.

Nobody would expect psychological analysis to support the central dogma taking the "God-the-Son" symbol as a reality.

Analysis, however, also cannot support the critical essays which were undertaken without any psychological method, such as for instance—to name only the most important—those of Strauss, Feuerbach, Renan. Those authors denied the symbolic value of myths, or if they accepted it—as Strauss did, for instance—it was only in order to bring them down to the level of vague daydreams of the primitive soul and not to see them as bearers of a terminology apparently enigmatic but extremely precise in its hidden meaning, the significance of which should be revealed through analysis. Whatever merits the intentions of those authors had, the results—often very valuable from a literary viewpoint—cannot be taken into account in a translation endeavor aiming to avoid all speculation.

From a psychological viewpoint, the most important criticism of dogmas is that of Freud, which was undertaken in his book *The Future of a Delusion*. For Freud, this delusion without a future was the belief in God.

Not only did he attack the supreme symbol, "God-the-Father," but he based his criticism on the analysis of the extra-conscious functioning. The tool of psychological criticism was created by Freud. Using this tool in the present work leads to results which are completely different from those of Freudian analysis. Thus, it is indispensable to spend some time studying the cause of this divergence in the analysis of the problem—undoubtedly the most essential—represented by the "God" symbol. There is no better ground to illustrate the essential difference in the study of intrapsychic processes by psychoanalysis and by the psychology of motivations. The fundamental error of psychoanalysis is to confuse the subconscious and the superconscious.

The Freudian theory, which was the start of all the studies of the extra-conscious depths, does not recognize the specific function of the superconscious process. It deems itself compelled to explain the "God" symbol through subconscious symbolism. The term "sub-conscious" is only a means of localizing the motivating intentions which are cut off from conscious control: fantasies of escape, pseudo-consoling delusions which, being repressed because overloaded with guiltiness, are obsessively clamoring for surreal satisfaction sought for in the empty games of a pathologically exalted imagination. Is the "God" symbol, as Freud claims, a product of repression, a pathological imagination, a pseudo-consoling delusion?

Stating our position vis-a-vis the Freudian conceptions concerning inner psychic functions or even mentioning his criticism of the "God" image would not be of major importance in this instance, if the following pages did not make use of his "repression-sublimation" terminology, compelling us to keep in mind that the meaning of these words—indispensable in the description of psychic dynamics—has been radically reversed. And this occurs precisely because repression and sublimation concern the dynamic relationship between the two extra-conscious processes (subconscious and superconscious), the latter having been neglected by Freud. The "divinity" symbol belongs to superconscious symbolism, which we have to demonstrate. Freud undertook to confront this symbol, which is central to all mythologies, through his pansexual doctrine.

Yet Freud deserves much credit for having discovered symbolic thought. It is no accident that the psychology of extra-conscious depths has from the outset looked for confirmation in myths, for example, the Oedipus complex. The supposition that myths do have a psychological significance has been voiced throughout the centuries. It has led to many attempts of interpretation which were devoid of method, and which in turn led to a radical aversion—a kind of anathema—against the exegesis of myths. In this respect, Freud's attempt was a renewal. It was no accident either that he attacked the "God" image, believing as he did that it was only a pure delusion, a by-product of repressed sexuality, a pseudo-sublimation.

Since "to repress" and "to sublimate" are commonly used nowadays in psychological vocabulary, and since everybody understands these words as Freud did, we have to study at length the causes and consequences that do not fail to have a disorienting influence on thought—as does any kind of confusion—all the more harmful in that we are dealing with the essential problem of human life.

The major error lies in the fact that Freud, neglecting—or rather being unaware of—the sublimative process or superconscious, replaces it with the "superego," which, he thought, is rigid, hypocritical, and moralizing. Now what Freud calls "superego" is nothing in fact but an "underego[5]": conventional guiltiness in the face of society's rules of the game.

The entire understanding of the inner motivating functioning and the whole method of deciphering mythical pre-science are based on a clear distinction between the genuine guiltiness of the superconscience and conventional guiltiness. The latter, far from being a psychic process, is nothing but the product of taboos of social origin.

According to Freud's pansexual theory, hypocritical taboos are opposed to the powerful libido. They repress it. From this definition of repression stems the Freudian concept of sublimation. For Freud, to sublimate means to oppose the hypocrisy of the social "superego" which is rigid and excessively severe, in order to magnify the libido: vital energy, vital impulse, supposedly rooted exclusively in sexuality.

All these Freudian definitions are due to his confusing the harmonizing superconscience and the "superego," which, in truth, is nothing but an "underego," its moralizing rigidity being caused by the subconscious and pseudospiritual obsession of a hypocrisy that in Freud's view exclusively concerned sexuality. Having nothing at his disposal but his great and brilliant discovery of the subconscious and its symbolical expressions, Freud uses them in his analysis of the "divinity" symbol, which compels him to see in it nothing but a delusion without a future.

It is indispensable to stress that in the following analyses, *"to sublimate" means: to reestablish the harmony of material and sexual desires; "to repress" means: to destroy harmony, to repress—through a false and vain self-justification—the guilty anxiety[6] of the superconscience*, the latter being a salutary warning attached to perverse motivations for the purpose of preventing their fulfillment.

These preliminary definitions and findings are in total conformity with the symbolism of the mythologies.

Mythical deities represent the harmonizing forces of the superconscious. The disharmonizing forces of the subconscious and the "monstrous" distortions of psychopathology due to the mind's errings are symbolized by monsters and demons that the heroes (symbols of the essentially combative man) should fight. Most mythical heroes, insufficiently helped by the gods (insufficiently armed with superconscious forces), perish in their struggle against subconscious temptations, which is a true symbolic representation of the real situation of man confronted with his own intrapsychic conflicts. Instead of analyzing the "God" symbol (which would have been impossible within the context of pansexual symbolism) Freud directs his entire criticism toward the belief in a real god, a belief which leads indeed to moralism. Dogmatic

---

5. This is a pun on the word "sur-moi," which means 'superego'; "sous-moi" is not part of the psychoanalytical vocabulary. It was coined by Paul Diel.

6. In French "angoisse" (German: angst). A more satisfying term would be "anguish," but the term "anxiety" has been used in all Anglo-Saxon psychoanalytical writings.

moralism is excessively opposed to sexuality, even in its healthy and natural form. Freudism suggests magnifying sexuality as a remedy (which
amounts to nothing else but reversing a dogma). Since Freud makes no
distinction between the "God" symbol and the dogmatic god, a pure
delusion to be sure, he is compelled to suppose that all the sublimating
manifestations of human life—the various cultures, all based on the
"divinity" symbol—are only by-products of repressed sexuality, a kind
of pseudo-sublime consolation for the guiltiness attached to sexual
pleasures. It remains true that Freud in his writings objects several
times to the conclusion that in his views the only salvation of future societies would be found in the sadistic and masochistic excesses of sexuality, even though this has now become an accepted belief, owing no
small foundation to Freud's confusion between repression and
sublimation.

Societies suffer from many other hypocritical taboos, which are not
only sexual but also material and, above all, pseudo-spiritual. The
meaning of myths, condensed in the "God" symbol, is precisely the
elimination of all the conventional—moralizing and amoralizing—taboos, replaced by the ethical law of the superconscious harmonization
covering sexual, material, and spiritual desires. Being—as we shall
see—of biogenetical origin, superconscience is the ethical force because as a law it is a spiritualizing force and as an imposition of harmony it is a sublimating force.[7]

God is not a delusion, God is a myth.

But is a myth different from a delusion? Does it actually have a hidden meaning reflecting human life? Is it really a superconscious image,
product of a more-than-conscious imagination, in which the biogenetically immanent meaning of life has been condensed?

Belief in the deities originated in myth. Only the latter relate the
deeds of the gods and credit them with feelings, will, intentions with
respect to men. The fact that the multiple gods were finally replaced,
concentrated in the image of an only God, is of secondary importance.
It follows that if the deeds of the multiple deities, as narrated in the ancient myths, had no hidden significance, the only God would also be an
idea devoid of meaning. Thus, there is no doubt in the choice between
the symbolic God of the myths and the real god of convention, between
a God endowed with a symbolic significance and a real god without any
deep symbolic meaning. In order to remove ourselves from this necessary choice which is imposed by the fact that the divinity is above all a
mythical figure, we would have to be able to explain where this certainty of the existence of a god, not a symbolically true one, but an anthro-
pomorphically personified one, came from. From revelation? Such an

---

7. For more details, see the chapter on Oedipus in *Symbolism in Greek Mythology*,
Shambhala.

answer cannot be refuted since it cannot be verified. Unfortunately, it gives birth to a new alternative which is far more dangerous. Since its nature is no longer purely theoretical, it proves capable of bringing about the most serious practical consequences: having to choose between blind belief and skepticism.

Our time derides the conventional belief of ancient peoples who believed in the actual existence of the deities. Present belief in an only God appears to be more advanced. However, skepticism, having destroyed the ancient gods, undertakes to do the same with the only God. Skepticism was always the reaction to the error of conventional belief. The history of all cultures is summed up in the creation of mythical images, their dogmatization, and their destruction by skepticism. Though it is true that in the past, psychological truth always had to take on a new form of symbolic expression in order to create a new culture, one cannot exclude the possibility that in a more enlightened future, the immutable truth underlying mythologies may at last become fertile without having to turn to an ambiguous expression. The history of the formation and destruction of mythically based cultures can only be explainable if one understands that it is the result of the conflict between the psychic processes: creative imagination (superconscious), affective imagination (subconscious) and critical thought (conscious). Since the historical process has psychic roots, it belongs to the realm of psychological analysis.

If it were possible to prove that only one symbol, and all the more so the central "divinity" symbol, contains a hidden meaning endowed with a deep psychological scope, would it not be highly probable that all the other mythical symbols had a psychological significance connected with that of the "divinity" symbol?

The pagan myths already dealt with gods who became men, and men who were sons of deities. To those fabulous beings who were half gods and half men (expressing the possibility of sublimation in man) were opposed monstrous beings (expressing the possibility of perversion) who were half men and half animals or—and the meaning is the same—animals speaking like humans, such as the serpent in paradise. The Christian myth, foundation of our present culture, is built on the story of a serpent talking like a man, symbol of the initial perversion (symbolically called original sin). The myth finally deals with a god-the-son, showing men the way to liberating sublimation. In this tale going from the talking serpent to god-the-son, all is symbol or nothing is symbol. If one does not want to believe that the serpent actually spoke, there is no choice but to believe that the divine filiation is also a symbolic one. It has become the norm to admit that certain biblical passages that are too obviously illogical, for instance, "the talking serpent," are symbolic. This is nothing but a subterfuge as long as one does not know how to define symbolic language and as long as one does not have a precise knowledge of the meaning of specific symbols. Besides which, to suppose that one individual passage has a hidden meaning means admitting that all the illogical passages might be symbols. The most illogical among the countless illogical passages of the texts is the image of a personal god.

Nothing is more surprising, more worthy of attention, than these seemingly absurd fabulations—mythical images—which have nonetheless kept up to our time their superconsciously formative influence on the human soul, and whose influence even if it is manifested in a distorted and superstitious way, continues to resist the skepticism of the scientific era. Would such a persistent influence on the soul not incline us to admit—were it only as a hypothesis—that these absurd fabulations have a basis of truthful inspiration? Such inspirations, which are a product of psychic functioning, do not cease to move the soul because they help the psyche to objectify itself, to superconsciously prefigure that which it can know through inspiration, that which is of the deepest interest to it, i.e., its own functioning.

Myths are the sign that since the most primitive times human beings have asked themselves the most important question that can be, the question of life's meaning: where does it come from and where does it go? What must one do to fill as best as possible this short span of life given to each of us, and which is all that the animated being possesses essentially and should perhaps not waste? As soon as one approaches the myths, the depths of life are perceived, yet the essential problem is rejected in the name of a skepticism justified by the powerlessness of philosophy and the social sciences to give a satisfactory answer. From skepticism, we go on to indifference. By way of contrast, such a question was imperative for primitive man. Closer to nature, more exposed to unforeseeable dangers from which he had no protection, he could not disregard it. However, since he was not able to ask the essential question in a logical way, he could not give it a logical answer. Asking it, or rather living it, with the full force of his vital impulse, he answered from the depths of his soul barely detached from nature; nature itself replied from within his being.

It is difficult for us to imagine how alive the mythical images and figures were for ancient man. Not only did he owe all his cultural life to them, but the myths were the core of all the events of daily life: mores, customs, even habits and manipulations of everyday work. Thus, rather than admit the absurdity of the myths, one is tempted to suppose that they contain a more or less hidden meaning behind their fabulous facade, their symbolizations and personifications, that meaning being purely subjective and affective. In the framework of such an interpretation, the only value of myths would be a first attempt of orientation in the outer world: they would have expressed nothing but the great manifestations of Nature which serve as the framework of human life, e.g., the seasons of the year, or which are threats to it, e.g., floods, droughts, storms, etc. Such events do indeed constitute part of the hidden meaning, they belong to symbolization. But this purely external significance of symbolization could not by itself have laid the foundation for even the most primitive culture.

History shows that the cultural life of all peoples starts with the creation of myths. They are the common source of religion, art, philosophy, and science.

Dealing with the gods and their relationships with men, myths are the expression of the ancient peoples' religious sense.

As far as art is concerned, even if myths are seen as purely fantastic expressions, fabulations devoid of any deep and truthful meaning, one cannot deny their aesthetic character. Moreover, they have been at the origin of all forms of art: music, dance, theater, literature, painting, sculpture, architecture.

The present work—in order to find the basis of the "God" symbol's hidden meaning—proposes to show that myths—products of the superconscious—are not only the expression of religiosity and art, but also a philosophy and the psychological pre-science of the ancient peoples. The criterion of scientific worth is truth and its exact formulation. If science in our time is far more advanced in the precision of its formulation than the enigmatic and symbolic expression of myths, it is far from being deeper than the profound truth of myths, encompassing the meaning of life in its entirety. Such a statement will undoubtedly seem shocking in a time so proud of its discoveries. Yet, would not one attain an even higher valuation of the spirit if it could be proven that truth has been inherent in the human soul since the beginning of its existence and that only its formulation changes with the passage of time, according to the spirit's growing consciousness, expressing the essential truth in an ever more conscious, logical, and exact way. Some may find such a prospect attractive, others may be repelled: indeed, what is attractive is not always true; however, what is repulsive is not always false.

Since the symbolic terminology of myths talks about the gods and the human soul, about the relationship between the gods and the soul (reward and punishment), it is important to understand the true psychological meaning of this metaphysical and moral symbolization common to all myths. Our investigation proposes first to determine how the "divinity-spirit" (spiritualization-sublimation) symbol was created, and then to follow the historical evolution leading from animism to paganism and then to monotheism. After which, it will analyze the supreme symbol of myths: the "only God," a symbol whose significance can be grasped only through a confrontation with the other metaphysical symbol, "the immortal soul" and its responsibility (freedom). It will stress the inseparable link between metaphysical freedom, which is a symbol, and moral freedom, which, though not a symbol, is not an actual fact but rather, a goal to be achieved. Thus, the investigation will lead to the analysis of the "God-the-Son" symbol, the expression of ideal freedom, the symbol of perfect sublimation. From all these analyses will finally emerge all the aspects of the symbolic relationship between God and man, the significance of the "God, judge of man" symbol or morality, symbolically imposed by "God."

Research—which by its very nature opposes belief—does not prevent anyone from believing; but belief cannot prevent anyone from researching. For this research, belief is in itself a psychic phenomenon, therefore a psychological problem. The endeavor to find a solution to this problem must be undertaken in all objectivity; it cannot be judged except according to its scientific value.

The foundation of this research lies in the mythical creations whose crowning achievement is the Christian myth; the foundation of belief in our time is the speculative explanation of this myth. Nothing could have been more desirable than to find an agreement between psychological translation and theological explanation. Since such is not the case, it was not possible to entirely avoid polemics. But the latter was used only as a means to an end: the search for truth.

Part 1

THE HISTORY OF
THE "DIVINITY" SYMBOL

CHAPTER 1

The Source of the "Divinity" Symbol

A. MYSTERY AND APPEARANCE[1]

If, one night we were to notice the presence of two or more moons in the sky, what a panic would ensue! We would take it to be the end of life and the destruction of the world.

What could be the cause of such fear?—A breach in the reign of causality.

Nothing indeed could be more terrifying than a breakdown of the reign of causality. If nature no longer obeys the laws, natural order collapses. And with the collapse of our belief in the natural order, there goes our trust in nature. If the causes of the event are unknown, its consequences become unforeseeable; moons, stars could come down from the vault of the sky, roll down to the earth, and threaten it with destruction.

Such an event, the most frightening that could occur, seems impossible to us, precisely because we do trust the laws of nature. The sustained endeavor of the mind—scientific effort—has deeply anchored in us trust in the regularity and stability of the natural environment.

But primitive man did not have this calming trust, this understanding certainty. He did not know the true causes of events and could not foresee their possible consequences. Surrounded as he was by unexplainable phenomena, haunted by unforeseeable possibilities, he could be filled with terror by any unusual event.

Such panic and mortal fear, constantly present in primitive man, who felt helpless in the face of nature and life, was the origin of religious feeling, itself the source of the creation of myths. The endeavor to overcome primitive fear by spiritualizing it—i.e., by transforming it into an understanding of its causes—marked the origin of religious and scientific life and it determined their evolution.

---

1. What the author calls "*l'apparition*," literally: the appearance, means the appearance of the manifest—the apparent—world.

Science is a late form of this endeavor. It developed when causally explanatory thought replaced the magical and primitive conjuration of fear. Science tries to overcome the underlying fear of life by means of its transformation into exact knowledge. But however efficient scientific endeavor can be in ousting the unexplainable, science will never be able to eliminate the essential cause of religiosity; what is unexplainable in itself, i.e. the unsolvable enigma which is the existence of life itself. Science can only explain the modalities of existence and merely demonstrates the lawfulness of their modifications.

Thus, the most primitive religiosity and most evolved science have a common origin: sacred fear, and a common goal: its progressive spiritualization.

Supposing that one day science will reach its ultimate limits, that it will be able to explain all the existing modalities and all the lawful modifications of the inner and outer world, the unsolvable enigma, the mystery, will not be eliminated in the process. The metaphysical questioning, the question without an answer, will impose itself with all the increased intensity of its fear: how is it that something exists, that a world, a universe exists lawfully regulated down to the last details of its modalities and temporal modifications? That man exists, that the human mind exists, that an inner psychic life exists.

The supposedly possible outcome of science would be a return to the metaphysical fear marking the origin of human life. But this return would be free from the original naivete. Scientifically admitted and accepted, sacred fear would necessarily be transformed into love of the unfathomable mysterious depth of life. Such a spiritualization of fear, its transformation into a science of life, will undoubtedly imply the understanding that mystery is not transcendent but immanent to life: that the world and life are the manifest appearance of mystery, and that this appearance is not an illusion, precisely because it is established in mystery which, in turn, is absolutely nothing other than an emotion of fear or love, immanent to the psyche.

The supposed outcome of science is only a fantasy. The understanding of the immanence of mystery—barring all speculation about its so-called transcendence—is possible in our time provided that the sciences decide to undertake the study of all the existing manifestations of mystery: intrapsychic life and the surrounding world. Intrapsychic life can be studied only through introspection, itself the only way to note the immanence of mystery: emotion in the face of mystery and its motivating force, which is the most essential phenomenon among all the existing manifestations of mystery.

The metaphysical problem regarding the existence or non-existence of God is wrongly posed as long as the social sciences turn away from the inescapable necessity to introspectively study the inner psyche. A proof can be found in the word "metaphysics," which means not accessible to the methodology of physical science. But precisely because the essential problem wrongly called "metaphysics" is in fact of an intra-psychic nature, its genuine solution is possible. It is—we can never stress this enough—the elimination of all metaphysical speculations and their replacement by the introspective study of the inner motivations. For not only actions but also thoughts are rightly or wrongly motivated.

Since the mind is the means of fighting the underlying fear of life, it is part of its nature to confront all that is unexplained (inner motivations) and even all that is unexplainable (mystery) were it only in order to clearly define the immanent cause of the impossibility of explanation. This is the only correct way of tackling the metaphysical problem. Science is unknowingly compelled to tackle this essential problem. But it does so only implicitly. Its attitude is a negative way of answering. But the latter—understood according to its motives—is far from being a valid denial of the essential problem. Aware that this question cannot have an answer, science makes of this finding its method: it excludes the question from the field of its research. This means that it recognizes implicitly that the principle of life's existence is unexplainable and mysterious. In order to talk about this principle, one is entitled to call it mystery, *provided that the word "mystery" not be hypostatized and mistaken for the name of an actual entity existing outside of the world*. The word "mystery" simply means the limit of the human spirit's competence.

Defined in such a way, the mystery (of the existence of the world and life) is indisputable. It is beyond all discussion. Its spiritual evidence must be distinguished from the sensory evidence of the world and the sensitive evidence of life. Mystery is the spiritual evidence since it is obvious to the spirit (which itself is nothing but a mode of existence) that the mystery of existence is necessarily beyond it.

All the studies in this book follow from and lead back to this spiritual evidence, thus defined for this evidence gave birth to myths.

Primitive man fought the fear of the environment with the help of his budding intellect, but the latter was as yet only pragmatic and utilitarian (for instance, it enabled him to make weapons to defend himself). His inventive imagination was supplemented from the outset with an explaining imagination, though the latter dealt only with the essential unknown. During the pre-mythical era of animism the two functions are interrelated. Explaining imagination—while fighting fear of the essential unknown—was equally used to moderate the fear of the environment, since it was not yet sufficiently controlled by intellectual invention. Pre-mythical animism is characterized by the attempt to surmount the environmental dangers through a primitively religious and magical conjuration. The various stages of this evolution will be studied in detail later on.

The mythical era is characterized by the fact that the struggle against essential fear is more and more detached from the struggle against fear of the environment. It acquires its own particular importance. The mythical problem—or hidden meaning of the myths—is fear in the face of the essential unknown and the effort exerted to conquer it.

From the evidence of the mystery of life and death, no exact explanation can be deduced; it only brings about the deepest feeling that can animate a human being: metaphysical fear. In order to free himself from this fear threatening to paralyze life, making it mortal confusion, an unlivable state, man (insofar as he becomes intellectualized) can be prompted to expel it from his imagination. Overintellectualization will make him lose the essential evidence of the unfathomable depth of life, and this loss is the essential cause of all the unhealthy distortions of life. But human beings can overcome essential fear by sublimating it, by incorporating it into the imagination, which in primitive times was possible only through a symbolizing form of imagination.

This meaningful endeavor—the mythical endeavor—is possible in spite of the fact that mystery is unexplainable, since mystery is not just mystery; it is the mystery of existence. All existence, life included, is its manifest expression, its apparent image so that life, through the imaginative and symbolizing function of the superconscious can obtain a truthful image of mystery with the help of the modalities of existence. But such an image is only comparative; while being truthful, it is not real. It has only a symbolic significance.

The historical proof of the superconsciously objective form of imagination is provided by the fact that the mythical creations of all highly cultured peoples symbolize the diversity of the motivating relationships between man and the gods, symbols of the mysterious depth of real life. According to the imagery of the facade, myths are often very different, though their hidden meaning is always indentical. All the myths deal with mystery. The interaction of the various cultures is far from sufficient to explain this conformity.

Fear of the *unexplained environment* is accidental. Its roots are to be found in unconscious imagination. Fear of the *unexplainable mystery* concerns the essential, the ethical meaning of fleeting life. Its origin is to be found in superconscious imagination, which, through the process of spiritualization, creates the symbolic image of mystery. With respect to human feelings, such a spiritualization is an elevation, a sublimation of fear. But with regard to mystery, spiritualization itself is but a downgrading process. Symbolic imagery brings the mystery to the level of the human spirit and its vital search for an explanation. This spiritualized and sublimated fear is manifested in the worship of a mysterious "force," primitively felt as a threat going beyond any means of defense and suggesting imploration. Such a sublimated fear transformed into worship characterizes religious feeling as expressed in images. The essentially unexplainable mystery—mysterious "essence" of life, as it were—having undergone a transposition on the imaginative level and being represented in the form of a purely symbolic image, has always been called "divine."

In order to understand the mythical process in all its inescapable consequences, free from any speculative component, we have to follow its development step by step.

The essential problem when transposed on the mythical plane appears as a question which originally is not reflective but merely emotional: "Who created the world and life?" The question "Who?" already contains a personifying anthropomorphism. The answer, which is also purely emotional, can only be a magically deep suggestion since the verb "to create," which is part of the question, presupposes a creative act. To contest the value of the symbolism contained in both question and answer would mean to commit oneself to formulating a question and give an answer devoid of any anthropomorphization, which is clearly impossible. One might as well say that the question and its answer both deal with the unexplainable, thus the answer adds nothing to the question. Their common significance is: *mystery is mystery*, a self-enclosed proposition that can lead to no explanatory development. Talking about a "creator" is not an explanation, but a metaphysical speculation, unless one admits that this is an image—or more precisely a symbol—produced by a comparison with human activity, the latter being able to create a preconceived product with a given matter. Symbolic anthropomorphization being admitted, the comparative image can be developed, but it is self-evident that one should not forget that all the details of the development are themselves nothing but images.

The image of the "intentional Creator" being a symbolic personification, the myth is entitled to choose a name; in all mythologies this name is "creating divinity"' Vishnu in India, Uranus among the ancient Greeks, Yahweh for the Hebrews, etc.

One must realize that every step of the symbolic development represents a danger, not for mythical imagination but for its intellectual understanding, which will attempt to introduce a speculative element, forgetting the warning that it is dealing only with personifying images. Having taken all possible precautions, one could phrase the subject matter under study in a pseudological way: "the divinity is the cause of creation." If the term "cause" is accepted for a logical concept, the divinity itself becomes a reality. One talks in images or abstract concepts and ends up believing in their reality. In this wavering between the logical and the symbolic planes, the initial evidence is definitively lost. Error leads irreversibly to the arid realm of speculation.

In order not to confuse the term "mystery" with the "creator" image, which is only too easily hypostatized into a concept, in order not to mistake it for a concept describing a mysterious entity, in order to conceive it in its genuine meaning, mystery must not be confused with a mysterious thing or with a mysterious being. Things and beings, just as relationships between things and beings (the world and life) are modalities of existence. Mystery is neither a thing nor a being existing outside of the world and life.

The relationship between mystery and its appearance, i.e., the spatio-temporal existence of things and beings, is mysterious in itself; it is neither causal nor voluntary. As soon as the relationship ceases to be mysterious, mystery itself ceases to be mysterious: it becomes the creating-being, a reality located outside of reality, a misunderstanding, a meaningless thought. (The term "mystery" is frequently used in theology and philosophy. But in those cases, it concerns a non-mysterious mystery. Since the term is not sufficiently defined, it is easy to slip from image to logic, and one is immediately led to explain mystery with the help of logical thought.) Mystery cannot be thought; it can only be felt emotionally. The slightest effort to think the mystery leads to explaining it, i.e., to eliminating it or to hypostatizing it (to making of it a thing or a being), to dogmatizing it. Insofar as one tries to think the mystery, one destroys the feeling of its evidence. The temptation to think the mystery explains why it is difficult to feel it and to be afraid of its evidence.

In order to prevent the confusion between mystery and an object located outside of the world, it might be better to call it "X," if such a term were not too abstract. "X" means nothing to the imagination; the term "mystery" arouses fear and its vital consequence; the task of spiritualizing it into images and of sublimating fear into a trusting love. From the fearful mystery "come forth" not only the living universe, but also the meaningful direction of life. One must be able to talk about the mystery, and, in order to do so, one has to use symbolization. This is the only possible method; and it is the method of myth.

What is important to understand is that myth—according to its hidden meaning—does not contain any supernatural elements; at least no supernatural elements that would be metaphysical reality.

The evolution of mythical life, historically embodied in cultural cycles, follows the development of this central symbol whose signification is mystery and whose name is "divinity." The central symbol is finally concentrated in the ultimate symbol "only God."

Such a concentration is defined as follows: since human thought "pierces the darkness"—the unexplained and its accidental fear—the human spirit is symbolically "the light." But the human spirit is never fully objective, ideal, absolute. By its very nature, it is prone to error and beclouded by the unexplainable. The ideal would be a spirit protected from error and able to reveal the very mystery of life. It would conquer all fear. Idealized human spirit is imaginatively projected onto mystery. Since mystery is the symbolically called "divinity," supreme divinity, the only God, imagined as a spirit shedding light on mystery and as the revelation of the meaning of mystery and thus of the meaning of life, becomes symbolically "the ideal and absolute Spirit." It is symbolically called the light of life. A "personal God-Spirit" conceived as symbolism is a truth. The comparative significance of this most evolved symbol is appeasing trust, faith in the mysterious *lawfulness* covering all that exists and all that can happen to man. In this meaning, it is possible to say that the man who possesses mythical faith is afraid of nothing. Symbolization expresses this trust, this faith in the lawfulness of the world by assigning to the divinity the role of metaphysical creator, and it expresses faith in the lawfulness of life by making of the divinity the moral lawmaker. The myth expresses in this way that the existence of the world and the lawfulness of life are both rooted in mystery. Faith, which must be distinguished from beliefs, by freeing men from fear unites them essentially. Mythical symbols, by expressing the possibility of this sublime liberation, create a cultural community because they add to the limitless immensity, to mystery which is the object of faith, a matter of religiosity, images enabling men to communicate within a same belief (religion: re-ligare or reunite). Science is also based on this faith, trust in the lawfulness, in the comprehensibility of the world which constitutes the starting point of its research, which without such a trust would lose its momentum.

B. MYTHICAL FAITH AND THEOLOGICAL BELIEF

One has thus to distinguish between *faith and belief* or—which amounts to the same thing—*religiosity and religions*. Moreover, one has also to distinguish the mythical foundation of the religions or *symbolic images from their speculative and superstitious explanation.*

Faith, being sublimated fear in the face of mystery, cannot be a simple belief. As far as mystery is concerned, the question is not one of belief or disbelief, for it is evident that one does not "believe" in fear; it is an immediate emotion, and its object, though undefinable in itself, is evident to such an emotion. Nevertheless, such evidence can be lost. But this is not a lack of belief; it is an incomparably more essential loss. The evidence of mystery, the emotion of fear, can be lost in the same way a blind person can lose the sensory evidence of the world of shapes and colors. The loss of the evidence of mystery is an amputation with a vital scope; it is the loss of the vital impulse, since this impulse is nothing else than the tension between the essential fear and its demand to find its spiritualization-sublimation, which is essential desire animating every being.

On the other hand, belief does not deal with mystery as such but with the facade of myths. Belief is attached to images mistaken for realities. One can believe or not in one or another set of images. Believing in one set of images excludes belief in other images. Each cultural cycle believes in another set of images.

Belief becomes superstition when it loses its infrastructure of faith, when the images being uprooted from mystery pretend to have an unjustifiable and senseless independence.

Faith is a psychic function; beliefs are its products. The function can be strong or weak; the product can be truthful or erroneous. The function is weak if it mistakes it own product—symbolic images—for the image of a reality that would exist independently from the psychic functioning. The function is strong if it can avoid such a fundamental error.

The "divinity" symbol does not only have the meaning of "creator" but also that the "judge of man." The gods are represented as meting out rewards and punishments. Such a moral significance stems from the same root as the metaphysical meaning. If the "divinity" symbol is the product of an anthropormorphic spiritualization in which sacred fear is appeased, it goes without saying that man, insofar as he participates in the appeasing vision, is thereby rewarded; this means that he is excluded from the reward, punished, when he forgets the call to spiritualization-sublimation symbolized by "the divine commandment."

Reward and punishment, symbolically issuing from the deities are therefore—according to the hidden meaning—immanent to life. They represent the mysterious lawfulness of manifest life, the law of harmony, and the conditions for its joyful achievement, in contrast with the law of disharmony and its inner discord: the feeling of guiltiness. The multiple gods symbolize the positive qualities of man. Their suggestive image confronts man with his genuine responsibility in the face of the mystery of life and death. Emotion in the face of mystery inspires ethical courage: oblivion of one's inferior self through love of one's essential self. Since the transcendent mystery—transcendent to human reason—can in no way exist actually and personally, the relationship between mystery and man (God-the-Judge) has not actual existence either besides that of its symbolic truth, which is psychologically real. Symbolism would have no hidden and truthful significance if the transcendent image of the god-judge were not founded on the immanence of the ethical law: responsibility based on the possibility of choice between sublimation and perversion.

This choice when transposed to the mythical plan becomes the distinction between good and evil that man inflicts on himself. Within the context of the myth, man is accountable to the divinity, since his choice will depend on the strength of his vital impulse and his vision of the mystery. Sublimation is never perfect. The divinity, the image of perfect sublimation (image in which fear—or evil—is dissolved), becomes thus the ideal measure (the judge) of the degree of sublimation or perversion, on which alone depends man's worth.

Just as the collective vision creates mythical images, the superconscious vision of each individual must be able to participate in the common vision through his personal faith. However, this individual participation may have various degrees, and when the faith of individual's weakens, all their activities are influenced. Fear of life which is insufficiently spiritualized-sublimated continues to manifest itself through various forms of dispersion that are characteristic of daily life (anxiety, worries, guiltiness, hatred, etc.). This is what the myth calls "evil."

Mythical images, on which individual faith leans, help to overcome fear also in its daily and dispersed form and they even help prevent such dispersion. This is called "good."

Thus mythical faith is not only an awareness of the evidence of mystery, it is also a motivating force. All feelings are motivating forces inciting to action. The essential feeling—metaphysical fear—incites to essential action which is sublimation (character formation), the superconscious complement of spiritualization (formulation of the guiding ideas). The latter in its mythically imaginative form creates the common vision of the directive aim: the divinity image. But this image would be compelled to remain a kind of imaginative theory if it did not have a function, which is to motivate essential activity, called "sublime." The task of sublimation is to actively accomplish, according to individual strength, the directive aim of life, condensed in the superconscious vision in the image of mystery, the "divinity" symbol.

Metaphysical fear has a sublimely motivating force, since through fear before life's mysterious depth, human beings feel how fleeting all their accidental feelings and the multiple desires they generate in fact are. Moved by the essential desire to overcome fear, stimulated by the collective image of mystery (divinity, representing ideally appeased fear), the subject, moved also in his activities, finds his inspiration in the need to subordinate the multiple desires to the essential desire, to harmonize them, which cannot be done unless he avoids their imaginative exaltation.

The image of mystery—the divinity symbol—through becoming the motivating center of sublime harmonization, acquires, in addition to the "creator" metaphysical significance, all the amplitude of its moral significance. The mythical phrase "to love God" means to be magnetized by mystery, not to be oblivious to the mysterious depth of life, not to be blinded by multiple desires (by love of the world) to the extent of losing the vision of mystery's evidence.

But the "divinity" image and its motivating force could not stimulate the individual sublimation of sacred fear if the details of sublime activity were not prefigured by myth in order to impress superconscious imagination, if the effort of active sublimation demanded from each man were not developed in images, were not also transposed on this very same symbolic plane where the divinity image is set.

For mythical faith to be culturally active, a detailed and moral symbolization has to be added to metaphysical symbolization: the struggle of the heroes against the monsters (perversion).

Now a detailed knowledge of psychic activity in its sublime and perverse (meaningful and meaningless) forms that must be included in the myth on its superconsciously symbolic plane is—on the conscious level—unfeasible without introspective psychology. The latter thus becomes the principle of the mythologies' traductibility. *Spiritualization-sublimation and its reverse—psychic perversion—constitute the entire contents of psychic life, the whole of motivation-reaction, psychic functioning which a scientific psychology capable of translating myth, a psychology of motivation must study.* The detailed translation of symbolic language into psychological terminology finds that besides metaphysical symbolization (God-the-Creator), the mythologies have a symbolization endowed with an ethical scope. In psychological terms, ethical values and non-values are superconsciously and subconsciously immanent motivating intentions, based on the laws of harmony and disharmony. Were these affirmations to be proven, they would explain the historical phenomenon which is perhaps—or undoubtedly—the most surprising and the most important of human existence: *the fact that the essential basis, not only of the ancient cultures, but also of our present culture—is mythical pre-science and that its collapse is the essential cause of decadence.*

Due to the supposed conformity of the myths' ethical symbolism and of lawful psychic functioning—conformity which is affirmed by the psychology of the motivating depths—it is necessary to set aside for a while the study of the "divinity" symbol and to go into more detailed psychological considerations. The purpose is to give a glimpse of the nature of psychic lawfulness. For it is only if such a lawfulness actually exists that the superconscious imagination of the myth can foresee it intuitively and transpose it to the symbolic plane.

C. MYTHICAL PRE-SCIENCE AND PSYCHOLOGICAL SCIENCE

Myth is not looking for lawfulness in the outer world; it is concerned only with the truth of the inner world: harmonization of activity or, rather, harmonization of the intrapsychic cause of activity: desires. The lawfulness of psychic life is not—as in the case with the outer world—a real fact: it is an ideal to be achieved.

It is therefore important to determine the essential difference between the lawfulness of the physical world and that of the psychic universe. The inner world is a temporal expanse, which unlike the spatial expanse is intention, inner tension, more or less impatient expectation.[2] Experienced time is not chronologically measurable. Its duration depends on the variations of patience. In the so-called "inner" world, nothing has a spatial presence. All is flight through the dimensions of

2. The French "attente" has the same root as "tension," "intention," "extension," "attention," "retention," stressing the common feature: the inner tension of desire in its different forms.

time: past, present, future. The present itself is nothing but an unceasing flight from the past into the future. The periodical awakening of hunger and sexual desire is what impresses in the psyche the subjective feeling of duration, of expectation. The satisfaction of these desires depends on the outer world and its objects, implying the necessity to often retrain these endogenous excitations without being able to respond immediately through a reactive discharge. This forced retention, this affective tension toward the object is subjectively felt on the human level in the form of desire, the fundamental fact of psychic life. At the human level, experiential time is divided into the three dimensions: past, present, future. *Past and future exist only in the imagination.* They are manifested in the form of memory and expectation of satisfactions or dissatisfactions. Imaginatively linking past and future, human desire creates a semiconscious feeling of a time that has become a continuous flow from past to future, with an imaginative load of anxious expectation. (Mythically speaking: the temporal is the principle of disquiet.) Since past and future originally exist only in the imaginative re-presentation, the disquiet of expectation is likely to be imaginatively exalted and to worsen into anxiety and fear, often pathologically exalted in overexcited ruminations. This harmful effect of imaginative exaltation does, however, have an immanent remedy. Imagination, in its natural form (when not pathologically exalted), is capable of drawing from the past lessons projected onto the future in the form of meaningful projects, using the present to conclude with the help of past causes future effects which are foreseeable and controllable. Imagination, instead of becoming exalted, becomes foreseeing intelligence insofar as it includes in its projects the reality of environmental obstacles and the reflection on ways to overcome them patiently.

However, experience drawn from the past in order to enlighten the future is not in itself sufficient to calm the basic disquiet of temporality. The individual submits to his fate insofar as he lives his desires and their unhealthy exaltation while endeavoring to overcome the latter more or less effectively with the aid of conscious reflection. The species evolves with time. The evolving psyche adapts finally not only to the obstacles of the environment (conscious function). Intellectual foresight in its turn evolves toward clairvoyance of the spirit. Utilitarian intellect can endeavor to fulfill any kind of desire without taking into account its real value of satisfaction. In this respect, the intellect remains partially imbued with imaginative exaltation. Evolution through time, seeking means of satisfaction that are more and more effective, must necessarily succeed in creating the superior process: the healthy valuating spirit. Its valuating function lies in the evolutionary necessity to objectivize, to organize the projects of the intellect, to harmonize them (superconscious). Affective subjectivity and its disquiet impatience, are appeased, thanks this objectivization. The psyche acquires—were it only sporadically—quiet, patience, the strength to master the retrained excitations: the desires; it becomes capable of living essential satisfaction: joy, sublimated fear. This is the evolutionary phenomenon—the feature which is characteristic of experiential time can be expressed in different terms: time itself changes. At the human level, it can become more and more homogeneous, detached from affective expectation and condensed or concentrated in the present. Homogeneity of experiential time, freed from the imaginative and self-exciting flight into the past or the future, enables the mind to conceive and to live in moments of concentration an objectified and de-individualized time. Freed even from the accidental; from the conscious self, the individual absorbed in his superconscious lives for shorter or longer periods in a state of presence of mind, of presence to the spirit, a state of inspiration which is the condition for an objective search for truth. The myth follows the evolution of time, of the temporal, up to its ultimate consequence: it deals with saints, sanctity, the sanctification of the man whose experiential times becomes total concentration in the present: patience, acceptance, harmony. The saint lives, as it were, outside of the temporal, outside of expectation and therefore of vulnerability. Past and future vanish. He lives in the "eternal presence." He enters into "eternity," the symbolic dwelling of mystery.

This all too terse analysis enables us to perceive that the temporal, in its positive form which *can be defined as psychic evolution* includes all the essential phenomena of the human condition, mythically and *symbolically transcended* in the "divinity" image. (For more details, see *La Peur et l'Angoisse* (Fear and Anxiety), central phenomenon of life and its evolution.)

Linking human activity to mystery, the harmonious connection of psychic life—condition for lawfulness—can only be defined if one takes into account the essential cause of activity: motives. Motives are the most characteristic phenomena in man; they are the essential property of the human psyche.

Motives are desires which are retrained and subjected, for the purpose of a future discharge, to the superconscious valuation of their promise of satisfaction.

Superconscious valuation is just. The superconscious valuates the promise of the desires and recognizes it as valid or not according to its capability of incorporation into a harmonious connection. But superconscious justice can be overwhelmed by the false promises of imaginative exaltation. This however does not do away with justice. The latter punishes with guilty dissatisfaction the falsely valuated desire in order to obtain from the conscious its meaningful revaluation. But the conscious can rebel. Instead of revaluating the desire under the control of superconscience, it stubbornly represses it so as to escape control. The punishment worsens. The repressed desire is incorporated into the ambivalent disharmonies of the subconscious and becomes subject to pathogenic distortion which can lead to the eruption of the repressed energy in the disguise of a pathological symptom.

Superconsciously immanent justice remains. The energy which is perversely retained through repression and transformed into motives of future senseless actions is never completely absorbed in the explosion of symptoms. It remains partially hidden in the subconscious and re-emerges towards the conscious in a muddled feeling of guiltiness liable to lead to despair with respect to one's wrongs. This essential cause of despair remains, most of the time, unknown to morbid introspection and its false self-justification. Yet, the muddled feeling of guiltiness because it is semiconscious, offers to introspective elucidation a chance of succeeding. The efficacity of introspective elucidation—which has always existed as "good sense," not to be confused with "common sense"—lies in the fact that, in order to be lucid, introspection must ally itself with superconscience so as to be able to oppose the false valuations of the subconscious with the positive, joyful, and harmonizing values of the ethical superconscience (which is what mythical pre-science represents in the struggles symbolically taking place "with the help of the deities against monsters and demons"). Every man unknowingly practices at times morbid introspection and at other times elucidating introspection. It is difficult to distinguish them clearly without the help of a science of motivations and the support of a therapist armed with such a science. When employed daily to purify the deliberation, lucid introspection clears up the muddled and semiconscious feelings of guiltiness and can even cure evident psychopathological states by depriving them little by little of their food: the imaginative exaltation of desires and anxieties in daydreams, this being the first step of subconscious life (for more details, see *Psychologie de la Motivation*).

All motives can be made conscious. But psychic functioning —the energetic relationships between the processes—can be understood only if one takes into account the fact that the effort to bring motives to consciousness leads most of the time to lies aiming to hide under a sublime excuse, the perversity of the acting motive. Every psyche tends to hide, though excuses which are consciously but false, the effectively acting motivation which is subconsciously repressed.

Activities are significant only through their motives. In order to improve them, one must go back to their intrapsychic and essential cause, i.e., motives.

Activites are good or bad (capable or not of constituting a harmonious and joyful connection) insofar as their motives are right or wrong, just or perverse, i.e., justifiable or not to the spirit and its endeavor to overcome the unexplainable, which in the case of motives is the unavowable. But even the unavowable motives—unexplainable because they are painful and more or less voluntarily hidden—the more or less subconscious motives, are also linked through the contrasting analogy of ambivalences. For instance, repressed guiltiness is the counterpart of vanity. Vanity is nothing but the tendency to repress guiltiness. The greater the vanity, the more deeply the guiltiness, any guiltiness, will be repressed. Vanity is repressing, guiltiness is repressed. Both are complementary as part of a common perverse functioning, and they are disharmonious and contradictory as vitally experienced. The former is overvaluation and excessive and lying self-satisfaction; the latter corrects this by undervaluation, obsessive self-dissatisfaction. Motivating energy thus pathologically split is paralyzed in a "dead-lock"; but starting with manifest and observable vanity, the repressed counterpole remains analytically discernible while being the unexplainable psychic element in every individual which causes his suffering. To be unable to admit something is an individual fault with respect to the essential principle of life, i.e., joy, the result of harmonization. Repression, the opposite of spiritualization, is the sign of an exalted fear of truth about oneself. It is a vital anxiety[3], a fault of the individual with regard to life: a vital guilt.[4] Its other name is vanity, since vanity is nothing but the inability to recognize one's faults. All repressed motives vary between these two counterpoles: guiltiness-vanity; their formal variability remains, due to this fact, lawfully united, harmoniously coordinated through contrasting analogy. Subconscious motives, in spite of their varying multiformity, constitute a pseudoharmonious and lawful connection. However, motives are not only lawful causes. They are also directly experienced feelings, and as a felling every perverse motive is an anxiety; all these multiple anxieties wind up forming psychopathological symptoms.

Since all the subconscious affects are lawfully tied by their common guilty vanity, the subconscious as a whole remains also lawfully and dynamically linked to all the superconscious motivations; the two extraconscious processes being on the one hand principle of healthy formation, and on the other hand, principle of unhealthy distortion. This dynamic and lawful link between ethical superconscience and subconscious can be called "antithetic" in order to clearly distinguish it from the ambivalent links of the subconscious. The superconscious antithesis concerns the difference between subconscious fear of the truth about oneself and superconscious joy of self-knowledge, essential problem of life.

The subconscious is nothing but vain blinding of the superconscience.

The words "superconscious" and "subconscious" are distinguished solely through their prefixes, the former meaning "more than conscious," and the latter, "less than conscious." The subconscious law of

---

3. See note on page 15.
4. See note on page 9.

disharmony affectively experienced as anxiety is a special case of super-conscious harmony and its joy. The lawful link between the two extra-conscious processes and the conscious process lies in the dynamics of potential transformation from perverse to sublime and from sublime to perverse. Vanity has only to be grafted onto the sublime for it to be downgraded to perversity, and this indicates the curative method. For vanities have only to be dissolved (which is unfortunately not very easy) to obtain a transformation of the perverse motives into positive energy. Guiltiness, a healthy warning coming from the superconscious, is an emotion endowed with motivating force which awakens every time the conscious undertakes a project likely to disturb the joy of harmony. Through guiltiness, ethical superconscience warns the conscious whose function is wavering choice, at times right and at times vitally wrong. The conscious may hear the superconscious call and give up the proj-ect, the indicted desire. But the conscious can also respond wrongly by repressing either the guilty desire, in order to thus falsly disculpate it-self (moralism), or guiltiness itself. Repression of *guiltiness* causes banal greed, the unscrupulous discharge of perverse desire (amoralism). As to the repression of *desire*, it transforms the guilty anxiety of the super-conscience into phobic anxiety, sterile remorse which, when excessively accumulated through repeated repressions, is obsessively discharged through subconscious oneirism, either through a symbolically disguised explosion of the perverse desire or through the symbolic illogicality of purification rites.

Moralism and amoralism are false attempts at harmonization; the former through repression of the guilty disharmony; the latter, through banal false justification which can go as far as cynicism.

All the secrets of psychic functioning and all the enigmas of symbol-ization are summed up in the finding that there is a law dynamically binding—through the right or wrong choice of the conscious—the emotional motivations of the ethical superconscience to the affectively distorted motivations of the subconscious.

Since the psyche as a whole constitutes a connection which is lawfully bound by contrasting analogies and anthithetic analogies, myth was able to express symbolically the lawfulness that is both manifest and mysterious, and it should be possible by tracing the analogical links of the motives to create a psychology of motivations capable of decipher-ing mythical symbolization.

Thus all the premises of the deciphering of symbolization have been established in a brief manner which prepares for further analyses. The method is based on a clear distinction between the facade of symbolic language and its underlying psychological pre-science.

The later analyses will aim to prove in detail the psychological pre-science of the mythologies, based on symbols of primary importance: creator divinity, judge divinity, son divinity. The misunderstanding of the "divinity" symbol led to metaphysical speculations hiding the essential theme which is shared by symbolic pre-science and the science of motivations: the problem of values and their biogenetical immanence. To understand the immanence of the ethical values and of their superconsciously moving motivating force is of a fundamental importance for the psychic health of each individual and therefore for the life of all societies.

In this respect, it is of utmost importance to point out, as a last preliminary note, a fact which is most astonishing and yet remains one of the least studied: the concordance of symbolic pre-science with psychological pre-science contained in the roots of the conceptual vocabulary of all existing languages. This extremely important phenomenon is hidden by the fact that concepts, worn by usage, are now nothing but conventional cliches. As an example, it was pointed out that the terms "affectivity" and "emotivity" are confused and understood as being synonymous. It is not superfluous to return to this point. For the difference in their meanings contains the key to the science of motivations and will be of great help in expounding it. Affect as well as emotion is a motivating force. But it would be erroneous, for example, to talk about emotional blinding. The blinding of the spirit is of an affective nature and its force is subconsciously motivating. The term "affective" implicitly contains "affectation," synonymous with vanity. On the other hand, the term "emotive" clearly contains the root "motive" and implies in the forms "moved, moving" the active dynamics, the "moving" denoting the emotional *grasp* over our body, soul, and spirit. It enables us to *grasp* the essential truth since emotion is aroused by the problem of life and death, by the mystery of life and death. Only man can scatter emotion into a multitude of affects. The animal lives only emotionally because the spirit is incarnate in him in the form of instinctive foresight concerning the conditions of its survival or its death (and even the conditions of the life and death of the species). An immanent biogenetical and instinctively profound phenomenon, emotivity is in man the *animating impulse* which "dies" if poured out, because of the exaltation of the desires, into a multitude of banal affectivities, or which is strained by being morbidly exalted toward the spirit. Fear in the face of *the mystery of life and death* is sacred emotion, true religiosity. Emotivity in the face of existence's mysterious depth is an intrapsychic phenomenon. The symbol of mystery, created by man and called "God," is thus necessarily also an intrapsychic pheonomenon and in us can be nothing but a form of superconscious emotion which is sublimely motivating. Now this sublimely motivating, or harmonizing, force is precisely the ethical superconscience which creates the myths. Hence the ethical motivations are, in accordance with mythical wisdom, connected with the metaphysical "divinity" symbol.

D. ILLUSTRATION OF THE PSYCHOLOGICAL PRE-SCIENCE OF SYMBOLIC LANGUAGE

It is necessary to illustrate now through the analysis of some symbols the analogical procedure of mythical symbolism formation as well as its lawful scope.

One of the most constant symbols, if not the most constant besides the "divinity" symbol, is the serpent. It is present in the mythologies of all peoples. In all mythologies, the serpent symbolizes non-spiritualized, non-sublimated fear, exalted imagination: guilty vanity, which is the principle of evil. The link: serpent-vanity seems at first view to be only an association of preconscious imagination. In truth, such a link has a far deeper significance. The cradle of mythical cultures is the Orient, where serpents are numerous. They crawl in the dust without the possibility of elevation. Their venomous bite is lethal. They bite by surprise, leaving no possibility of escape. How could primitive man have known that these characteristics—transposed to the psychic plane—apply to vanity? Vanity is lack of sublime and spiritual elevation (affective blinding). Man is the prey of vanity and he does not foresee the danger threatening him. The venomous and painful bit of the serpent is, on the psychic plane: the sting of remorse, the torment of repressed guiltiness which is nothing else than vanity. The consequence of the "bite" of the pathologically inhibiting remorse is, symbolically speaking, "death of the soul." The primitive association makes a point by point comparison between the bite of the serpent and the nefarious consequences of vanity. In truth, the association is a superconscious analogy. In order for such an analogy to arise, the primitive psyche had to know the characteristics of vanity, and this was not possible without a superconscious pre-science of psychic life. The historical fact of the "serpent-vanity" symbolism (as of any other symbolism) demands therefore that we accept the mysterious superconscious function: intuitive vision and its symbolic expression.

In order to better illustrate the depth of mythical pre-science, we have to demonstrate the use of this analogy by mythology. It uses it as the starting point of a connection of harmoniously developed analogies which enables us to symbolically express the lawfulness of the psychic functioning.

Myth, in order to be able to represent through the "serpent" symbol all the analogies between the sublime and the perverse (that it could foresee only superconsciously) uses a device. It adds to the real serpent attributes that turn it into a fabulous being. For instance, a being which is half serpent, half man; or a human (or divine) being who can turn into a serpent; or, quite simply; the tamed serpent, the dead serpent symbolizing victory over vanity. (The device is not a contrivance but an imaginative "compression" such as is also characteristic of dreams.) Thus the serpent can become the symbol of spiritualization-sublimation. For instance: the tamed serpent becomes the attribute of Asclepius, god of health, which expresses the close link, the equivalence between sublimated vanity and psychic health. (The entire medicine of ancient peoples was originally based on the influence of the psyche over the body, an influence which is undeniable in principle though it is often superstitiously interpreted. The tamed serpent pouring its venom into the cup of salvation, symbol of sublimation, remains today the emblem of medicine.)

However, there are lawful analogies that are still far more surprising, superconsciously foreseen by mythical symbolism and expressed through the "serpent" symbol. In order to make the veracity of mythical representation tangible, it is necessary to first stress the importance of vanity in psychic life. The science of motivations finds that vanity is the distortion of the spirit; it is the spirit itself in a distorted form, it is the affective blinding of the clairvoyant function called spirit. Vanity prevents the spirit from fulfilling its essential task, i.e., to grasp the meaning of life which can be found only in the inner world. Vanity, repressing the necessity of this endeavor, prevents the spirit from carrying its research to the limits of the inner world, to the point where elucidating introspection comes up against mystery. Vanity is thus connected to mystery and the fear of mystery. It is repressed fear, perversely appeased (hence its power of seduction); it is the vital fault (vital guilt) which, due to repression, is scattered into multiple feelings of guiltiness, multiple anxieties which can often not be expressed except subconsciously, in the language of dreams, in pathological symbolism (hence its torment). Vanity—taken in its deep meaning—vanitas, vain, vacuous—is the primary cause of psychic destruction: the principle of evil.

In the biblical myth of Genesis, representing the perdition looming over human nature, the essential cause of perversion—vanity—is personified by Satan "the prince of evil," in the guise of a serpent. He is the negative form of the spirit, the fallen spirit, the "fallen angel," fallen because of his own guilty vanity: the vanity of the human spirit (the tempting demon) wanted and still wants to eliminate the supreme principle of life, i.e., sacred fear in the face of mystery. According to the myth of Genesis, the motivating force of vanity is the essential cause of all failures: the fallen spirit. Hypostatized into an idol (wanting to substitute himself for the motivating force of the superconscious), Satan is expelled from the sublime sphere. He has become the seductor of man, the subconsciously motivating force leading to oblivion of the call of the "spirit" (the essential desire) and to the exaltation of multiple and earthly desires represented by the apple, symbol of the earth. Satan-the-serpent (symbol of the vain seductibility of man, symbol of the temptation to exalt the desires) whispers to man his lying promises (symbols of the false promises of subconscious satisfaction). Having become guilty to having eaten the apple (having preferred the multiple desires to the essential desire or call of the "spirit"), the being who has become conscious, man emerged out of animality, is from now on subject to the principle of evil, subject to vanity. He is thereby exposed to inner suffering: Adam, symbol of nascent humanity is expelled from Paradise (symbolically speaking, he has lost animal innocence).

It is tempting to give here another illustration of the psychological pre-science, which mythical symbolism is.

In Greek mythology, the supreme deities are Zeus and Hera. The supreme couple symbolizes spirit and love, the ideal goals of spiritualization and sublimation. (What could have pointed out these psychological truths to the primitive people living in Greece when the myths came into being, but superconscious imagination?) The way to reach the spiritual and sublime goal is the harmonious connection of the guiding ideas, the motivating forces leading to the harmonious connection of actions. The myth expresses this psychic lawfulness through personifying it by deities who are descendants of the spirit "Zeus." The divine son of Zeus who rules over the harmony of the soul (over the harmonious connection of the motives) is Apollo. Since achievement of harmony of the soul is the condition of psychic health, Apollo is also the supreme deity of health. As long as harmony of the soul, perfect sublimation, is not achieved, the only way to come close to it is through an intuitive vision of the effort one must undertake. This intuitive vision is wisdom, the effort of spiritualization in its practical form. The myth personifies the inseparable relation between intuitive vision and harmonious achievement by a brother-sister bond. The sister of Apollo is Athena, symbol of wisdom. The condition for wisdom is a ceaseless struggle against the discord between desires. Athena symbolizes the combativity of the spirit which, through its victory, leads the way to the vision of the ideal sphere. Athena is the symbol of the intuitive vision which, when combatively carried into effect, leads to victory, of wisdom (the latter is imagined standing behind the hero in crucial moments or moments of hesitation, inspiring the right decision). Athena, inspiratrix of wisdom, symbol of the intuitive vision leading to the combat for harmony, symbol of spiritual and sublime intuition, was born, springing arms and all out of the head of Zeus, the spirit. It would undoubtedly be difficult to find a better symbolic definition of intuition.

E. THE MYTHICAL ERA AND THE HISTORY OF THE LIFE OF CULTURES

These few examples enable us to perceive the nature of the mythical vision and of its importance in the general history of human life. The myth is an inner psychology expressed through symbolic terminology. Mysterious lawfulness, the principle of pre-human and human existence, is represented by the supreme divinity. It is important to know that the essential truth is not only to be found in monotheism but is already present in polytheism. The ethical principle, the impulse towards harmonization imposed by the superconscious spirit, is symbolized by the "son of the supreme divinity." In Greek mythology, his name is Apollo. The disharmony of desires, their imaginative exaltation, is represented by the lawful principle of evil, in Greek mythology by Hades, brother of Zeus. Their kinship represents the two aspects of the ethical principle, the superconscious law of harmony and the subconscious law of disharmony. Each mythical symbol represents an aspect of the motivating functioning of the psyche. It is thus conceivable that such a symbolic pre-science—the superconscious vision of the myths—was able to create and sustain cultural eras and nothing else could have done it.

As long as successive generations superconsciously understood the symbolic truth, individuals guided by the vision, by the common faith in the enigmatic truth hidden behind the images (guided by the sublime motives derived from them, by right value judgments determining activity) were able to constitute a cultural community which evolved toward maturity. It is only when the symbols were mistaken for plain realities that the culture was condemned to decline. However, it must be realized that at the origin of every culture the sublime and the perverse were present: sublime imagination creating and understanding myths and perverse imagination turning them into superstition. Thus every culture, precisely because its values are only formulated symbolically, carries in itself from the outset the seed of its decline, and that seed will fatally bear fruit. From the outset, faith is love of mystery, superconsciously dreamed and analogically perceived through symbols and images. It is an active love preferring joy, harmony of motives and actions, to imaginative exaltation, to pleasures. Superstition is defined by exalted love of images. Primitive man already created not only verbal images, but figures, statues. He implored the statue to protect him against fear, against essential disorientation, and he brought his offerings, symbols of his intention to sacrifice earthly gifts, desires attached to earthly goods. Imploration and sacrifice are thus imbued with symbolic meaning, as long as the statue retains its symbolic significance. But there is a tremendous risk that the significance be inverted, that the offering be understood only in the form of trade, of buying grace; that prayer—addressed to a statue stripped of its mysterious significance—ask for nothing other than protection against the vicissitudes of life and that the requested benefits be only pleasures. Since the vicissitudes of life alternate with the pleasures, it is always possible to believe that the prayer was heard. Belief becomes blind, attaches itself to the statue, the image, and turns it into an idol.

The collapse of faith leads to the collapse of meaningful activity. Activities lose themselves in multiple and senseless, inverted and perverted directions. Erroneous ideals are formed. Ideologies clash and become heated to the point of fanaticism. Falsely motivated and disoriented activities mutually inhibit and exalt each other. The primitive and salutary sacred fear degenerates into panic. The confusion of disoriented life dislocates the life of societies and the integrity of individuals. Spiritual disorientation goes with ethical disorientation and causes the collapse of values. Confusion and its resulting panic are more or less felt by all the members of society, giving them the feeling of having missed the meaning of life, which is a characteristic of declining epochs. Confusion splits up into multiple anxieties and countless worries which are but the negative side of exalted desires whose affectivities, in blinding the spirit, are degraded into inhibiting anxieties. Such an inescapable threat of falling back into a pathological aggravated fear, into panic-stricken disorientation, is the living and painfully experienced proof of the immutable truth. Values and non-values—possibilities of harmony and of disharmony—rule over everything that exists, independently of the human spirit. But the function of the spirit is to discover them. The task of the spirit is to formulate and reformulate them in more and more precise ways until reaching the understanding of their superconsciously and subconsciously immanent lawfulness. Such a lawfulness is not theoretical by any means: it rules over the destiny of every man even to the least details of his daily life. The details depend essentially on the inner motivation of the individual, prefigured in ancient times by mythological symbolization. Without this, human life, from the start of its biogenetical emergence, would have definitely collapsed into fear of the unexplainable and fear of the unexplained environment. Nowadays, fear of the environment is above all fear of the unexplained causes of the disorders of social life and its subconsciously motivated inter-reactions. The essential cause of social disorder is the loss of sacred fear: the despair of a life which—through derision—has lost its meaning and its value.

The overintellectualized man of our time tends to ignore the superconscious foundation of life. Vacillating between blind belief and intellectual reasoning, he has unretrievably lost the depth of mythical faith. He will not be able to find anew the depth of mythical emotion except by deepening the rationalization of the symbols. Only a complete rationalization of the symbolizing pre-science—an understanding of symbolism—will be able to bring him back to the true meaning of faith: spiritualization of fear in the face of the mystery of life and death.

Reason is not intellect.

Rationalization is not the same as intellectualism, and the latter alone is totally incapable of envisioning mystery and understanding faith. True rationalization, on the contrary, has an analogous parallel-ism with faith. While the purpose of faith is the sublimation of fear, the purpose of reason is its spiritualization. The spiritualization of reason-ing aims to attain a reasoning capable of grasping the meaning of life, no longer needing to dream about it in a primitive and symbolic way. Rationalism is scientific trust in the strength of human reason and its ability to eliminate progressively all that is unknown and the attendant fear insofar as it comes from the outer world (the unexplained) and the inner world (the inextricated). Its strength lies in the trust that reason is, in principle, capable of explicating all the modalities of existence: in-ner life and outer world. Its lucidity includes the understanding that there is a limit to reason. But this limit is not "God," this limit is mys-tery. God is the symbol of mystery and the supreme task of reason is precisely to understand the significance of this symbol which is itself nothing more than a modality of the inner world. True rationalism will fight any false metaphysics, any explanatory and dogmatizing meta-physics. It does not deny mystery and does not explain it. But it denies an actual God by explaining the God-symbol. It fights dead belief, in order to sustain living faith. It leaves room for its cultural complement, i.e., true religiosity. On the other hand, intellectual doubt is only the ambivalent complement of false religiosity. In wanting to avoid dogma-tizing metaphysics, it winds up falling back into it; for it leads to a spec-ulative affirmation about mystery: the affirmation of its non-existence. It asserts that the existence of life is not a mystery. Or, at least—since such an affirmation is too senseless—it pretends that the most frighten-ing evidence of life—the mystery of its existence and of its lawfulness—is of no importance in life. Which is just as senseless.

The mystery of existence and its fear which has to be spiritualized are revealed only to human beings, craving a surety which cannot be attained but by means of explanation. But the totality of life is imbued with mystery and its fear, and animal life itself is compelled to over-come fear and suffering, through a kind of spiritualization: instinct. The vehicle of all evolution is suffering, which can be overcome only through adjustment to the demands of life. Satisfactory adjustment (the aptitude to live) is the most elementary biological phenomenon which is common to animal and human life. It is the bridge which, by the way of evolution, links human life to animal life (we shall see later on what capital importance mythical symbolization gives to this evolu-tionary link). The instinctive adjustment of the animal can be defined as a foreshadowing of the spirit, since it implies a "finality" which is still unconscious but already vitally meaningful. Since it is an uncon-scious foreshadowing of the spirit, the preconscious adjustment makes possible to overcome by way of evolution the dangers of life which, without it, would be lethal. It leads toward intellectual and conscious life, since the intellectual forms of the spirit also have the task of over-

coming fear in the face of vital dangers which without such an understanding adjustment might become lethal. The most evolved function
of the psyche—spiritualization of metaphysical fear, the creation of the
"divinity" symbol—is a form of superconscious adjustment not only to
the accidents but to the meaning of life.

Besides the metaphysical symbolism regarding the mystery of creation, the theme of all the myths is the biogenetical situation of human
beings in life, and this situation is determined by the fact that conscious
beings, men, are suspended between unconscious and superconscious
life. They started from unconscious life and must evolve toward an ever
more lucid, conscious and superconscious life.

Man's biogenetical situation in life can be defined as follows: the distinction between animal and human life, i.e., the intellect, is an intermediary form between an animal's means or orientation (instinct) and
man's most evolved means of orientation, the superconscious spirit
which must itself become conscious. Man has lost instinctive surety
(hence his fear) and must seek spiritual certainty, which can be found
only in lawful truth. Through instinct animals are adjusted to the inescapable demands of their environment; through intellect men alter
their environment, they adjust it to their needs. This entails the danger
of exalting their needs, a nefarious consequence of intellectualization.
Hence man must, with the help of his spirit, adjust his needs, not only
to the environmental accidents, but to the mysterious lawfulness, the
essence of life, the meaning of life.

Animals, unlike men who have become conscious, are biologically incorporated in the meaning of life. They rest in it. Guided by instinct,
they do not have to choose; they cannot stray. Animals take part imper-
turbably in the life of the spirit, even though the latter is only unconsciously expressed in them through the capacity for instinctive adjustment (evolutionary drive) and through all their bodily organization.
Unlike animals, man can betray the spirit. The intellect contains the
nefarious temptation to abandon the meaningful direction of life, to go
counter to it, to ignore the "call" of the "spirit." Man must choose between "spirit" and earth, between essential desire and multiple desires,
between essence and appearance. This is his dangerous dignity: his
responsibility.

Myths express symbolically the essential history of the human being,
of the human species, of mankind: his departure from instinctive rest
in the preconscious spirit of animality (paradise) and his ideal goal: superconscious reunion with the spirit inherent in life, with the lawful
and mysteriously evident meaning of life: joy, the opposite of fear
(heaven). The myths also narrate how all the sufferings stem from fear
(symbolically speaking, the punishment inflicted by "the spirit"), due to
confusion, the errors made by man and mankind during the evolutionary voyage of life, through time, through the temporal.

But besides this moral significance which is biologically founded, myths have a metaphysical significance. There are two manifestations of the world and life which can awake—at least fleetingly—in every man, even in the most spiritually blinded man, the awareness of the evidence of mystery, the metaphysical fear: a starry sky and death. There is no one who (in spite of immediate concerns and conventional securities) has not been aroused, however vaguely, by the sight of the sky and by death, to mythical fear, fear which is the source of the metaphysical questions concerning the creating principle and the animating principle: the responsibility of the animated being toward the creating principle.

After having studied the immanent origin of the "divinity" symbol, which is inseparable from the origin of mythical symbolization as a whole after having established the principle, indeed the necessity, of the translatability of the myths grounded in the human mind and its functioning, after having proven that mythical symbolization hides a definable meaning, we have to study the historical evolution of the central "God" symbol.

This historical part of the present book will involve us with ethnology and sociology. The latter disciplines have accumulated a wealth of details about the life of the peoples who created the myths. They also attempted to fit the details into frameworks. In order not to get lost in a maze of details, it is necessary to avoid any polemic regarding these theories; not that one can ignore them or underestimate their importance, but for reasons connected with the theme of this work and its methodology.

The theme is not basically historical but psychological. The methodology is not to compare historical details (neither is it a critique of other authors' comparisons).

For the psychology of motivating inner life, which is the key to symbolism, there is only one principle which could make it possible to lawfully arrange the details of life in general and also the details of the life of the tribes and peoples who created the significant images culminating in the "divinity" symbol. This arranging principle is fear in the face of mystery. We have to demonstrate that the historical evolution of mankind and its past stages are essentially characterized by the production of a symbolization, becoming more and more lucid, concerning the evident mystery of life which is imaginatively represented by the divinity. Evolution leads from animism and its multiple "spirits" to the multiple deities of the pagan myths and finally to the conception of the "only God," "spirit" of life symbol.

CHAPTER 2

The Evolution of the "God" Symbol

A. THE PRE-MYTHICAL PERIOD: ANIMISM

A perfect spiritualization of fear could not become possible before the most evolved period of the mythical era. At the beginning fear was not yet sublimated-spiritualized; it was only conjured away. This conjuration of fear is the characteristic of pre-mythical and magical animism.

Animism can be considered as a theoretical vision (albeit entirely based on the feeling of fear), and magic is a practical application of this vision. What animism aims at is the cause of events, i.e., their explainability. And what necessarily brings about even the most primitive causal vision, in which the causes are imagined as secret intentions—is the mysterious organization of the world and its stability manifested even through the temporal changes in objects and situations, a phenomenon we call causality.

Animal life is already based on the causal stability of the world and of its changes (events). The animal acts as if it knew causality. For instance, when it leaves its lair, it is sure to find the same forest, unchanged, with all its familiar details, and when it becomes aware of a change—for example, when it smells a certain odor—it becomes frightened or aggressive, it looks unconsciously for the cause of such a change.

Insofar as concerns the search for causes, primitive man is unlike the animal owing to the fact that he no longer lives from excitation to excitation; he is aware that every new excitation is received by one same being, the fundamentally unchangeable being he is, and that the reactions come from the same being, yet remaining as though linked in him through memory.

Excitation and reaction—the contents of subjective life—become the prototype of the explanation of causes and effects which are objectively perceived. Primitive man believes that the objects react (produce effects) because they are excited. Perceived causes and effects are interpreted as if they were intentional excitations and reactions. Primitive man projects his own motivating intentions not only onto animals but also onto inert objects. Individually motivated intention is the main difference between the human being and the animal. Through this intention, excitations and reactions which are unconscious and instinctive in animals (experienced in the global form of an inescapable situation) are in man linked in a new way which is more refined and less inescapably compact: they are reflected in the psyche. Man is not only preconsciously animated as is the animal (animal = animated being), *man is aware of being animated*. This awareness of animation is the decisive step marking the evolutionary separation between human life and animal life. However vague the essential awareness of animation was at the origin of human life, primitive man already reflected about his inner intentions, he thought them over, he deliberated in his mind before acting. The evolution of thinking beings will consist in thinking with increased clarity about the intentions which animate man half-consciously, so that the motivating intentions become more and more conscious. However, primitive man is already a half-conscious being: he has become an "I". He opposes this "I" to the world and its excitations; he finds himself in opposition to the world and opposes his reactions to the world. Thanks to his motivating intentions, he can produce changes in the world, and it is not so surprising that primitive man tends to think that any modification of the world, even an external one, works through intentions. Intentions are what animate him, and he believes that everything is—like him—animated with good or bad intentions.

The animal can only submit to the variations of the environment; the most primitive man begins to look more or less consciously for causes in order to foresee causal changes and to be able to direct them to his advantage. He has a vague and subjective idea of causality but not of lawfulness (at least not mechanical lawfulness). Since for him all cause is intentional, everything becomes for him a whim. The intentions that surround him enigmatically (the "spirits") can take hold of and animate any object (the objects which above all seem animated to him are those endowed with unexplainable physical motions: lightning, clouds, wind, running water, etc.). The intentions that the primitive suspects everywhere—since they can take hold of any object—can also use him, his own body; he is never completely confident of being himself. (This is the first root of his fear; but it is not the deepest one. It is only an individual and effective fear, though it will bring about the deep emotional fear, the metaphysical fear.) *From affective fear magic will arise, and from metaphysical fear religion will arise*. Since the two forms of fear (in the face of the environment and in the face of mystery) cannot be separated, magic and religiosity are linked together, and religious belief in its superstitious and culturally regressive form will be, throughout the course of evolution, the most imbued with magical elements. The reason for this—according to what has just been said—is that primitive man did not perceive physical lawfulness and believed only in capricious intentions. Modern man conceives physical lawfulness; but the lawfulness of intentions, of motives, escapes him. He projects intentionality not onto the objects of the environment but onto the beyond and remains inclined to believe in a supreme intention, somewhat capricious, endowed with feelings of approval and disapproval, which would oversee human behavior, meting out rewards and punishments. Or else, he tends to believe—which is another superstition—in the absence of any lawful meaning in life, and thus of any responsibility. In the latter case, the individual hypostatizes consciously and in a banal way—and no longer unconsciously and magically as was the case with primitive man—his own disoriented intentions: his own whims.

Since primitive man is never completely confident of being himself, since he is more or less constantly afraid that alien intentions will take over his body and his soul, nothing matters more to him than to subdue to his own purposes the alien intentions which, he believes, inhabit the world. Because, due to his underlying fear, his confused imagination, he is very highly suggestible even in his deepest intentions, he believes that "the intentions" surrounding him—the objective causes and effects—are also suggestible and can be influenced. He attempts to subjugate them through magical rites and ceremonies.

For primitive man's attempts at explanation, the intentions he believes are inhabiting the world become good and bad "spirits," a result of the projection of his own spirit, its strength and its weakness, onto objects and beings. He strives to influence the spirits he has thus projected, through incantations and threats, in order to stimulate his own strength and appease his fear. This magical procedure achieves precisely the desired result. Rituals and ceremonies exert—metaphorically speaking—an influence on the good or bad spirits. Since all these spirits are only the projections of his own psyche, primitive man, exalting himself through rituals, incites his own spirit to believe so firmly in the power and the reality of his projections that the influence, thanks to his suggestibility, will soon become manifest. In this way, for instance, sicknesses may occur or disappear as if they had been sent or cured by good or bad spirits (in the same way, hysterical people can imagine and suggest to themselves actual illnesses, since psychopathological phenomena are in certain respects a regression toward primitive life). Primitive man's explanation of the influence which has become a psychic reality remains an imaginative one. But this imaginative explanation is based on a true psychic fact: suggestibility. The explanation is not objectively true, but it is subjectively veracious. Like any veracious explanation, it contributes to overcoming fear. It cannot, by its very nature, objectify and sublimate fear, but it conjures it away, and so finally takes on a real value: a power of transformation over the motivating constellation of the psyche. This is precisely the definition of imaginative, imagic or magic power. Such a culture, primitive though it may be, is therefore coherent, stabilized, closed in itself.

Animism is a first attempt to overcome fear through understanding, and the latter, although illogical and imaginative, is already psychologically veracious because it has an effective influence upon the inner motivations.

In animism and magic there is an element of utilitarian explanation, primitively conscious (the search for causes) merging with an element of superconscious explanation (the struggle against fear).

One can never stress enough the necessary distinction between utilitarian intellect and spirit, which is the principle of culture, the difference between the conscious and the superconscious functions. The first cultural manifestation of human beings—animism—cannot be understood in its true significance without such a distinction. If life were progressing only through a successive evolution from unconscious to conscious, with no ethical superconscience, the first man would have only been a superior type of monkey, better adjusted to the environment than the other primates. Neither the erect posture nor the use of the hand and of tools—signs of a budding utilitarian intellect—would definitely distinguish him from animality. The Neanderthal man is not yet a genuine man, even though he is an ancestor of man. The first man appears during the era of the reindeer (Magdalenians). What defines him as a man is not the emergence of the conscious but the dawning of conscience: the superconscious process, an adjustment not only to the environment but to the meaning of life: the vision of a universe of the spirit (even though such a vision is as yet nothing but that of a world inhabited by spirits, the animist vision and its complement, magical technique). *Only with superconscious vision, with the vision of a meaning to life, with the dawning of conscience (thus of guiltiness) will the naiveté of the animal be transformed into responsibility and will there emerge a being who is superconsciously aware of his responsibility in the face of life's meaning: the human being.*

To create any animal species the evolutionary tendency does undoubtedly make use of mutation, but the mutation through which superconscious life emerges out of the evolutionary tendency has a unique importance which can be compared only to that which separates animal and vegetal life. These two decisive mutations open deep gaps between the vital manifestations, though it remains true that successive evolution is the bridge uniting them all. Animal life comes out of vegetal life through the necessity to adjust to the circumstances of the environment by locomotion, and locomotion with its correlate—perception at a distance—prepares the evolution toward aperception, the characteristic of conscious life. The conscious being emerges from animality through the necessity to adjust no longer only to circumstances but to the meaning of life. The evolutionary bridge unites vegetable and animal life up to the thinking animal. Thus there are forms of primitive life which barely allow us—through a mere morphological distinction—to know whether we are in the presence of a vegetable or an animal; in the same way the evolutionary bridge unites human and animal life and there are forms of superior life that make it difficult to say through mere morphological distinction (fossil skulls) whether we are in the presence of man or beast. (The Neanderthal man is no longer an animal, but he is not yet a man.)

The decisive mutation from animal to man could not have been caused by the utilitarian element of conscious life—the progress of instrumental technology—but only by the explosion, brought about by conscious life, of the metaphysical problem: *the concept of death inseparably linked to the mystery of life.* Besides the objects surrounding primitive man which can become magically frightening, death, the inexhaustible source of sacred fear, already opens to magic imagination a metaphysical realm. As soon as life starts to be reflected in the now conscious psyche, the limit of life, i.e., death, becomes conscious and foreseeable. The primitive psyche is so deeply frightened in the face of the mystery of life because the mystery of animation inescapably includes the mystery of death. Foreseeing death compels the being that has become conscious to become aware of the depth-height of life and of its mystery. Only this extraordinary event, namely, the irruption of death into conscious life, was able to bring about such total upheaval, the most decisive of mutations: the need of orientation toward the meaning of life.

Any type of fear, even fear of environmental accidents, comes from emotion in the face of lethal danger. Its sudden inrush can—already at the animal level—cause panic and thereby loss of the means of defense. The metaphysical fear of man is no longer brought about by environmental accidents but by the permanent lethal danger, mysteriously inherent in life. Metaphysical fear is an emotional fright through which life that has become conscious is likely to lose the benefits of evolution and which can paralyze the adaptive defense defined by the utilitarian means of the intellect. Mutation from conscious to conscience is the evolutionary answer to this danger, which occurs at the most decisive moment of evolution. *The mutation from conscious to conscience creates man,* a being capable not only of feeling sacred fear, but of vanquishing it through spiritualization-sublimation, the first historical manifestation of the latter being animism, the most primitive form of religiosity.

Animism projects animation—its only means of explanation—not only into the actual environment but into the non-existence that follows death. In accordance with the procedure of all magical explanations, even a dead man remains actually animated. This magical and animistic compression dealing with the mystery of life and death—the central problem of religiosity—is the most difficult to uproot from the human psyche. It remains the danger of dogmatic interpretation of all the evolved religions, even though the latter are based on the pure symbolic expression of the myths, which, according to its hidden meaning, was able to go beyond magical realism.

In animism, the dead continue to live bodily. They lead, outside of the world, a life of shadows. They can come back and haunt the living as ghosts. They are intentional spirits living in the other world, who can become incarnate and come back to earth in order to fulfill their intentions, whether benevolent or malevolent. In order to insure for themselves the benevolence of the dead, the living must remain in sympathetic contact with the dead ancestors, they must go on feeding them, they must placate them with sacrifices. It has been historically proven that the magical expression of the mystery of death, i.e., *ancestor worship*, is present without any exception among the most primitive peoples; it is the origin of religions. It cannot be absent from any people's background, no matter how primitive they are, because it is the crystallizing core of social and cultural life. The men of the hordes and primitive tribes are essentially distinguished from animals by their fear in the face of the mystery of life and death. Already in the prehistorical and premythical era of animism, fear of death was the origin of religious beliefs, and these beliefs were inseparably linked to the ethical imperative.

The first image of a divinity was that of the father-ancestor deified after his death. In animistic belief, the ancestors—and especially the patriarchs of the tribes (whose members were all linked by kinship)—went on after their death to live in body and spirit in another world from which they intentionally kept watch over their children, the members of the tribe. The deified and immortalized father-ancestor represented the personification of the ethical ideal. The image of the dead ancestor endowed with all the virtues (moral strength) survived in the memory of every member of the tribe and thus exerted on the life of everyone (recognized as being fleeting) a suggestive influence that was superconsciously motivating. The members of the tribe, united in a common belief, had to be worthy of the deified ancestors in order to themselves become, after death, admissible to the celestial abode. Now the superconsciously motivating ethical imperative linked to the image of the deified father-ancestor had, for the primitive man of the animistic era, a very precise significance.

Animism is the belief in good and evil intentions scattered throughout nature and finally projected onto the supernatural sphere of an afterlife. The animating intentions were considered good or evil depending on their favorable or unfavorable effect on the existence of the tribe that was surrounded by lethal threats frequently demanding the sacrifice of life in fights with enemy tribes and against monstrously dangerous animals—for instance, the bisons that the tribe had to hunt to obtain its daily food. The ancestor was deified because he had had the courage to die in the body rather than in the soul. Flight in combat—and even the slightest sign of cowardice—was considered as proof of secretly evil intentions leading one to prefer the pleasures of bodily life to the survival of "the immortal soul." Legend relates the deeds of the fabulously idealized ancestors. From generation to generation, the sons had to obey the will of the ancestors, told and finally hypostatized by the legends, so that they in turn could enter after their death into the legend of immortality.

The animistic cult of the deified ancestors is the foundation of religiosity. During the mythical era the deified ancestor-father of animism will become the Spirit-father, God-the-Father, and all human beings are his children, worthy or unworthy of him depending on the motivating intentions which animate them. The fabulous legends of animism are foreshadowing the mythical fables. During the mythical era, the main stress is no longer on the physical courage which was, however, already founded on ethical courage during the animistic era. This underlying ethical courage, the intrapsychic struggle against subconscious motivations opposed to superconscious intentions (symbolized by the deities), will during the mythical era become the underlying meaning which will then be not only legendary but symbolically veracious. The themes of all peoples' mythologies are the conflicts of inner motivations, symbolically represented by the facade of heroic struggles.

In this respect, it will be highly informative to stress that the central theme of "life and death of the animating impulse" such as it existed in the framework of animism at the beginning of mankind also remains the symbolic theme of the biblical myth of the evolutionary genesis of the thinking being, a myth belonging to the late period of monotheism, the acme of symbolic thought.

The biblical myth symbolizes the theme of "life and death of the animating impulse" with the image of a Father-God who reveals himself to Adam by indicating—symbol of human superconscience—the danger to be avoided. Adam, the first man, still living in the Paradise of animal innocence though already endowed with foreseeing intelligence and thus exposed to responsible choice, had to take care not to eat "from the fruit of the tree of knowledge." The "forbidden fruit" symbolizes the nefarious consequence of conscious life which tends to forget the spirit because of an excessive love for "the fruits of the earth:" the imaginative exaltation of earthly desires, the danger of intellectualization. Adam, symbol of nascent mankind, had to choose between the spirit and the earth. He chose the earth, the earthly desires represented by the apple. Mankind will always tend to prefer the fulfillment of earthly desires to the call of the superconscious spirit, a tendency called by the myth "the original sin of human nature." Now this sin, being hereditary because transmitted from generation to generation (the sin against the superconscious spirit), is psychologically speaking "the banalization[1] of the human spirit" which—mythologically speaking—is "the death of the superconsciously animating impulse" (death of the soul). This is the central theme of all mythologies, and also the New Testament: from this banal fall, man should rise. He should rise, straighten up, which is symbolically speaking "the resurrection" of the vital impulse. From the "death of the animating impulse," man should be reborn during life and not after death. He should be reborn from the adamic temptation.

The purpose of deciphering symbolization is to eliminate all metaphysical speculation. Bodily death belongs to the sphere of unfathomable mystery as much for symbolic thought as for conceptual thought, be it logical or analogical. The "soul" symbol is the mythical personification of the animating impulse. Belief in the immortality of the soul has the same scope as the animistic legend dealing with life after the death of the body. All these preliminary findings call for a more detailed explanation which will be the theme of the second part of this book. On the other hand, it is important to stress immediately that the capital error of dogmatic exegesis is based on a confusion between the "soul mystery" and the "life and death of the animating impulse" a symbol which—like all mythical symbols—belongs to the realm of inner motivation and to the biogenesis of the human psyche. This fact is clearly indicated in the myth of biogenesis (the story of Adam), which shows just as clearly that the evolutionary genesis of man does not in the first place concern the evolution of somatic morphology but above all the evolutionary genesis of the inner motivating functioning of the psyche.

From the point of view of the evolutionary mutation of the thinking species, the adamic fall is the condition for elevation. The fall proves that intellectualization is insufficiently adaptive and that spiritualization is needed, as the only way to overcome exalted suffering and its fear. Conscious intellect, which is biologically insufficient (or—which means the same—spiritually guilty) demands the full development of the sublime process: of the ethical conscience and of its desire to be fulfilled (essential desire). Opposed to the exalted and multiple desires, only the essential desire can define the meaning of life: immanent morality which is nothing other than the—biologically founded—effort of this essential fulfillment, the harmonization of desires. The mythical punishment (eviction from the paradisiac rest) symbolizes a biological fact: the emergence of the conscious being, subconsciously tempted and superconsciously called to evolve toward the mastery of desire.

---

1. Diel diagnoses banalization—a state generally considered as normal—as a form of mental illness never before diagnosed. Banalization attributes an excessive importance to material and sexual desires, which are considered as the sole meaning of life.

Banalization is the ambivalent counterpart to the neurotic forms of mental illness characterized by the convulsion of spiritual desires and the inhibition of material and sexual desires.

(The specific difficulty of this book resides in the necessity of using the language of error in order to fight against error. Symbols such as "God," "Paradise," "original sin" have a deep significance. But usage, mistaking symbols for realities, has given to these terms an erroneous meaning which has perdured and which threatens to invade the very effort of correction and thus perturb it. Since it is impossible to guard against this danger of confusion by introducing a new terminology, it will be unavoidable to warn against it again and again, even at the risk of repetition.)

Already in animism, the forerunner of the mythical era, the *bio-psychic foundation* characterizing mythical symbolism—the essentially evolutionary and mutational relationship between man and animal—has a fundamental importance.

Primitive man does not yet distinguish himself clearly from the animals. Animals are—biologically speaking—the ancestors of man (totemism). The animistic conception reflects this truth that the human being is the evolved descendant of the animals, but that he has lost the instinctive surety, the instinctive rest in the meaning of life (paradise) and is exposed to fear. the animal ancestor becomes the magical semblance of the divine, i.e., the contrary of fear, the magical sign of self-satisfying life. Magical and totemistic deification of the animal ancestor (culture of the hunters) will finally be replaced by the magical deification of the man ancestor, by the cult of the dead (culture of the shepherds) and then evolve during the mythical era toward the symbolical deification of man, the fighting hero (culture of the farmers). The ideal, becoming more and more precise, is sought no longer in the preconscious past of evolution but in the superconscious future. Since man has become a reasoning being, he has to become a reasonable one. Having lost unconscious surety, the conscious being is fated to disquiet. This is at the same time a sentence and a privilege. He has been expelled from paradise, but called by the spirit; he must seek the reasons, the causes of phenomena and events. Since the possibility of finding a link between causes and effects is now available to the reasoning being, he can live in truth which sustains joy. But causes are manifold and difficult to discern; they are often only suppositions which open the way to error, a source of fear. Primitive man, whose reasoning is still weak, is afraid of the dangers entailed in his vocation, of the difficulty in opening a path in this new world of the spirit which has been given to him, in the world of causes and effects. Because of his fear, the world of the spirit seems to him to be magically animated and threatening; he mistakes acting causes for spirits. During the very first stages of animism, when society barely constituted, is still limited to isolated families, primitive man shows an attitude which indicates his desire to seek refuge in the state of instinctive surety out of which he has been expelled. Not only does he idealize and deify the animal, he identifies himself with the deified animal, he mimics it, believing that through magical sympathy he will acquire, recover the serene strength of the instinctive spirit animating the animal. Mimetic magic comes before ritual magic.

However, apart from the peace and encouragement brought about through suggestion by even this most primitive form of magic, it remains inoperative. The animal, though deified by the imagination, is in fact often fatally dangerous; it is itself a source of fear. The regressive identification with the deified animal is only a pre-religiosity. It can help in checking sacred fear, but it cannot protect against fear of the environment, which, even though it is less deep, remains all the more close and pressing. It is true that primitive man defends himself against this too immediately real danger with the achievements of his budding intellect, which teaches him means of attack and defense. But metaphysical fear, fear in the face of death, remains linked by association with the actually dangerous animal and compels him to resort to a new form of magical defense. He fights against this danger through rituals of exorcism or through taboos forbidding him, for instance, to touch the magically frightening object, to kill the sacred animal, or to touch the fatally dangerous animal with weapons that have not been magically consecrated. However, the taboos often deal less with actual dangers which can be more or less observed and foreseen than with imaginatively exalted dangers. Taboos by association or transference can be projected onto any kind of object, within any type of situation, which in their turn, become frightening. The most innocuous objects, the most natural situations soon become taboo, a sign of the confusion in which man does not know where is the danger that he feels is constantly threatening him. The danger becomes profuse and ubiquitous. Fear is no longer inspired by the aspect of objects but by the hidden and invisible quality, the magical power projected onto objects, situations, men. The natural complexities of life—being conjured away only in the imagination—are made even worse by superstitious complications. For instance, certain individuals can be declared untouchable—actually or sexually—if the taboo is grafted on an imaginary difference of a totemistic nature. The taboo itself, through the fear of transgression it inspires, becomes a source of superstitious fear harmful to life in its most mundane aspects.

Animistic culture, no matter how self-sufficient and coherent it is, falls into decadence under the accumulation of superstitions and shows itself incapable of arresting fear. It must surpass itself and can do so only through the evolution of its fundamental principle: the concept of multiple "spirits" and their deification.

Magical realism must evolve toward mythical symbolism. Animism would be condemned to lose itself in a ritualistic technique which—to the extent that magical faith is weakened by excesses and abuses—

would not even be subjectively motivating, if animistic belief had not explained the world through the principles of life, the essential found in every man: the mysterious principle of animation. Thus even this most primitive explanation contains the original principle of an analogical and metaphorical truth which will become the starting point of mythical symbolization. In order to understand how myth was created, it is absolutely necessary to study primitive society characterized by animism and magic.

"Created" by metaphysical fear, human life develops on three planes which must be distinguished: individual, social, and cultural planes.

These planes overlap, since society is a complex of individuals and their traditions, and culture—orientation toward the meaning of life—is the essential condition for individuals to be united within a society. (A common source of error stems from the fact that the term "society" means at times living society (all individuals) renewing itself from generation to generation, and at times the cultural tradition uniting the generations.)

The evolution of the human being cannot take place unless social institutions enable him to become not only a civilized *individual* but also a cultured *person* (in the mythically deep sense). Even today, the civilized individual is shaped by the social environment; but we must not forget that the essential evolution of societies, their culture (to be distinguished from utilitarian civilization), is due to the spontaneous creations (the ideas and ideals) of personalities who are superconsciously inspired. Sociology, based on the study of primitive peoples—in which the distinction between individual and person is not yet clearly established—tends to minimize the difference between civilization and culture and to see human beings as if they were totally determined by their social environment. Yet even the life of the most primitive peoples remains unintelligible without such a distinction which transposes onto the social plane the essential truth, the discernment of the conscious and superconscious processes: intellect and spirit. This fundamental discernment means that the study of human life must be based on the unconscious process of animals, and completed by the investigation of superconscious and subconscious motivations. To understand social life—even in its most primitive forms—one must take into account the biological fact that it is an evolutionary consequence of the gregarious instinct of the superior animals, and the psychological fact that human society must be not only civilized but also cultured, lest it fall into decadent banalism. Leaving aside for the moment this possibility of perversion, we can say this: civilization is an intellectual formation; culture is a spiritual one. Civilization is the organization of the outer world (social life); culture is the organization of the inner world (personal life). Civilization's aim is to fulfill the multiple desires; culture's, to fulfill the essential desire. (There are animal societies, which are instinctively civilized (bees, ants); what is totally missing from animal life is culture.)

Primitive man is only a member of a family or tribe (just as the animal is only a member of a species). He is an individual, but he does not yet have a personal importance. His still embryonic thought is imaginative. And to his imagination corresponds his suggestibility. The latter is manifested not only in autosugestion—the principle of magic—but in heterosuggestion. Suggestibility unifies the members of the tribe as instinct unifies the members of the species. The opinions expressed by the other members of the tribe, as well as their actions—and above all their cultural actions—do not awaken in primitive man criticism and doubt, but certainty and the pleasure of resting in public beliefs and opinions.

Imaginative suggestibility unites not only the living members of the tribe, but also the past and future generations.

In order to be able to constitute a cultural society (a human society), suggestibility must gather around an imagination that is assured of the deepest common response; this point of crystallization is to be found in sacred fear and its appeasement, sought in imagination about the meaning of life and death. Therein are united the autosuggestion of the individual and social suggestibility. What the subject suggests to himself—through superconsciously imaginative intuition—is in conformity with the intuition of the other, of all the others. Concrete imaginations, the images thus expressed, bear on the psyche of all.

The cultural foundation is the basis of the essential history of mankind and of its development.

Sacred fear in the face of the mystery of life and death founds the first stage of cultural formation, the mother-cell of society: the family who sacrifices to its ancestors. Having thus become cultural cells, the various families linked by kinship unite around a patriarch who is the living representative of the dead and deified ancestors imagined as still belonging to the clan and insuring help and protection (matriarchy is only a variation on the same theme). All the clans then unite in a same cult, and the head of the tribe formed by the merged clans is no longer the patriarch but a priest-magician, keeper of the formulas used to conjure both good and bad spirits, performer of the rituals through which one can contact the dead and deified ancestors.

However, though temporarily appeased through traditional rituals and the common cult, fear will not fail to reemerge. The cult creates social institutions. As it sets into superstition, the religious institutions become rigid and dogmatizing. No longer linked to the cultural vision and its meaning, they become unable to maintain collective life. Society becoming more numerous, and culturally influenced through contacts with tribes of alien mores, can survive only by transforming its institutions that have become inadequate. Since the metaphysical imaginations concerning the afterlife of the ancestors and the institutions of the cult have formed all social institutions, the latter can perdure only through new dogmatic interpretations that are more and more rigidly imposed. The cults are enlarged, and the primitive magician makes way for a whole caste of magicians and sacrificers. They are the ones who know the secret will of the conjured spirits who have turned into tutelary divinities, and who explain the belief in an afterlife. Every member of society must show himself worthy of an afterlife through his unshakable belief in the efficacy of ritual ceremonies; from this stems the concept that everyone will be judged by the deities according to his belief in the taboos which are little by little senselessly multiplied.

The merit of the individual is no longer personal (courage and combativity of the animating impulse) and it is not yet in conformity with the essential conscience: it is not a harmonization of desires, later perceived through the hidden meaning of myth. The individual merit of the animistic era in its decline is nothing but conformity to traditions, to historical conscience which, through magical transference and the minor importance attached to the individual and his life, can be in total opposition to essential conscience, though the latter was already present in metaphysical fear. The primitive animistic metaphysics of the barely deified multiple spirits goes together with the primitive morality of the magical rituals (human sacrifice, anthropology, etc.).

As the animistic era enters into decline there already appears more and more clearly the danger inherent in social life, the consequence of the conflict between civilization and culture: the cultural superstructure crumbles, the metaphysical vision is set in superstition, and nothing remains save a traditional infrastructure which has become mere convention. If, at the beginning, metaphysical feeling was able to create for itself an institutional framework, the institutions wind up seizing power, thus stifling the emotivity and motivation that gave birth to them. The two representatives of power and rule appear: the representative of the power exerted on outer life, responsible for the upkeep of social institutions, i.e., the king; and the representatives of power ruling over inner life and its imaginative beliefs, namely, the priests. Their function is justified as long as the laws they impose remain the crystallizing center of the effort toward spiritualization-sublimation fighting against fear. This fight is the axis of metaphysical ideas and moral ideals, the mainstay of culture. But the two institutions become the framework of a senseless domination. Having forgotten the meaning of power (a means to achieve the essential goal, which is to arrest fear), they wind up transforming the means into an ultimate end; they want power for its own sake and, if possible, unlimited power. The two forms of senseless power emerge: perverse external domination—tyranny— and perverse internal domination i.e., prejudice in all its forms and especially religious prejudice—superstition. Since both are aiming at unlimited power, these two forms of perverse domination inescapably fight against each other, and this compels them more and more to compromise with respect to the deep meaning of their institution. Their rivalry, upsetting the foundations of social life, destroys its summit (cultural life) and brings about disorientation and a return of fear; however, this fear can only become the stimulus of new efforts of orientation. The animistic era will evolve toward the mythical vision. In its turn, the mythical era will be subject to the same involution. Tyranny and superstition remain today the great dangers of social life. The most ancient myths foresaw such a danger in their symbolic language. They gave a great importance to domineering perversion and the outburst of fear toward which it leads society in a regressive trend.

On the basis of this analysis, the evolutionary step leading from animistic culture to mythical culture can easily be defined: the individual becomes personified. Fear is overcome in the struggles of the mythical heroes symbolizing the ethical task of harmonization to be carried on all through life. The superconscious motivations are represented in the form of deities, the subconscious motivations are symbolized by monsters. The helpful or hostile spirits—scattered throughout nature in the animistic conception—are replaced by the spirit animating man: his own vitally meaningful or senseless intentionality.

The suggestive force of traditions is the foundation of beliefs from the animistic era onward. But suggestive transmission in itself could lead only to an unshakable belief in any affirmation, be it true or false. In order not to be superstition from the outset, the most primitive faith must already be characterized by another element, opposed to suggested and impersonal belief. Now the magical animation of objects is precisely a personification. What animism and its personification of objects suggest to the individual is in fact what he carries in himself, what he feels in the deepest way, what makes of him a living and active person: his own desires and their interior tension toward satisfaction, which is the origin of the motives for his actions, be they meaningful or senseless. The primitive and magical personification of objects was in this respect a psychic transference whose secret intention was already in animism the requirement to bring order among the desires lest one incur guiltiness in the face of the intentionality of the natural environment (the anxiety of arousing the hostility of the spirits projected onto the objects).

What matters here is to understand in depth the evolution of religiosity which already started during the animistic era, since intentionality was projected not only onto the natural environment, but also and above all onto the deified ancestor, who, being a transcendent and supernatural judge of his sons and of the tribal community, is the first foreshadowing of the divinity-judge, a symbol which is shared by all mythologies. Beliefs—whatever their imaginative foundation—can, up to and including our time, carry out their guiding function only if they prefigure the ethical requirement: the auto-harmonization of each individual's secret intentionality to be achieved in this life. This essential requirement was already underlying in animism. The magical thought of mankind's childhood still confuses object and subject: it turns the object into a personified subject. The whole meaning of evolution is to make of the subject and object, an objective being, personified not only in the imagination but actually and actively. This is nothing other than the intrapsychic endeavor of spiritualization-sublimation.

This transformation of the imaginative personification of the object into a demand for active auto-personalization of the subject will lead to the evolution of magical culture toward mythical culture. In order to accomplish this, the personalization imaginatively projected onto the objects by animism is withdrawn from the object and concentrates anew in the subject. Magical projection, the primitive form of explanation of life and its activity, splits into two forms through this reconcentration in the subject: a form of imaginative explanation purified from magical confusion and thereby becoming pure image or symbol; and a form of vital activity which will no longer be a conjuration of the personified object, but the lawful formation of the subject.

Personification remains, even in the most evolved cultures, the root of all metaphorical truth, of all poetry. For prelogical and symbolic thought, it was the only way to express superconscious truth. It makes up the vision of the mythical era which is both poetical and religious. In order to become the tool of the mythical pre-science with respect to intentions, it must go beyond the stage of animistic projection which makes of personification a magical reality. (The tendency to mistake poetic, magical, or symbolic personification for a reality is inherent not only in the primitive psyche but also in the childish and the sick psyche.)

The evolution from the realism of the magical formula to the symbolism of the mythical image was already dawning toward the end of the animistic era.

At the very beginning of the animistic era, the barely conscious human being confronted the most banal environment as if it were a mystery. Forest and plain are seemingly animated by noises, by animal cries that exalt the disoriented imagination. We have stressed that, little by little, primitive man emerges from this initial lethargy due to magical personification. Insofar as the environment becomes a known reality, the imagination begins to purify itself from its personifying realism. The hunter knows how to read every trail and every noise; he connects them with their actual causes. Yet, among the hostile forces he feels are surrounding him, even if they become more and more susceptible of evaluation, there are many remaining too dangerous for the available means of defense. Even if those dangers are connected with actual causes, the imagination cannot rid itself of their frightening hold; it fantasizes on this richly suggestive basis. Serpents, for instance, whose bite brings sickness or even death, are no longer immediately seen as evil spirits. The regular link between the consequences of the bite and the real fact of an encounter with the animal is understood, and the consequences of the bite are no longer perceived as an unexplicable event, inflicted by an evil spirit as a form of punishment (for instance, when a taboo has been violated). On the other hand, the fact of having met the serpent is now imagined as being the punishment. The hostile spirit sent the serpent, a real animal. The serpent remains—partially— an imaginary creation. It is, as it were, split into an image and a reality. Thus there is only one step to go for this separation between magic and reality to become mythical image, for the serpent to be seen as the symbol of the evil spirit within man.

On the plane of the mythical evolution that is starting, the "serpent" symbol is no longer connected with the fact of an actual bite and its consequences, sickness or death. The serpent represents vanity, and the inflicted bite symbolizes repressed guiltiness: remorse whose consequences are the illnesses of the mind or "death of the soul." These psychically immanent punishments do not concern the accidental fault— the violation of a social taboo—but the essential fault of human nature: false motivation, the principle of which is guilty vanity. In order to be able to represent the details of right and wrong motivations, symbolic language will invent fabulous nonexistent animals: half animals and half men, or half men and half gods.

But, in order for the magical personification of animism to become the symbolic personification of the myth, for the attention to be detached from the outer and be focused on the inner life, complex conditions have to be met.

One fact is worthy of notice.

At the end of the animistic era, there is already a spate of confabulations dealing with good and bad spirits and containing the seeds and elements of myth. However, these stories are still too imbued with purely subjective accidents connected with certain places and events which are important only for such and such a tribe. Myth will use symbolization and personification only in order to express the objective truth concerning the meaning of life.

B. THE MYTHICAL ERA

1. POLYTHEISM

a) From Animism to Polytheism

In the mythical era, understanding goes beyond its magical form and splits into a manifest symbolic image and an underlying significance.

The significances include all the affective and emotional subconscious and superconscious motivations, since they are all connected in emotion in the face of mystery. Sacred fear is the ethical motive of spiritualization-sublimation without which fear is only a negative spirit, a vital anxiety. Since the hidden meaning of the myth relates to the ethical effort (the struggle against the evil spirit—the falsely motivating intentions—in man), symbolization becomes able to compare the weakness of the human spirit with the image of perfect clairvoyance, though the latter is a pure ideal, a pure symbol: the deities as personifications of the positive qualities immanent to the soul and spirit of man. Through this confrontation of the unhealthy and the perfectly ideal states, myth contains the possibility of speaking symbolically about what man is and what he should be. In the intention of symbolism, which has become a description of the intrapsychic conflicts, man should—for his own essential good—fight with the help of his own positive intentions, represented by deities, against his own perverse intentions—evil because they are disharmonizing—represented by demons and monsters. This achievement becomes a natural task, symbolically imposed by the deities. Animism wanted to set free from the evil spirit, fear, vital anxiety through projection and conjuration. Myth—while being expressed only in a symbolic way—aims at anxiety and disquiet in the inner life of man, their true abode. Disquiet with its often frightening torment, becomes the vital guilt of man due to the non-achievement of the ideal state. To express this symbolically: disquiet, punishment for the guilt, is presented as being inflicted by the "divine" principle. In order to purify himself from vital guilt, or evil spirit and free himself from torment, man must undertake an inner task—the objectivization of the blinding affect of fear: its spiritualization-sublimation.

The mythical era is thus different from animism in that magical conjuration is replaced by the symbolization of an intrapsychic endeavor, whose aim is to overcome fear more effectively. This endeavor finds its mythical expression in the form of heroic struggles against frightening dangers, monsters of the dark, symbolizing the horrors[2] of affective clouding. The symbolic deification of the ideal state is thus completed by the other typical symbolization of myths: the hero and his struggle against monsters representing his own subconscious intentions.

But this essential difference between animism and myth has a preliminary condition in another distinctive feature which gives to symbolization all its scope. The magical fear of the animistic era and its conjuration concerned the dangers of the earthly environment as subjectively interpreted, while during the mythical era fear becomes objectified. Emotional attention overcomes fear in the face of the immediate environment. By freeing itself from it, it encompasses a larger and

2. See note on page 15.

more remote environment. The impressive unknown is not only the earth and its swarming masses, but also the heavens with their rhythmically regulated, lawfully ordered manifestations. Metaphysical fear in its more or less disoriented form, the fear of death, which was already characteristic of animism is complemented by the mystery of the frightening lawfulness revealed in cosmic harmony. Spiritual and sublime, the emotion inspired by this new and tremendous form of the unknown is the condition for any high culture going beyond animism: religious worship, aesthetic wonderment, and scientific astonishment. Worship, wonderment, and astonishment are the sublimated forms of fear.

For the metaphorically true fabulations of the myths, personification and symbolization are only the tool necessary to express this sublimated fear, transformed into worship.

The focusing of attention on the cosmic environment was prepared by the periodical changes manifested in the direct environment, though caused by stellar motions, the seasons of the year. Being earthly phenomena that influence and even determine all the conditions of human life and at the same time consequences of the stellar motions, thus linking direct environment and cosmic environment, these periodical and seasonal changes compel the primitive spirit to take the evolutionary step leading from animistic explanation to mythical explanation. This cultural evolution is complemented on the social plane by the transformation from tribes of shepherds to agricultural peoples.

In the Eastern countries—cradle of our culture—the year is divided into a period of drought followed by a season of rains. In the symbolic language of the myths, drought is imagined as being a hostile deity. In order to vanquish this nefarious deity, heaven and earth, personified as divinities, have to unite, to "get married." Rain acquires the meaning of see; it symbolizes the fecundation of mother-earth by father-heaven. The sun, appearing as if rejuvenated after the rainy season, is imagined as being a benevolent deity causing vegetation to flourish and seed to rise. Wheat and bread become symbols of a gift from "heaven" and acquire the significance of "food for the spirit." The whole year and the cycle of "sowing-to-reaping" are imaginatively represented as a struggle between a former hostile deity (drought) and the rejuvenated solar deity (reappearing after the rainy season, after the union between father-heaven and mother-earth). Son of the union between heaven and earth, the sun is celebrated as a victorious deity. But the rejuvenated sun dies every year and the struggle starts again year after year. (The institutions refer frequently to seasonal symbolism. In certain primitive cultures, the king who represents the solar deity is dethroned or killed every year and replaced by another king venerated as a god during the year of his reign.)

In a more evolved mythical period, "heaven" becomes a symbol of spiritual elevation, and rain, falling from the sky, a symbol of the fecundation of the spirit. Even clouds are encompassed in the symbol of the spirit. The symbols begin to take on a moral significance going beyond the cosmic and seasonal significance. Thus the myths of a more evolved period can no longer be understood if one omits this transfiguration of the cosmic event into a moral meaning.

Once the moral significance has been acquired, a complementary and inverse significance is added: the punishment of the earth by the spirit who is outraged by the immorality prevailing on earth. The earth is purified, the sons of the earth are punished by the flood.

The spiritual scope of this formerly seasonal symbolization reaches its acme in the image of a virgin-mother (condensing the symbolic images "mother-earth" and "desire-earth"). The image adds to the character of vegetal fertility—through the intermediary of the symbolism "fruit of the earth": means of satisfaction of natural desires—the moral character of innocent purity, the opposite of exaltation of the desires. Fecundated by the sun who has become the father-spirit, the virgin mother-earth gives birth not only to vegetal life, but to the life of the spiritualized being: the victorious hero of the myths. Symbolization is finally concentrated in the symbol of an earthly woman (Mary in the Christian myth) who, symbolically fecundated by the spirit (in the form of a cloud) gives birth to the unique man, totally purified (incarnation of the spirit), light of the world. While being on the plane of reality "son of man," i.e., a real man (son of Adam), he is on the symbolic plane "son of God." What matters is not to confuse the two planes. His name "light of the world" denotes that he is a symbolic transfiguration of the ancient solar divinity who previously ruled only over vegetal life. Since the solar deity in its primitive form had to fight against the dryness of the earth, the divinity symbol, transposed on to the evolved plane, will call for struggle against moral impurity or dryness of soul. (The same symbolization is to be found in various pagan myths without any declaration that the son of the earthly woman and the solar deity finally become "God-the-Spirit" is "real god." The union is a symbol and the symbolism means that the son of the mythical union will be an exceptional hero not only—as many others—a fighter for the spirit, but a mythical victor. The parallelism between the various mythical fabulations has always been stressed by mythologists. It is far more important to understand the underlying significance running through mythology from polytheism to monotheism, proof of a common superconscious language. In Greed mythology, already the victorious hero, Perseus, is the son of an earthly woman, Danae, who has been impregnated by the spirit-deity. Zeus takes the shape of a cloud and the fecundating seed is symbolized by a rain of gold. The latter stresses the spiritual significance of the cloud and rain symbols. Gold, having the color of the sun, is the symbol of spiritualization-sublimation. (It must be added that only the gold color has such a significance. Like almost all symbols, it can have an inverse meaning; gold as a material treasure means the opposite of spiritualization; attachment to earthly desires and their imaginative exaltation.)

The evolution which ended by elevating the seasonal symbolization to the level of the moral plane can be understood in all its inescapable necessity only by taking into account that the sun, center of symbolization (since it is the predominating phenomenon of the stellar manifestations and their consequences), does not only determine the cycle of the seasons through which it rules over vegetation; the sun also *rules over the day-night cycle, which lends it its illuminating function, its specificity in symbolizing the spirit, i.e., the illuminating function of the human psyche.*

The successive phases of mythical evolution are characterized by the growing predominance of the "sun-spirit" symbolism, representing superconscience, thus by a more and more spiritual underlying meaning and therefore by a progressive prevalence of the ethical scope. The interpretation of myths has always had a certain rather strong tendency to overestimate the importance of the seasonal cycle to the prejudice of the daily cycle. This is not surprising. Indeed, if symbolization—using the illuminating role of the sun—opens up the deepest meaning of the "sun-spirit" analogy, namely its moral significance, this new aspect does lead to the danger of meeting a difficulty in understanding which will remain impossible to overcome as long as psychology has not provided a means of translation: the analysis of the various psychic processes.

b) The Two Phases of Polytheism

(1) PREVALENCE OF THE AGRARIAN SIGNIFICANCE

Since the sun will always symbolize ever more clearly human superconscience to the extent that the real sun will finally be completely superseded by the symbol of the idealized spirit, by the "Spirit" symbol, the mythical era is divided into two main periods: paganism and monotheism.

The monotheistic period is itself divided into two phases, characterized by a difference in the evolution of the "spirit" symbol, these two phases being clearly distinguished (at least with regard to the cultures that influence the Western world) by the cycles of myths related in the Old and New Testaments.

In accordance the above, it is unavoidable to distinguish also in the polytheistic period two phases, characterized by considerable difference.

The agrarian meaning of the first phase is more allegorical. The ethical signification of the second phase, concerning the conflicts of the inner motivating functions, is the characteristic feature of symbolization. This justifies the concern to stress—briefly—the historical fact of the transformation of agrarian allegory into ethical symbolism.

The solar deities, center and acme of the pagan myths, symbolize in the first phase—as we have just explained—the actual and seasonal benefits of the sun: the fecundation of the earth; and they symbolize in a second phase, paving the way for monotheism, the daily benefits of the illuminating sun which has become the symbol of the illuminating spirit: the fecundation of the soul and spirit by the solar deities which have become entirely surreal symbols, symbols of the superconscious function (sublimation-spiritualization).

Discerning the two phases of polytheism is too important a step to omit a more detailed illustration.

Greek mythology, for instance, was able to create a cult endowed with a highly symbolic significance: the mysteries of Eleusis. In them the two phases of the agrarian and ethical pagan culture have overlapped, though they remain discernible. The core of the mysteries of Eleusis is the mythical story of the abduction of Persephone, daughter of Demeter, by Hades. Demeter (terra-mater) is the goodess ruling over the earthly and seasonal fecundation, i.e., the yearly cycle from sowing to harvest: the grain must be buried in the ground to become ear and bread, gift of Demeter. This seasonal cycle from sowing to harvest becomes the core of the mysteries of Eleusis, since it lends itself to the symbolization of the fate of earthly desire: its repression and its sublimation.

Here is the tale of the myth: Hades, god of the underworld, abducts Persephone while she is listening to the song of the Sirens (symbol of imaginative exaltation) and takes her to his underground abode: the subconscious. On the basis of this double significance—buried grain and repressed desire—the agrarian and psychological images become intertwined, then finally give way to the ethical significance which is the meaning and goal of the initiation to the mysteries.

Zeus (the Sun) intervenes and Hades is compelled to partially give up his prey. Persephone (on the plane of the agrarian myth: the buried grain) leaves the underground abode for a half-year: protected by mother-earth and father-sun, the grain becomes the ear of wheat providing men with earthly food, satisfying the most natural needs. The myth symbolizes—under this most primitive significance corresponding to a first agrarian phase—material benefits; it celebrates the gift that man receives from mother-earth and father-sun. But no myth is content with symbolizing the materiality of life which, in any event, has an underlying moral aspect: gratitude for the satisfaction of bodily needs being the perfect opposite of the immoral principle, irrational exaltation of desires.

If this underlying relationship is such that it suggests the need for a more complete translation of the myth in order to discover a deeper significance, we must—before studying it—stress a complementary and significance aspect which has a higher scope: this version (the most primitive one) is already endowed with a metaphysical symbol, inseparable from the moral meaning of life: the mystery of death. Like the grain, man is buried after his death, and like the grain he "rises again"—according to the oldest belief—from this burial. The myth symbolizes belief in immortality. Hades, brother to Zeus, is the judge of the dead (the significance of immortality will be translated later on). Now this metaphysical symbolism also leads to the moral significance, i.e., the psychic, psychological one: there would be no point in imagining a judgment of the dead if man had no other task in this life than to feed on earthly bread. He must precisely undertake the task of living not only for "earthly food" or—which leads us back to the central formula (the symbol of "original sin")—of not exalting material needs in a senseless way. It thus seems indisputable that in addition to its immediate meaning concerning the most urgent necessity of life (its material sustenance or bread) and its remote and metaphysical meaning (the mystery of death), the abduction of Persephone—to come back to the central myth around which Greek religion will finally crystallize—must (or at least should, in principle) contain a moral and psychic significance. Only this psychic significance—characteristic of a second phase in pagan culture—will ensure the predominant importance of the mysteries of Eleusis. Now grain, wheat, bread—actual earthly foods—are in all myths and cycles of myths, symbols of the food of the soul and spirit, i.e., they symbolize the condition for the productivity (fecundity) of the soul and spirit, the condition (food) for sublimation and spiritualization. (The hero of the Christian myth calls himself "bread of life" because his truth nourishes the soul and spirit.) The brain which becomes ear, symbolized by the fate of Persephone, also contains this spiritual significance.

The moral meaning is contained in the myth of the abduction, since Demeter symbolizes not only the seasonal fecundity of the earth but also earthly desire. The myth thus becomes capable of expressing the two fundamental "adventures" of desire: exaltation-inhibition ending in repression (represented by the abduction) and sublimation-spiritualization ending in liberation. The attributes of Demeter are not only wheat but also all the fruits of the earth. As in the case of the apple in the myth of Genesis, the fruits of the earth are the symbols of the satisfaction of earthly desire. This satisfaction can be preverse or sublime. The significance includes Persephone herself, who is a "fruit" of Demeter, since she is her daugther. The fate of Persephone thus becomes the symbol of the central phenomenon of human life, symbol of the conscious and multiple desires and their transformations caused by the interaction of the various psychic processes. From the desire-principle (Demeter) characterizing all life—even unconscious life—comes conscious desire, which is only to easily multiplied and exalted: "Persephone" who becomes exposed to subconscious perversion (abduction) and this includes the possibility of warding off perversion thanks to the op-

posite reaction, super conscious sublimation. The adventure of Persephone contains these two possibilities: the abduction symbolizes repression; the rebirth (resurrection) of Persephone (the ear) symbolizes
desire emerging from repression, thanks to the spiritual reaction (with
the help of Zeus), awareness of the error and the guilt.

In order to perfectly understand these relationships which are fundamental for the myth as well as for life, we have to take into account the
functioning of the psyche: human desire is conscious only with respect
to the coveted object (man knows that he desires this or that), desire is
not conscious—at least most of the time—with respect to its causes
which, being themselves psychic activities, are motives (to be distinguished from external aims which are stimuli from the environment).
To make the motive of desire conscious (and not only its yearning for
the object) is to make it more-than-conscious, superconscious; it is to
become master of the desire through its spiritualization. On the contrary, through repression man becomes unconscious even of the object
of his desire. The latter can become forbidden through the force of the
feeling of guilt which attaches itself to the exalted desire and inhibits it.
The energy of desire, exalted on the one hand and inhibited-repressed
on the other hand, can be transferred to an object that has no attraction in itself and is often even a cause for anxiety (because of the ambivalence "attraction-guiltiness," i.e., exaltation-inhibition). Desire thus
becomes subconscious, having lost sight not only of its true motives, but
even of its real object. Now the object—ersatz for the subconscious desire—the falsely coveted object, while being a cause for anxiety (because of guilt feelings), is no less attractive than the real object was; on
the contrary, it becomes an obsession (because of the transferred energy which has become uncontrollable). Obsession (insatiability) is thus at
the basis of all subconscious distortion. One can perceive on the one
hand the torment (punishment) which can result from the subconscious
transformation of desire, and on the other hand the paramount satisfaction which will reward its superconscious transformation. One can
also conceive the vital importance of the symbolic representation of
these psychic relationships. Symbolism, though it was not adequate to
touch and strengthen the conscious, was thus all the more capable of
impressing and inspiring the superconscious of the psyche which was
more primitively but also more sublimely suggestible.

At Eleusis three ears of wheat were shown to the initiated person prepared by the teaching of the priests. This teaching concerned undoubtedly the meaning of the myth of Persephone, which moreover was surrounded by many mythical episodes, variations on the central theme.[3]
Showing the three ears of wheat would have been meaningless if it had

---

3. See chapter on the mysteries of Eleusis in *Symbolism in Greek Mythology*, 1st ed. (Payot,
1954; Shambhala, 1981).

not been a symbolic concentration of the significance of the initiation, a significance which (leaving aside the dogmatization to which any official religion is subjected) could only concern the symbolic transformation: wheat—bread—food for the soul and spirit. Three is the sacred number, symbol of the spirit, and the grain risen from the burial (death of the soul) having become an ear of wheat, symbolizes sublimation. Symbolically resumed by the showing of the three ears of wheat, the teaching of the priests and the initiation to the mysteries of Eleusis, concerned the metaphysical mystery and the moral reality: sublimation-spiritualization of the desires through which man can himself become a fertile being (the ear of wheat).

To say that the myth "acquires" more and more moral significance could lead to a misunderstanding about the mythical phenomenon in general. It is important to realize that the moral significance is present as an underlying element from the outset of the mythical creation, otherwise it could not have been already contained in this primitive version of the myth of Persephone whose translation has been schematically given. But the growing predominance of the moral significance often brings transformations to the myths—were it only by the addition of details—and they are extremely significant, compelling the translator to seek their moral meaning, since in the seasonal and even metaphysical interpretation the additions would only be trimmings lacking any significance. In this myth, for instance, Persephone is abducted while listening to the song of the Sirens; in another version, while picking narcissi. The Sirens symbolize the seductive aspect of exalted imagination; the narcissi are one of the symbols for vanity. These symbols acquire a genuine meaning only if they are psychologically interpreted: desire (Persephone) is subject to repression (abduction) when it lets itself be seduced by exalted and vain imagination. This significance is stressed and justified by a whole complex of additional details. Persephone having been abducted, desire having been exalted and repressed, she becomes the wife of Hades, god-king, symbol of the lawfulness of the subconscious. (Hades wears a helmet that makes him invisible, symbol of repression.) The children of Persephone, wife of Hades, are the Erinnyes, symbol of repressed guiltiness. It would be absurd to say that a psychic phenomenon (guiltiness) comes from Persephone and Hades if the latter did not themselves symbolize psychic phenomena. And indeed they symbolize the psychic phenomena whose consequence is guiltiness; they "give birth," mythically speaking, to guiltiness. In accordance with the lawfulness of subconscious functioning symbolized by Hades, exalted and obsessive guiltiness (Erinnyes) is the consequence of a repression of desire (Persephone). But the psychological significance goes much farther and all the way to its extreme consequence, completing the lawfulness of the subconscious by that of the superconscious: man, when pursued by the Erinnyes (prey to guiltiness) will find refuge only in the temple of Apollo, god of harmony (sublime liberation). On the facade of the temple, there is an inscription "Know thyself": acknowledge your guilt).

This moral significance of the mysteries is clearly assumed in a second phase (the first phase being the agrarian meaning). The mysteries of Eleusis become—in their deepest and complete sense—a true pagan foreshadowing of the monotheistic and Christian myth which will express the common contents in a much deeper, clearer and wider way. This kinship of the two significances is historically documented: the first Christians made a connection between the mysteries of Eleusis and their new belief. The reformer of the mysteries of Eleusis, the one who amplified their moral significance is a symbolic figure: Orpheus. The ancients made such a close connection between Orpheus and Jesus that the two were even confused at times. According to the mythical fable, Orpheus started as a worshiper of Dionysos, symbol of disordered passions, of the insatiable frenzy desires, symbol of the explosion of the subconscious process ambivalently opposed to repression (Hades). Dionysos does indeed become a central figure in the mysteries of Eleusis; he even takes the place of Hades, which is made possible by the complementarity of the symbolic significance. However it is said that Orpheus finally got reconciled with Apollo (he gave up the erroneous ideal of banal explosion for the ideal of sublime liberation or—as the Christian myth will put it—he resurrected from the death of the soul). The Orpheus-Jesus connection is thus in fact an Orpheus-Apollo-Jesus connection. Jesus, spiritual light of the world, is thus connection with Apollo, the solar god who in Greek mythology bears the same role of illuminator.

(2) PREVALENCE OF THE ETHICAL SIGNIFICANCE

After having given an illustration through examples, we have to trace a theoretical development of the most significant stages in this evolution of mythical symbols, the true keystone for the understanding of the "divinity" symbol.

It has been shown previously that in a first phase of the pagan culture, imaginative attention, barely detached from the direct environment is not yet an objective contemplation dealing with the law of nature, harmony, the immanent meaning of life. The characteristic feature of this first phase is that fear is insufficiently spiritualized. Cosmic life does not yet impress man through its objective order. The attention is drawn to stellar motions only because of their influence on earthly life (the seasons of the year) and their consequence for the bodily life of man (cycle of sowing and reaping). The sun is raised to the rank of deity thanks to its real benefit: the fecundation of the earth. In this respect, the sun is worshiped, among the Greeks, in the guise of the ancient deity Helios.

But Helios loses his importance little by little. He is superseded by Apollo. Helios symbolizes the fertilizing sun; Apollo signifies order and harmony. First cosmic order, then harmony of the soul. He is not the fecundator anymore, he is the illuminator. First came actual illumination by the sun (Helios), then finally symbolic illumination: the spirit.

The rhythmical succession of day and night, however important it is for the life of the body, could not inspire mythical creation, if it were not connected to the deepest source of symbolizing imagination: sacred fear in the face of the unknowable and fear of the unknown to be fought by the elucidating spirit.

The harmony of stellar motions inspires much metaphysical fear in the face of the unknowable origins as it induces the mind to seek the causes presiding over manifest harmony. In this respect, the immutable stellar harmony becomes the symbol of psychic harmony to be attained. The star of day and the star of night become symbols of the inner conflicts between the lucidity of the superconscience and the blindness of the subconscience.

The sun actually and symbolically brings the day, the light; it chases away the unknown and fear. The moon brings the night (in primitive imagination). Its insufficient light wraps all objects in a vague glow giving them a fantastic aspect. The moon symbolizes a significance diametrically opposed to that of the sun: it becomes an evil spirit, a hostile deity.

The earthly and multiple spirits of animism start to concentrate into two groups of solar and lunar deities, benevolent and malevolent, which is a preparation for monotheism characterized by the "God-Satan" duality, principle of good and evil.

The origin of this progressive transfiguration is in fact a triple constellation: sun, moon, earth, because it is evident that the earth, abode of man, is included in the symbolization which represents the fate of man. The duality imposed by the "benevolent-malevolent" contrast remains predominant since moon and earth have a kindred symbolic significance. Moon and earth are equally opposed to the sun since perversion is precisely characterized by the exalted attachment to earthly desires. The "moon" symbol is often replaced by the "earth" symbol, the earth being mythically imagined as begetting beings rebelling against the solar principle (in Greek mythology, for instance, first the Titans, symbols of the wild forces of nature, and finally the intellectually rebellious being, Man, son of the Titan Prometheus). But, according to the depth of the symbolic truth, the malevolent principle is never totally and irreparably opposed to the benevolent principle which is predominant to the extent that it penetrates even its opposite principle, the latter thus remaining fecundable and vincible. Thus the "sun-father" symbol is at the same time opposed and bound to the "moon-mother" symbol, the latter having the same significance as 'mother-earth," so that the two symbolisms become only one, or at least are able to replace each other. In this way, the lunar deities become finally underground (infernal) deities.

Polytheism is characterized by the fact that the deities of the light, just like the deities of the darkness, beget a whole genealogy of children representing the diversity of the superconscious qualities or the subconscious perversions of the human soul. The "filiation" symbolism enables to indicate clearly and in detail the psychic fact which is expressed as follows: on the plane of inner motivations, positive and negative qualities "beget themselves" by the way of consequence. Thus, the force of spiritualization has as a consequence the harmony of desires: Apollo is the son of Zeus. The harmony of desires, in order not to fall prey to the disharmonizing temptations of the subconscious, must be sustained, complemented by the combativity of the vital impulse symbolized by Athena, herself daughter of Zeus. Myth therefore represents the indispensable psychic complementarity of harmony and the combative impulse by making Athena the sister of Apollo. The various forms of symbolic kinship are significant for the various character constellations, consequences of the lawfulness ruling the motivational functioning of the psyche. Hades, symbol of the subconscious lawfulness, is analogically akin to the lawfulness of the superconscious functioning represented by Zeus: Hades is the brother of Zeus. The most frequent symbol is that of filiation. Man, son of an earthly woman, can be symbolically "son of a deity" if the chief feature of his character is such and such a quality symbolized by such and such a deity. The victor of Greek mythology, Perseus, is the son of an earthly woman "Danae" impregnated by the spirit Zeus. The fecundation is symbolized by rain falling from heaven. This is one of the most ancient symbolisms: Uranus, spirit-father, impregnates Gaea, terra-mater, with the rain falling from heaven. Like all ancient cosmic or agrarian representations, the impregnation of an earthly woman by a spirit deity finally acquires a significance endowed with a psychological bearing. In this deep symbolic understanding, the birth, and the achievement of the hero Perseus, son of Zeus and victor over Medusa (vanity), is analogically comparable with the birth of Jesus, symbolically "son of God."

Being symbols of intrapsychic qualities, the deities are invisible. They live in a place imaginatively located "behind" the heavens. The image of an invisible abode has the same significance as that of a dwelling located—as it often is—on the summit of a mountain. This is the first indication of a "beyond," a symbolic "Heaven."

But precisely because the deities represent human motivations, the symbolizing imagination can become bold enough to anthropormorphize them. All these deities, projected in a remote abode, have the superhumanly magnified characteristics of man. And since their *raison d'etre* is the symbolization of the conflict between the psychic pro-

cesses—the personification of the qualities and shortcomings of man—
the deities are symbolically endowed with a human body while the animistic spirits were the occult forces of nature, having the power to take
possession of a body.

According to the symbolization of the pagan mythologies already,
the deities taking human form can come down on earth and bring mortals their help and message.

Man, for his part, can also enter into contract with the deities and *the
only really valuable contact is the achievement—depending on each man's
strength—of the qualities symbolized by the deities.* Since human nature is
weak, the contact has been sought since the very beginning of animism
in rituals and ceremonies of sacrifice. During the pagan period too,
man implores the benevolent deities and attempts to placate the malevolent ones, by sacrificing the first fruits of the earth; but he offers as a
token of gratitude the first fruits of the harvest and this sacrifice does
not have the significance of an animistic ritual, i.e., magical conjuration. Sacrifice, taking on a much deeper meaning, becomes a symbolic
action. It is true that nowhere else will the real meaning be so easily distorted; even so, through all the superstitions, the offering will symbolize renunciation of earthly goods (the promise not to exalt the desires),
an expression of the preference granted to the "divine" principle. In
this way man hopes to become worthy of the manifold goods (fecundity) imagined as having been scattered on earth thanks to the kindness
of the gods. The symbolic expression of sacrifice is meaningful only if
the gratitude symbolized by the rituals influences the daily complexities
of life: if it implies at the same time acceptance of refused gifts (poor
harvest) and gratitude for granted abundance. Sacrifice, during the animistic era, does not ask for individual well-being (which too easily ex-
ceeds natural and actual needs), but for the well-being of the whole
people, the material foundation needed for its existence; the same is
true of the first phase of monotheistic rituals. The object is, first, the
harvest, but also peace, victory in battles against neightbors, etc. One
of the most important objects in these prayers for the general well-being is public health, protection against epidemics. And it is then that
the significance of the sacrifice starts to become individualized. The religious authorities are asked to perform in order to obtain the cure of
such and such a sick person. First the cure of people whose life is of
public importance, and finally everybody's health; first bodily health
and finally *psychic health, which characterizes the second phase of polytheism.*
At the outset, physical and psychic health are not conceived as being
strictly distinct from each other. Harmony of psychic life is seen as a
condition for physcial health. Thus the solar deity who ruled only over
material and public well-being (Helios) becomes the god of health and
harmony (Apollo). Sacrifice itself undergoes a new deepening in its significance: the symbolic offering of earthly goods starts to signify that

man, every man for himself, must guard himself from the exaltation of his needs, that he must purify his own desires from exaltation so as to become worthy of approaching the divinity who is the symbol of the just satisfaction of desires. *The divinity is no longer, in the first place, a being who metes out collective well-being and material fulfillment for the needs of society; it is more and more the symbol of the essential satisfaction of the individual, the satisfaction of the essential desire of each man.*

During the first phase of polytheism, the two moral principles of good and evil were not as yet clearly constituted as implying an attitude on man's part with respect to the divinity. Good or bad meant nothing more than the helpful or hostile intention of the deities toward man. Or, rather, toward the community in which the individual was as yet nothing but a more or less indistinct member bound to take part in the maintenance of the material conditions of social life.

In the second phase of polytheism, the essentially different feature is that the relationship between the individual and society begins to be reversed. The total submission of the individual to conventional taboos is, after all, nothing but a relic of the childhood of mankind (close to animality, in which the individual is nothing but an indistinct member of the species). It is quite clear that the fate of evolved societies composed of a growing number of individuals depends above all on the integrity of the inner life of each and every individual. During the second phase of polytheism, paving the way to monotheism, guilt feelings begin to become individualized. With the reversal of the relationship between society and man, the relationship between man and the divinity is also reversed. *Man no longer feels that he is totally dependent on the good or bad intentions of the deities toward him; what matters is that his own bad intentions be transformed into good intentions toward the deities.* This sublime transformation endowed with a liberating force depends on the personal will of man, on his own inner deliberation. Individualized guiltiness concerns the inner motivations of man. In this way the projection of motivating intentions onto the "providential divinity" image—which still persisted in the first phase of polytheism—begins to reconcentrate in its emotive source: the ethical superconscience which creates images.

This evolutionary procedure is far from being conscious. The naivete of popular beliefs perdures. The new ethical dimension is, however, clearly indicated and historically substantiated by the fact that in all pagan cultures there appears the institution of a new cult, the "mysteries" entrusted with a teaching which—while it remains symbolically veiled—attempts to arouse in its initiates the awareness of their own ethical responsibility in the face of their own destiny.

The cults of the Mysteries had one common goal: initiation to the mystery of life. The initiates were led to perceive the immanence of justice, symbolically projected onto the deities. The rituals of the Mysteries were meant to arouse in the initiates the animating impulse out of its somnolence in the conventionalism of popular beliefs so as to enable them to achieve, for their essential good, the harmonization of their own motivating intentions.

Here we must stress vigorously that there is nothing occult in talking about a mysteriously animating impulse[4].

In this respect, we must clearly define the terms "soul," "animation," and "impulse," in order to avoid confusion of a spiritualistic as well as of a materialistic nature. "The soul and its fate after death" are not realities, but personifying imaginations as are all mythical respresentations. They are metaphysical symbols belonging to the mystery of life and death. Animation and the individual vital impulse, on the other hand, are existing realities, psychic phenomena, the truth underlying the "soul" symbol.

The evolutionary impulse of harmonization and reharmonization is naturally immanent, immanent to the whole of nature, to life in all its forms, to human life in the form of ethical superconscience and its individually evolutionary impulse, which are mythically symbolized by the "call of the spirit" to struggle against the perversion of subconscious involution.

Mythologies are not vain speculations but explosions of truth. Confronted with this explosive truth, it would be only vanity, a failure of the subconsciously motivated mind, to take refuge in metaphysical speculations (absolute spirit and absolute matter), the former making a reality out of the "soul" symbol and the latter denying the actual existence of the animating impulse. The absolute does not exist and any reference to it is a metaphysical speculation. Neither theological spiritualism nor the materialism of the sciences of life can bring a valid solution to the ethical problem. The former gets mired in moralism and the latter in amoralism.

The emergence of the more and more clearly—though symbolically—formulated ethical problem in *the second phase* of polytheism is an evolutionary step superseding the naivete of *the first phase* which did not take sufficiently into account the vain feeling of guiltiness of the individual. What is individualized guilty feeling in its essential form, if not emotion in the face of the mysterious lawfulness of the motivational functioning in each individual psyche? Fear in the face of the mystery of the cosmic universe shifts to the intrapsychic universe and becomes guilty fear in the face of the unfathomed deeps and dark areas in the psychic life of each one of us.

Breaking away from the background of mythical life, there appears during the second phase of polytheism an understanding going beyond symbolizing imagination: astronomy. In evolving, science will seek an impersonal law. However, what is this objectively formulated law if not,

---

4. See note on page 5.

after all, another way of expressing the principle that myth calls "divinity"?

Mythical workship does not aim at the search for the objective formulation of laws as astronomy starts to do; its concern is with personal emotion, which is both overwhelming and reassuring in the face of the immeasurable greatness of the mysteriously "superhuman" organizing spirit. This spirit creates and maintains the tremendous rhythm of harmony in the material universe complementary to the universe of desires and inner motivations, in which harmony, though constantly perturbed, imposes its law. It imposes it in the form of a more-than-conscious feeling of guiltiness, still vague and undefinable, but all the more constraining in that it encompasses the entire existence of the individual. Ever since the thinking being has lived and as long as he lives, he will be moved in the face of the mystery of life and death when contemplating the starry sky. In these all too fleeting moments, the vital impulse is roused from its somnolence. Full of sacred fear, man becomes aware of the evidence of his ephemeral existence, feels the mystery in the face of the perceptible manifestation of the mystery which animates him too, feels the guilty vanity of his daily life, devoid as it is of vital impulse.

But individual and genuine guilty feelings are too easily forgotten, overwhelmed by the collective guilty feelings of moralism and its excessively good intentions which are vain and fasely justifying, or stifled by the vanity of the excessively evil intentions of banalism looking for superiority in the complete absence of scruples. In both cases, emotion in the face of the depth of existence implying its height—theme of the genuine religiosity of myths—is lost to the extent that it cannot awake either through the contemplation of stellar harmony or even through the essential guily feelings of the individual in the face of the disharmonies of his own life.

Essential and genuinely individualized guilt feelings (which, to be genuine, has to be superconsciously immanent to each individual) is manifested on the religious plane of the relationship with the divinity or rather, with the image of the divinity, through the superconsciously motivating influence which is the animating impulse. The individual, in keeping with his vital impulse, is the bearer of emotion in the face of mystery, whose permanent presence rules over his activity. Sacred emotion moves him in the slightest details of his daily life: it is incarnate in him. Prayer addressed to the superconsciously immanent divinity image is therefore actually addressed to oneself, to one's own superior self, to one's own animating impulse, to one's own ethical superconscience. Since the beginning of mankind, prayer was autoimploration. A suggestion to remain courageous in the face of the unavoidable temptations of daily life. Rituals are only a means to reinforce the autosuggestive force of the image of mystery, i.e., the divinity. The loss of the superconsciously individualized feeling of guiltiness—the essential loss—is the conventionalization of the mythical image, projected outside the psyche in another world mistaken for a reality. The deity is no longer implored for the essential good of the individual (the harmony of motives); it is finally implored by each individual for his own material well-being. Instead of becoming personalized, i.e., of conforming voluntarily with the psychic lawfulness represented by the divinity—or to put it more clearly, instead of harmonizing the psychic processes and thus the desires—man will always tend to want only to individualize himself in a conventional and excessive manner by exalting his desires. He will expect the divinity to satisfy his individually exalted desires.

In the second phase of the pagan era, the motivating cause of *cultural decadence* is rooted precisely in the fact of the individualization of guiltiness, which, as any evolutionary progression, bears in itself the danger of involution—or as the myth puts it, fall is the consequence of elevation when the latter becomes vain. This mythical truth is based on the psychological fact of the lawfulness of motivational functioning, lawfulness which is summed up in the relationship between guilty feeling and vanity. Being egocentric over-elevation, vanity is the product of a repression of guiltiness and it is in a vicious circle the means of repression through its tendency to self-justification.. *A feeling of self-dissatisfaction, guiltiness in its individualized form, implies an intensified self-dissatisfaction which can become the motive for a just elevation precisely insofar as guiltiness is consciously understood as a dissatisfaction of the ethical superconscience, but which on the contrary, becomes a motive of vain self-elevation—in other words, a motive of fall—precisely insofar as liberation is sought for in the deceptive satisfaction of the inclination to repression.*

However, in the evolutionary process, elevation remains the essential goal. Fall is but an accident. Its terrifying consequence includes the possibility of becoming the motive for an intensified effort of evolutionary elevation.

The most characteristic feature of the successive decadence of cultures is not the manifest and spectacular destruction of their superannuated cultural infrastructure. The essentially characteristic feature is the fact that the aging of cultures and the horrors of their agony become the motivating cause of a slow effort acting secretely with the aim of recoverying—with the help of a more evolved formulation—the immutable ethical truth: demand for harmony which is biogenetically founded, and thus superconsciously immanent to the human level. It is the immutable meaning of life, *mythically called "eternal truth."* Just as the "dead in the soul" individual must be born again, so the cultures whose soul is dead must also be reborn to "life eternal": to life in conformity with the eternal ethical truth. Just like mystery, the immutable ethical truth is not subject to the law of temporal life. But temporal life, in spite of the possibilities of aberration, and precisely because it is rooted in mystery, is essentially positive and evolutionary *in its forms of expression*. Mythical faith evolves into a new symbolic formulation of the truth which is mysteriously immanent to life. It evolves toward faith in an only God, called in the Old Testament *"The Eternal" because he is the symbol of the eternal ethical truth immanent to the psychic functioning*.

In order to pave the way for an approach to the acme of mythical evolution, we must recapitulate briefly the stages leading to the summit of symbolization.

From the two phases of polytheism, it is important to distinguish clearly the three periods in the history of the "Divinity" symbol: animism, polytheism, monotheism.

The thinking being, who at the beginning of his mythical evolution was only a trembling creature abandoned in the midst of an incomprehensible and frightening environment, became as the spirit awoke in him, the center of nature and of mythology: the comprehensive center, reflecting the whole of the universe, a mirror in which life and universe attempt to attain their own understanding. The living being, lost and insignificant in the universe, becomes through evolution the meaningful axis around which the universe gravitates. This is the highest dignity of man. To the struggle against the adversity of the surrounding nature was added the inner struggle against the very nature of man and its affective beclouding, a struggle aimed at the evolutionary achievement of his supreme dignity in which, again, the interior sun (or spirit) and the interior light (understanding enlightenment) are his best guide and protector.

2. MONOTHEISM

The third period in the history of the divinity symbol crowns the mythical evolution.

Monotheism also has two phases, delineated by the Old and the New Testaments.

The two testaments complete each other. They contain, symbolically represented, the essential history of the human species, the evolutions and involutions of psychic life which has become semiconscious: the victories and the defeats in the conflicts of the inner motivational deliberation which is the common theme shared by animism, polytheism, and monotheism. The radical differences is that monotheism condenses the conflicts in the law of superconscious harmony (only God) and the law of subconscious disharmony (Satan).

The Old Testament narrates the history of the people symbolically chosen by the only God (actually chosen because they were the first ones to conceive the monotheistic vision). The text relates a real history interspersed with symbolism: the covenant with the Almightly (vision of the eternal truth) and the countless relapses.

The New Testament shows that in the midst of the decadence of peoples and cultures, the individual can be "born again" to the meaning of life.

The advent of monotheism is codetermined by an accidental and external fact: the progress of civilizations. The agrarian peoples of polytheism have become the founders of powerful empires. Such a transformation took place long before Israel had become, in its turn, a kingdom after its slavery in Egypt. It is not impossible that the monotheistic culture of the Hebrews could have been influenced by the Egyptians who already knew a supreme deity: Amon Rashunter. Whatever the case may be, the influence could only have been codeterminant because the myth of the covenant dates from the time of Abraham. The fact remains that only the Hebrews created a genuine monotheistic myth, already established in the time of Moses, and turned into a theological system when Israel was a powerful kingdom (though it was relatively weak and constantly threatened by the great powers of those days: Egypt, Assyria, Babylon). In the large cities, riches piled up, multiplying the temptations of banalizing pleasures, but a new plague appears: the clashes between the cities which envy one another's wealth. This inspired the prophets to remind the rebellious peoples of the meaning of the covenant and the foreseeable consequences of breaking the convenant, i.e., essential perdition, loss of the vital impulse and the danger of losing the strength and courage to resist the assault of the enemy: "God will give the people who forget the covenant into the hands of the foes." This prophecy came to pass—as much historically as it did essentially—and prepared the advent of the prophet Jesus. But the people were awaiting only a messiah according to the flesh, who would free them from the Roman yoke, while he was the messiah according to the spirit, whose kingdom is not of this (banalized) world.

Since there are not multiple deities and multiform monsters, the conflicts of motives are not represented by the exteriorized battles of the pagan myths' heroes.

The prophets of the Old Testament, while referring to the "covenant and break" symbolism, already explained clearly and in plain words the causes and effects of the people's banalization. "Vanity of vanities, all is vanity!" exclaims Ecclesiastes. The prophets do not lay the blame for the vain fault on a more or less abstract society, and their warnings, while addressed to the entire people, are meant for each individual so that he would not use the general perversion as an excuse and as a vain justification of his own share in the common guilt. This individualization of guiltiness is most clearly expressed in the Psalms of David.

In the Christian myth, the individualization of guiltiness reaches its acme.

(In the polytheistic mythologies—especially in Greek mythology—the different shades of temptations are specified with the help of a multitude of heroes, each one of whom fights his own predominant temptation represented by some specific monster. Most of the heroes die, which shows the difficulty of victory in intrapsychic conflicts.) The Christian hero does not attack some specific temptation but the principle of all individual temptations: vital guilt, the innate weakness of human nature, the sin of Adam, which, because it is individualized in each man, becomes the guilt of the world and the responsibility of each individual for common suffering. By fighting against the guilt of the world in himself and talking openly about the intrapsychic conflict, the Christian hero unveils the meaning that had been hidden in the symbolic struggles of polytheism. But there is more: by talking openly about his own struggle and victory, he unveils the principle of the introspective method: "Be constantly on your guard because he (Satan) is always prowling around you." He is always around because the whole world neglects the essential struggle so that everyman individualizes the common guilt[5] and makes it impossible to attack by justifying himself vainly through the perverse state of the world, thinking himself to be its innocent victim. "We see"—as is said in the Bible—"rather the straw in our brother's eye than the beam in our own." (in our introspective eye).

In this respect, nothing is more important than to understand clearly the difference between vital guilt, the guilt of the whole world and individualized guilt, the vain guilty feeling of each man. This distinction is the key to symbolic language because it is the key to understanding the inner motivating functioning.

Vital guilt is the imaginative exaltation of desires (material and sexual desires)—the forbidden fruit of the tree of knowledge—the banal greed of desires making man the enemy of man. *The individualized guilt,* the guilty vanity of every man is defined by the ceaseless false self-justifications of one's own vital guilt—one's imaginative exaltation of desires—whether these imaginations be banally fulfilled or hypocritically hidden: repressed by the moralism of the Pharisees. What the Christian myth unveils is the immanent punishment of the common fault: every feeling of guiltiness is through false self-justification projected in the form of accusation of others who indeed, since they are also falsely motivated, are included in the vital guilt which is shared by all. But everyone uses the accusation of others as a self-excuse under the pretext that he would be perfect and faultless if only the others were not unfair to him. Self-justification finally becomes self-glorification. Everybody tends to see himself as the only just person in an unjust world. Thus it is perfectly natural that in the end all the supposedly just men, by blaming one another for injustice, wind up not only in imaginative but in real and active aggression. The justifying pretext will be at times the principle of banalism (to abuse others in order not to fall prey to their

---

5. See notes on page 9.

abuses), and at times the principle of inquisitorial idealism (to attack others, eliminate the unjust in order to purify and improve the world). The message of salvation of the New Testament—according to its real significance—might reveal itself as being the only just solution.

If the moral problem finds its exemplified and explicit solution in the biblical texts, the metaphysical problem, on the other hand—mystery—continues to be symbolized by God, continues to be personified, to be superconsciously dreamed. The myth, while expressing realistically and not only symbolically the moral meaning through the prophet Jesus, reserves symbolic expression for the unfathomable mystery of life and death. In a unique instance in the history of mythology, the Christian hero himself tells in symbolic terms "the intentions of God" with respect to mortals, a symbol for the real intentions in the human soul.

Here is the myth told by Jesus, absurd in its facade, as were all the ancient mythologies: "I am the son of God the Father come down from heaven to bring to mortals the message of joy and salvation." This message, falsely, textually understood and proposed, is known by everybody, believer or unbeliever. It is in fact the main cause of unbelief because it deals with the promise of a life after death. God himself would have decided to grant grace and pardon to the sons of Adam. From now on, all men will continue to live eternally after their death, some in Heaven, the others in Hell, depending on the merits or demerits of their life on earth.

If God is a symbol, if the filiation is a symbol, the intentions of God with regard to men are also symbols, grace is a symbol, and the message of joy will also have a symbolic meaning. To find its hidden meaning, it would suffice to introduce, instead of bodily death and eternal survival of the individuals, the symbolic "death" of the animating impulse during life and the rebirth during life to the eternal ethical truth. It really seems that this is the only meaningful solution, for if death—as the Bible says—came because of the sin of Adam and if that death had been the death of the body, we would have no choice but to believe that if Adam had not disobeyed God's commandment, he would have been immortal. It follow that God, by forgiving the sons of Adam for the sin of their ancestor, had to reestablish earthly immortality. But human reasoning—as we know—is powerless when it tries to shake beliefs that are too solidly rooted.

One should therefore try to see if it is possible to find an irrefutable proof of the error in theological reasoning.

The answer is in fact implicitly contained in all the preceding analyses of the evolutionary history of the divinity symbol. We shall therefore try to clarify even further the symbolic implications developed until now, so as to reach the conclusion which will have to show how the evolutionary destiny of mankind is expressed in the symbolism of monotheism, and this will necessarily introduce new elements.

In view of the importance of this subject, we must regroup and expand the symbolic elements that have already been brought to light by the evolutionary history leading from animism and polytheism to monotheism.

The purpose of the preceding developments was to eliminate metaphysical speculation due to the literal interpretation of the texts, in order to replace it with the biogenetical immanence of the ethical problem and the superconscious immanence of emotion in the face of mystery.

Man created his idealized image, called "God," and the myth will say that man was created in the image of God. The myth is right in saying this because the spirit analogically and lawfully developed the superconscious image called for by the mystery of existence: the vision of an only God conceived in the image of the spirit of ultimate truth, symbol of the meaning of life, symbol of the essence of life.

Just as the ancient deities were not realities but symbols, the only God is not a reality. He is a symbol. His symbolic origin goes beyond polytheism and is lost in the ancestral obscurity of animism: he is the father-ancestor who has become the father-creator of all men.

The true significance of the "only God" symbol is the very same as that of the ancient symbolisms. But the truth is hidden in it under its most evolved form.

The multiple spirits that animism projected onto each being and each object are condensed in a one and only Spirit, creator and organizer of the universe. It is still, as was the case with animism, the projection of the human spirit and its intentionality, i.e., an anthropormorphic explanation of the mysterious intentionality found in all nature and ruling all natural phenomena.

The "only God" symbol combines the moral and metaphysical meanings. Being the symbol of manifest creation, God is metaphysically personified and becomes, symbolically speaking "the Creator." He presides over the inexplicable and mysterious fact (which can be expressed only in dream and image), the patent fact that mystery became apparent; that a world "emanated" from it, broke away from mystery and that it bears in itself the stigma of this divorce: the initial discord between spirit and matter, to be transformed into concord and harmony. The moral aspect deals with the fundamental opposition between the essential desire of reunion and the carnal and multiple desires that are only too often imaginatively and vainly exalted: principle of evil personified by "Satan," the anti-God. The latter does not preside over creation, does not take part in the "creative act"; God did not create evil: evil is the indispensable condition for the duality of existence, for the initial discord defining existence. The whole problem of existence is to overcome the discord, which can be accomplished only by an interpenetration of spirit and soma-matter. Their progressive interpenetration is the principle of evolution. The opposition between spirit and flesh

will be overcome in evolution through the actual fact that the spirit becomes materialized—or, to put it in other words, that matter becomes
spiritualized, or, as the Christian myth expressed it, *"The spirit becomes
flesh": the spirit becomes incarnate."*

This is an entirely new symbolism, characteristic of the Christian
myth exclusively. The chief error of dogmatism is rooted in the misunderstanding of the "incarnation" symbol.

The "incarnation" symbol and its misunderstanding preside over all
the sacramental rituals: baptism, communion, confirmation, and above
all the Mass and its claim to transform bread into spirit, the host into
the real body of Jesus.

Relics of the magical rituals of animism and the purification rituals of
polytheism, the sacraments remain based on very ancient symbolism:
bread and wine, food for the spirit and soul. During the Last Supper,
the meaning of the symbol used by Jesus as a sign of his ultimate be-
quest is all the more moving. His disciples could not have entered a
state of grace by drinking wine and eating bread. They did so only
through the teaching they had received and through their own vital impulse leading them to follow—within the limitations of their own
strength—the example of their master: *Purification of the apparent self in
order to achieve the essential self.* Only this active self-sacrifice can open
the gate to the "kingdom of heaven," the imaginary place where all
fears are vanquished, where imperishable joy rules, symbolically called
"eternal."

Crowning achievement of mythical life, the Christian myth is based
on the symbolism of the incarnation of the spirit. Jesus, a unique man,
illustrates through his actual life the symbolic truth of the myth. The
hero sacrifices actually and totally his apparent self to his essential self
through which he is united to the essence of life, symbolically speaking:
to the "Father." The entire life of the hero is just this essential and sublime consecration. Through this complete sacrifice, through the sublimating purification in conformity with the quasi-superhuman impulse,
the meaning of life becomes manifest, the lawful essence appears. The
spirit of life, i.e., the clearest expression of mystery or, symbolically
speaking, the "Word" of God, becomes incarnate, appears through the
activity of a human being. "God was made man." But these symbolic
affirmations lose all their deep truth when they are mistaken for realities. The hero of this experienced myth is—as the myth says—son of
God and son of Man: son of Adam. He is man become "son of God,"
man who has vanquished the demonic tendency (subconscious) and who
has accomplished the divine tendency (superconscious) of human nature. He is the symbolically "deified" man, the "God-Man." He
"comes down from heaven," i.e., leaves his solitary concentration, his
superconscious contemplation (heaven), the fullness through which he

could be self-sufficient, and he delivers himself to men still prey to the demonic tendency. He delivers himself to the apparent world and its suffering, to errors, to darkness. He takes upon himself all the suffering, all the fear that the world can inflict. He bears, carries, the whole guilt of the world. But all the suffering by which the world—prey to the demon—wants to affect him, cannot essentially perturb his rest in the meaning of life, his sublime joy. He remains living trust, love embracing essence and appearance, mystery and men, life in its entirety. He vanquishes the darkness and its demon, fear. He is the mythical light chasing the darkness away. Since he is a real man, he is the mythical hero who has become a real example, symbolically "the One who was sent," and the "son" of God, he who through the sacrifice of all earthly desires vanquishes all earthly anxiety, he who through the total sacrifice of his apparent life, reconciles erring appearance[6] with the ultimate meaning of life, with the essence of life, with the symbolically "divine" principle. He reconciles man with God. He shows that all sources of fear are powerless if the individual listens to the superconscious call, if he knows how to fulfill the essential desire, pursue essential satisfaction, the most intense joy; if he is inspired by perfect trust in life, by unshakable faith in mystery. The spirit of God (the meaning of life) is incarnate in him: it has become a motivating force. The mythical hero who is no longer a mere symbolic fiction but the actually exemplary hero, an actual person, gives us to understand the way to salvation and the possibility of this way. Being the definitive victor over life and death (of the soul), victor over human vanities, victor over darkness and fear, he gives us to understand the victory is a superconscious potentiality immanent to life, just as much as the initial weakness personified by the myth of Adam.

The meaning and the purpose of the analysis of the divinity symbol leading to the analysis of the "only God" symbol go far beyond the indispensable polemic against established beliefs.

The purpose is to prove the power of symbolic language and its psychological pre-science.

In this respect, analyzing the symbolism of the Christian myth is only a special instance and the underlying polemic of this book has, as it were—compared to the essential purpose—only an accidental importance due to the fact that the dogmatization of the Christian myths is the present foundation of Western culture.

The analysis of symbolic language and its evolution was up to this point, based on the past history of the central "divinity" symbol leading to the "incarnation" symbol belonging exclusively to the Christian myth, the central symbol of the gospels.

---

6. See note on page 23.

When further pursuing the psychological meaning of mythical language, it will thus be indispensable to concentrate on the "incarnation" symbol, which is the most evolved one, so as to show that, like all the other symbols, it contains a secret reference to the inner motivating functioning of the psyche. At first view, it does seem evident that if the symbolism of the "incarnation of the divine spirit in man" contains a hidden meaning, the latter—expressed in psychological terminology—could only be the incarnation in man of the evolutionary meaning (harmony), an achievement due to the authentic impulse of an exemplary man capable of vanquishing the weakness of Adam (vain temptation), the supreme spiritualizing force whose result is represented by the "sanctification" symbol (does not the hero say, "I have sanctified myself for you!"?).

If it could be proven that such is the meaning of the "incarnation" symbol, we would have no choice but to admit that the study of motivations is the key to the understanding of symbolic language: that symbolic language contains a pre-science of the inner motivating functioning from the pre-mythical era of animism right up to the completion of the mythical era.

The historical fact remains that the superconscious creation of the "incarnation of the only God in the only man" closes the mythical era, since it is impossible to reach a higher degree of expressive intensity in symbolic language.

The incarnation is the central symbol of the myth of the *divine trinity*, which is the most evolved form of the "divinity" symbol.

The post-mythical era is essentially characterized by the rule of dogmatism, a systematization based on the textual interpretation of the trinity myth, the prologue of the gospel of John.

In order to grasp in all its fullness the meaning of the "incarnation" symbol, it is thus dispensable to decipher, phase by phase, the myth of the trinity, a long and arduous but extremely rewarding task.[7]

The only purpose is to stress the truth of this book's thesis, namely, the existence of a psychological pre-science in the symbolic language of myths as proven by analyizing the evolution of the divinity symbol.

The analysis of the divinity symbol would be incomplete without a deciphering of the most evolved symbolism: the trinitarian divinity of the New Testament.

It would be impossible—though we do regret it—to undertake this deciphering without further polemics against established beliefs. Yet even the deciphering of the "trinitarian divinity" symbol and its confrontation with dogmatization—the essential error cutting across all the post-nythical eras—will not exhaust the meaningful depth of the "only God" symbol. It will be necessary to devote to its detailed deciphering a special chapter in the second part of this book.

---

7. See P. Diel, J. Solotareff, *Le Symbolisme dans L'Evangile de Jean* (Payot, 1983).

C. THE POST-MYTHICAL ERA

1. DOGMATIC SYSTEMATIZATION

Immediately following the completion of mythical life by the Christian myth's hero, the secret truth of symbolization starts to be lost. From then on, human life and culture—especially Western culture, which is directly influenced by the Christian myth—are nothing but the history of the fear due to the metaphysical and moral uncertainty that dogmatism vainly attempts to contain, and of the ceaseless spiritual fight against the error of dogmas, a fight which defines the essential history of the West.

After the death of the victorious hero, both the tradition of the example and the metaphysical myth had to be safeguarded, i.e., the history of the real life and the symbolic explanation of that life's significance—a symbolically veiled explanation narrated and bequeathed by the hero himself and related in the biblical texts. The institutions that were established for such a purpose, the churches, wanting to avoid the possibility of individual errors, of interpretation of the symbols according to personal inclinations, saw only one way to reach their goal: to deny the symbolic significance and to understand the texts verbally and literally. Such a position could not fail to arouse considerable opposition; for a long time, it was in conflict with vague and non-methodical attempts to search for a plausible meaning in the enigmas of the texts. Such attempts were suppressed by means that are well known. Verbal exegesis won the day. One has to admit that in the absence of an understanding of the inner motivating functioning—indispensable for deciphering the symbols—dogmatization was the only means to put an end to disputes over interpretation. However, such a means, which was insufficient to safeguard the unity of the church as a social institution, was extremely dangerous for the church as the guardian of the essential truth. In order to cover up the nonsense and incoherence of verbal acceptance, dogmas had to be invented which considerably transgressed against the principle of fidelity to the texts, leading to the schism between the Roman and Orthodox churches. Within the Roman church itself, the quarrels that at one time concerned the way of interpreting the texts turned more and more into disputes about the validity of such and such a dogma. This made it necessary—in order to safeguard the unity of the institution—to issue decrees telling people what they had to believe in order not to be struck with anathema, a frightening tool of the church and its growing power. In its zeal to obtain blind belief, the ecclesiastical hierarchy let itself be pushed to fanaticism, to the most extreme cruelty, thus putting itself in a position of patent contradiction with the moral foundation of the mythical teaching. The misunderstanding of the message provided a supreme justification: torture and execution were justified as saving the "immortal soul" of the victim. The later consequence of dogmatic intolerance and its promises of a finally purchasable immortal life (indulgences) became a new cause of protest within the church: Lutheran Protestantism leading rapidly to the creation of new and numerous churches, independent from one another, and all separated from Rome.

The facts are known. However, it is not superfluous to sum them up briefly so as to highlight the common cause: the misunderstanding of the myth of the trinity and of its central symbol, the "incarnation."

What unites all the churches that originated in Rome, in spite of their diverse theologies, is the erroneous interpretation of the message of salvation, understood as a promise of individual resurrection after death when the injustice ruling over the earth ("vale of tears") will be erased by a transcendent justice, having nothing in common with the concept of human justice, since both reward and punishment are immeasurably exalted in an eternal life in heaven or in the fire of hell.

The decay of dogmatic beliefs is manifest in our time through the existence of numerous sects or small groups, each of whom is armed with its own theology. Truth is not determined by the number of believers within such or such a sect, since the truth exists quite independently from the vote of majorities or minorities.

Doubt has never ceased to oppose blind belief, within the churches as well as outside their doctrines; but the hope of a future freed from dogmatic obscurantism has never ceased either. Is it not true that the decisive stages in the search for liberation are engraved in the memory of history through names witnessing to the hope of enlightenment: Renaissance, Reformation, the century of Enlightenment? Nowhere has the truth—which existed before dogmatization and is perduring—found a more striking expression than in the New Testament; "Let the light (of superconscience) shine in the dark (of the subconscious)." (This same significance was prefigured in the inscription on the pediment of the temple of Apollo, god of harmony and psychic health: "Know thyself." To know oneself is to know even the secret motives of the multiple forms of one's vain confusion.)

The historically necessary institution of official religions contributed to keeping alive the memory of the living example and to maintaining an interest in the texts relating the authentic myth. Thus, in spite of dogmatization, mythical truth was able to reach and touch souls endowed with a genuine religious force, since within the church true faith never died entirely. Nevertheless, dogmatization never achieved its main goal, which was unification, having finally provoked not only contradictory theological systems but the overwhelming doubt of our time.

Though the dogmatization of the biblical texts was a historical necessity, since the existence of a symbolic language was unthought of at that time, the fight against dogmatic error is no less—and even more—a historical necessity. It might perhaps be fairer to point out that it was not so much the existence of symbolization that was unforeseeable but the possibility of having the tools necessary to discover a valid solution to its enigma. History has known many attempts to do so, and they were all based on the hypothesis that the hidden meaning should be of psychological significance. However, the idea that the deities themselves could be symbolic figures was almost always absolutely excluded. We do not intend to enter into the details of those attempts whose results were so disappointing that they wound up discrediting the mythical fables. On the other hand, it is important to stress emphatically and with admiration that the main purpose of the works of Plato—the acme of Greek philosophy—was to prove that the deities are symbols of superhumanly idealized qualities. One wonders through what hidden motive the finding of this essential truth by one of the greatest ancient philosophers—whose works are still studied today in their slightest details—has not aroused all the interest that the existence of symbolization imposes on the human mind. All the more so that, without the slightest effort of deep analysis, the psychological significance of the deities is beyond dispute in Greek mythology. To give only a few examples: Zeus symbol of the spirit, Hera symbol of love, Athena symbol of wisdom and combativity of the vital impulse, Apollo symbol of harmony. Without insisting on the motive that prevented the acceptance of such evidence (the impossibility of approaching symbolic pre-science without a preliminary study of the psychic functioning), we must stress—to the credit of certain theologians—that it has now become almost common to admit that certain passages of the texts—for instance the talking serpent—might well have a symbolic meaning. However, if one image may have a symbolic meaning, could it not also be true that other details which are difficult to accept as realities may also be symbols? However, it is not enough to admit—were it only one symbol—without knowing precisely what a symbol is in general and without being able to say what a particular symbol means.

But the main difficulty in proving the existence of a symbolic language comes from a quite different complication: the obligation of a polemic against two solidly entrenched fronts. This must be brought up since the hidden meaning of the myth of the trinity is just as opposed to theological theism as it is to the atheism of life sciences and their theories of evolution. The underlying meaning of the myth is precisely the history of the evolution of psychosomatic organisms and not only of the soma-matter. This is contrary to what the materialism of sciences of life claims when—to oppose as radically as possible the belief in a real god and in his intentions with regard to man—it denies all intentionality, not only the evolutively manifest mysterious finalistic intentionality of nature in its entirety, but also the no less manifest motivating intentionality of the thinking species, thus downgrading evolution to the level of a game of chance and turning man into an automaton.

These preliminary remarks are indispensable, since the need to analyze the symbol of the trinitarian divinity makes possible a decisive development in the study of the "divinity" symbol which has thus far been necessarily based on the study of its historical origins. All the preceding analyses were aimed at awakening the awareness of symbolization's importance in history of cultures. But in fact, the superconscious and pre-scientific explosion of the essential truth does not concern solely the mythologies of the past. It goes beyond imagination. We all know—superconsciously—the meaning of the mythical dreams of the past, since we use their most ancient symbols in our own dreams. Our dreams are superconscious warnings, individualized myths in which we are the fighting heroes struggling against the wrong motivations of our daytime errors. Just as the mythological heroes (fighting against their perverse intentions represented by monsters and demons) often die by suffering—symbolically speaking—the "death of their animating impulse," we too can be faltering heroes in our dreams which turn into nightmares if in our daily life we fall into the "monstrous temptations" of conventional banalism (sin of Adam) while repressing our feeling of guiltiness. Who are we? This is an unfathomable mystery. In our dreams we live outside temporality. Not only is the dreamer using the most ancient symbols, but all the long forgotten details of his own past life are also present to him. All that which is repressed is unmasked by the introspective look. Spectator of his defeats as well as aware of their most hidden motives, the dreamer is at the same time the judged culprit and his own judge applying the laws of immanent justice. If this is the case, the other half of our fleeting life, our waking life and its often subconsciously motivated activity is but banal conventionalism, daydreaming, torpor, beclouding of the mind through ceaseless self-justifications.

It could be true that in the state of nocturnal dreaming we are outside of temporality, united to mystery, in a quasi-supernatural superconscious state, though it is a natural one because it is included in the secret of the inner psychic functioning. The symbol of the divine trinity contains the answer since it contains—summit of all mythical symbolization—the answer to all the problems of existence, summed up in the symbolism of the "incarnation of the spirit." Its dogmatic interpretation is the central knot of the theological system. It will not be possible to untie it without further amplifying a polemic, painful in itself, but beneficial if we want to seek the truth.

2. THE MYTH OF THE TRINITARIAN DIVINITY

The trinitarian symbol is the theme of the prologue of John's gospel. According to its true symbolic scope, the prologue contains all the aspects of the Christian myth. All the later developments in the analysis of the "only God" symbol will be helped by its deciphering.

The symbol includes three persons: God-the-Creator, the Word, and the incarnate Word, mistakenly seen by dogma as real and supernatural persons. In accordance with the preceding studies, the deciphering will have to prove that, here as elsewhere, the supernatural is a pure metaphysical symbol whose hidden meaning is *the natural meaning which is immanent to temporal life.* The work of deciphering will necessarily be lengthy because it is not enough to simply affirm propositions but they must be controlled step by step through a constant confrontation with passages of the biblical text that are themselves incomprehensible without reference to the hidden meaning of the central myth of the divine trinity. The meaning of the trinitarian myth is mainly condensed in the "incarnation" symbol, which, so far, has hardly been encountered. It is thus necessary to point out that the phrase "incarnation of the spirit" used in this work of deciphering will mean absolutely nothing more than manifest organization of matter, i.e., division of labor between the somatic organs: harmony. On the human plane, "incarnation" means the requirement of self-organization and self-harmonization of the psyche by the human spirit. The essential cause of actions being inner tensions—superconscious or subconscious motivating intentions—the incarnation of the spirit means harmonization of the conflict of motives, which is impossible without an elucidating autocriticism.

These definitions having been established, it will be possible to proceed with symbolic exegesis. The method is to seek the meaning hidden by the supernatural facade. If the supernatural is but a pure metaphysical symbolization, it ensues that the hidden meaning is *the natural meaning, immanent to life.*

The supernatural persons of the trinity myth represent—in conformity with the underlying meaning of all mythical symbols—*functions* that are immanent to manifest existence. The difference is that the symbolic persons of the "divine trinity" are metaphysical images, i.e., they do not concern—contrary to most symbolic figures—the motivating functions of the human psyche, but *the mystery of all existence and of its evolution leading to the emergence of the thinking species.* Dogma talks about a process of filiation supposed to be actually immanent to the nature of a "real god," and it introduces Jesus, a real man, in the bosom of God from whence he would have issued—as the second person of the trinity—since the origins of the created world, sitting next to his father and finally coming down to earth to bring to mortals the promise of immortality.

Let no one see in this terse summary any irony, but only the recording of an error whose consequences reach into the very least details of the dogmatization of the texts.

Here is the summary of the symbolic exegesis:

I- God is the mysterious meaning of life, *the first person of the trinity.* But he is not temporal life characterized by ceaseless modifications. He is the "unchangeable substance," or, in order to avoid this phrase which is too reminiscent of a material existence, he is the "essence" of life, though not its logical or physical essence, which would still be part of manifest existence. He is the mysterious, metaphysical, and symbolic essence. The phrase "Essence" (Soul-Essence, Father-Essence) will have throughout the meaning given herewith. In the same way, the phrase "Creator" is a symbol, made by way of an idealizing symbolic comparison with the intentional courses of man's voluntary activities.

II- Yet the mystery "exists." It exists for the human spirit in the manifest form of the universe. Universal existence is the *appearance*[8] of mystery, symbolically speaking: the creation of the "Creator." Just as man reflects, thinks, before making a material object, "God-the-Creator" is imagined as having thought before the creation of the material universe. The spirit of God is incarnate in it, materialized. The manifest appearance is thus "the Spirit of God": the "Holy Spirit," symbol of the manifest and mysterious organizing intentionality found throughout all nature. Since all symbols are made by way of idealizing human qualities, symbolization exempts God from the imperfection of human desire, which is compelled to wait for its satisfaction. God pronounces his creating intention, "Let the world be," and the world is. The existing world is the Logos or *"Word pronounced"* by God the Creator. In God—according to symbolization—the creating intention (the Spirit), the creating act (Word), and the implementation of the intention the appearance or manifest universe are one. All these meanings are included in the symbol of the *second person of the Trinity*: the Logos, the pronounced Word of which it is said that it was from the beginning with "God," because for symbolism, the temporal world, the "Logos," starts to exist with and through the "Word of God."

The most characteristic feature of the existing world is temporality and its duality: appearance-disappearance, life-death, composition-decomposition, harmony-disharmony. But in all temporal modifications, the "Spirit of God," the incarnate Holy Spirit (principle of organization and harmonization) is always being reincarnated anew through all the stages of manifest evolution and will continue to manifest itself in the future. World and life are summed up in the evolutionary thrust, in the progressive spiritualization of living beings, an objectivating spiritualization going from animal unconscious to human consciousness and superconscience. "Spirit," "Logos," or (it means the same thing) "Incarnate Word" thus mean the mysterious aspect of the manifest evolutionary thrust, the *animating impulse*, mysteriously active and evolutionarily motivating through time, through temporality: continuous creation. The preconsciously organizing and harmonizing spirit, "incarnate since the beginning," kindles, "lights up" life and finally "enlightens" it.

---

8. See note on page 23.

Now according to the Christian myth, the "incarnate Word," being in a constant state of incarnation—evolution—will lead back the living creation, the creature, to the creating principle, to the "Father-Essence" out of which it "emanated." In this form—future evolution—"the Logos," "the Holy Spirit" becomes the Paraclete, the symbol of mankind's effort towards an ever greater lucidity and understanding of the superconscious truth called "eternal truth," whose symbolic abode is "heaven." The mythical heaven is certainly not a real place. It is the symbolic location of the final reunion between the creation and its "first cause" (though the final union is imaginable only through a hyperbole following its directing line without ever reaching it).

III- In creation and in the course of evolution there appears the conscious being, partially enlightened though his enlightenment can be extinguished (the subconscious whose symbolism, opposite to heaven, is hell). But among the conscious beings, among men, there appears a unique man who is fully evolved, who has overcome the subconscious temptations. Having overcome the subconscious hell and its guilty torment, he ascends symbolically "to heaven" (the superconscious) from which he symbolically comes down to earth in order to bring to men the message of his achievement and of the joy which animates him. The evolutionary spirit of creation, the "Word of God," became fully manifest in him, became incarnate. Since the Logos, the "Word," is incarnate in him, his own word, his message is "the Word of God." He does all that his father (the Word of God in him) tells him to do: he is—as he says—one with the Father. He is "the light of the world" because the incarnate Spirit enlightens him. But the spirit is only individually incarnate in Jesus. *The third trinitarian person is not Jesus but the universal value of his achievement:* Christ, the Logos (the evolutionary impulse existing throughout all nature), the Holy Spirit (evolutionary progression toward an ever greater spirituality) can become on the human plane an effort of spiritualization-sublimation. At the highest degree of intensification, the "incarnate Word" in the man Jesus—the eternal truth that he exemplified—will become *the guiding ideal of mankind, the evolutionary ideal* which is only directive but which is a superconsciously active motivating force. *The third trinitarian person is Christ,* the Messiah, the personification of the message brought by the man Jesus. The image opposed to the dogma of the trinity demands a more developed analysis.

Polemics here are only an indispensable means of demonstrating, in spite of the rule of dogma, the moving and sublimely motivating meaning of the texts, i.e., the message of joy, meaning of the gospels.

The greatest obstacle being dogmatic interpretation systematized in the theologies, the method of deciphering seeks the hidden meaning of the message of joy which can only be the essential destiny of each man and, more generally yet, the destiny of the thinking species *whose only salvation lies in truthful thought about life: understanding of* "eternal truth."[9]

From what has already been proven, it follows that the myth of the trinitarian divinity predicts the directive path of future evolutions, going beyond the stage presently reached by the thinking species. The sanctified man brings—as it is said in the Bible—the purified appearance to his father. But this symbolic return of the appearance is—it must be stressed in order to eliminate any sentimentality—only a hope, approached in infinity: it is neither perfect nor absolute. The sanctified one, being not a god but a man, is not absolutely perfect in spite of his quasi-superhuman vital impulse. The appearance will never be perfect either. There is no absolute in temporality, which is the very principle of relativity. Its guiding ideal is perfectioning, i.e., continuous evolution. *The third trinitarian person is hope.*

Hope symbolized by the third trinitarian person is the possibility of rebirth of the animating impulse during the life of the body. Whose rebirth and rebirth to what?

Jesus dies in the body in order not to die in the soul: he resists the "powers of the world" until death. And he resists for the life of the only truth and not for any fanaticism. His example is of eternal value, an "immortal" example whose accomplishment, symbolically personified, as "Christ," lives forever in human memory, though it is periodically forgotten due to misunderstanding.

Being a mortal man, Jesus actually died, and his lifeless body underwent decomposition. But the impulse that animated him, Christ—the truth he taught—will rise again from the tomb on "the third day," according to the texts. The figure "three" is in numerical symbolism the symbol of the spirit: truth will become clear in a distant future when men, understanding the message of joy, by making "Christ be born again" in themselves, will be reborn (from the "death" of soul and spirit, from the incapacity to understand), from banal conventionalism, cause of the "death" of the vital impulse. More significant yet: the "death of the soul" is the sin of Adam, symbol of the perverse seductibility of human nature: every man can, during his lifetime, be reborn from the "death of the soul" (Romans 6:13: . . . offer yourselves to God, and consider yourselves dead men brought back to life.")

The "third day:" the rebirth of all mankind is symbolized by the myth of the Parousia. It is, according to the symbolism of the texts, the "last day" (of the world in its perverted form): the day when "Christ," the truth, will appear through the clouds (of darkness), the day when

---

9. Human destiny, symbolically represented by the trinitarian deity, is also present in the theogony of Greek mythology: Chaos, symbol of mystery; Uranus, the creating god; his son Chronos (time) representing the animal realm, preconscious life; Zeus, son of Chronos, symbol of the law ruling over human destiny (see chapter on theogony in *Symbolism in Greek Mythology*," (Payot, 2d ed., 1966; Shambhala, 1981).

"Heaven" (joy) will come down to earth, where the "dead in the soul" will be reborn to life in eternal truth.

The myth of the Parousia foresees the remote day when mankind will be reborn from the banalization which is the conventionalization of the spirit. Paul, in the First Epistle to the Corinthians 15:54–55: "When this perishable nature (subject to perverse temptations) has put on imperishability (the strength to resist temptation), and when this mortal nature (exposed to the "death of the impulse that should animate it") has put on immortality (life in eternal truth), then the words of scripture will come true: death (of the soul) is swallowed up in victory. Death, where is your victory (victory over the souls since the victory over the bodies has not been abolished)?" "O death, where is your sting?" (verse 56) "Now the sting of death is sin." What a mistake to believe that on "the last day" the deceased, rotten for centuries, will emerge in the flesh from the ground in which they were buried. This is a twofold error, since—according to the misunderstanding of the message of joy—the soul leaves the body at the very moment of death and rises instantaneously and directly to a heaven imagined as being located over the clouds. It is even a threefold error. For it seems quite clear that, according to the promise of dogma, not only the soul but the actual person such as he or she lived on earth, would continue to live eternally in "a transcendent heaven" or in "hell," which is imagined as being underground.

It would be superfluous to add proofs to what has already been proven. But because of the extraordinary power of condensation, which is an exclusive feature of symbolic language, and because the themes are so complex, it will be useful to sum up and elaborate on their meanings.

Being a real man, Jesus cannot be a person of the trinitarian symbol. He dies and does not come out of the tomb. What is reborn from the tomb—not from the tomb of Jesus but *from the tomb of the misunderstanding of his message—is the understanding of his message.* The meaning of his message of joy is that *in the midst of the decadence of a people (the "chosen" people), every man can individually and during his life on earth be reborn from the fallibility of human nature* symbolized by the sin of Adam, can resurrect from the Fall and stand upright.

Jesus, a real man, was himself exposed to diabolical temptation, which is symbolically attested in the gospels of Matthew and Mark. His rebirth from the temptation of Adam is symbolically represented by his baptism in the Jordan. This symbol of purification is—according to its underlying significance—identical to the symbol of the "incarnation of the Word." The identity is symbolically attested: the Word, second person—or to put it differently—the sublimating spiritualization, the "Holy Spirit" appears in the form of a dove (symbol of purity and purification) to witness to the fact that Jesus is his beloved Son, that the intensity of his impulse for purification will go beyond that of other men.

The "Holy Spirit," the manifest Logos, the Word of God, the second person *thus calls him his son*: "This is my beloved son." If Jesus were the second person—as the dogma pretends—the Word would become the son of Jesus. Jesus is neither the second nor the third person of the trinitarian image. He is "the beloved son of the Spirit" because, *man among men, he sanctifies himself through the effort of his own vital impulse*; otherwise his achievement would have no exemplary value. Dogma stresses not the life of Jesus, an example without peer, a guiding value as long as mankind will endure, but the death of a real god who would have come down from a real heaven in order to redeem mankind from the sin of Adam by sacrificing his life. Indeed this is what the texts say. *But the text, because it is symbolic, is entitled to have an absurd facade.* In it, all is symbol: Adam is the symbol of faltering mankind, Christ Jesus is the symbol of mankind in evolution. Hence comes the meaning of the message of joy in all its greatness: *human nature is not only weak, it is also strong*, man can fall, become prey to subconscious temptations, "die in the soul," but through the strength of his superconscious impulse, he can be reborn out of "death," arise, resurrect during his lifetime from death of the soul. Jesus is neither the third person of the trinity nor the second person. Jesus is a mortal man; *his achievement* is immortal. This achievement is not death on the cross, but the entire life of a unique man, the only one who through the strength of his vital impulse was able to "incarnate the Word." The vital impulse dies with Jesus. The achievement of his impulse will come out of the tomb of systematic mis-understanding. This achievement—forever exemplary—is symbolical-ly personified by two names: the message of joy symbolically represent-ed and called "Christ"; and the importance of the message for the future of mankind, the Paraclete. The trinitarian divinity represents *the principal stages of appearance in evolution: past, present and future.*

1. The origin, God the creator, symbol of mystery.
2. The manifest appearance of mystery: the Logos, the pronounced Word, the Spirit of God-the-Father; continuous evolution, progres-sive incarnation of the spirit, leading to the incarnation in the man Jesus and to his misunderstood message.
3. Future evolution in its essential aspect, the Paraclete, the Comforter, the consoling truth; the age-old effort of the sons of Adam to bring back Christ (the truth) from burial in error, and thus to resurrect themselves from the "death" of the spirits and souls, on the remote day of the "Parousia."

Is it not in this meaning that Jesus tells the apostles when he sees them moved by the certainty—perfectly foreseeable—of his soon-to-come death, death on the cross (punishment for rebellion), a fate which he knew was going to be his, "I will send you the Paraclete"? This means: your emotion proves that you will not die in the soul; my word will be incarnate in you. The promise was fulfilled on Pentecost when the Holy Spirit became incarnate in them, when instead of letting themselves slide and fall, they decided together to die in the body rather than betray the word and "die in the soul and spirit." That decision became motivating for their entire life.

In order to prepare the conclusion, it is indispensable to mention that there are two meanings to the symbolism of "filiation": one is the filiation within the trinitarian divinity (such as has been specified) and the other, the filiation—much more frequent in the texts—stressing the difference between all men, sons of God, and Jesus the man who is symbolically deified and becomes thus, in comparison with all other men, "the only son of God."

Now the popular image of a relationship of filiation between the divinity and man goes back to the beginning of time when the father ancestor was worshiped as a providential deity, supposedly watching magically over his children and imposing on them the tasks they had to perform in order to become worthy of his benevolence. The survival of the magical layer of the extra-conscious still exerts today its suggestive influence. The idea of a providence remains the strongest pillar of belief in the dogmas. In this respect, one must take into account that in the flowery languages of the Orient, cradle of the myths, the term "son of" was barely symbolic. It was rather a metaphor indicating the morality or immorality of the person and the meaning: "you behave as if you were the son of the lotus, son of a jackal, etc." In this vein, Jesus tells the Pharisees, "You are the children of Satan." In a meaning which is closer to symbolism, all men are sons of God: creatures of the creator. They should be so in their character, even in their most secret motivations. When Caiaphas asks him, "Are you the son of God?" Jesus answers, "It is you who said it." (How can you, high priest, not know that we are all children of the creator and that we must be sons worthy of the father?)

The confusion between trinitarian filiation (which deals with the—symbolically personified—successive evolutionary functions) and metaphorical filiation (dealing with the real character of man) is one of the main causes of theological confusion.

The meaning of the "trinitarian divinity" symbol, supernatural according to the facade, deals with the most essential natural phenomenon: the evolution not only of matter but also of spirit, represented by the "incarnation" symbol.

Such an acknowledgement downgrades *neither the divinity*, whose highest significance is mystery, *nor the human spirit*, whose highest manifestation is the superconscious creation of symbolic language, a language used even by the hero of the Christian myth in order to express his message.

Rationalizing symbolization by understanding it according to the letter leads to the wildest and most fanciful affirmations, especially when one rationalizes the summit of all mythical productions: the symbol of the trinitarian divinity. The whole mythical depth is destroyed if the Word, according to dogma, is taken for an actual person: Jesus, seated since the beginning at the right hand of the Father, deciding finally to encase himself in a robe of flesh in order to come down to earth. Everything becomes natural and clear when one introduces the symbolic meaning: the Word (the evolutionary meaning) is incarnate in a real man; the real man (the flesh) becomes the manifestation, the achievement of the sublime meaning of life. The Word remains a symbol and the man remains a reality.

The symbol of the trinitarian divinity is the mythical vision of somato-psychic evolution: the progressive incarnation of the spirit.

This translation, which is at the same time natural and deep, links up with the deciphering of all the other symbols of the Christian myth and of the polytheistic mythologies in a harmonious connection, joyful and moving and able to satisfy both the most deeply religious soul (capable of freeing itself from dogma) and the most highly scientific mind, capable of freeing itself from the materialistic dogma of the sciences of life, whose evolutionist doctrines pretend that life emerged from inert matter, a thing which even a real God—if he could exist—could never have done.

3. RELIGION AND PHILOSOPHY

The decadence of the mythical cultures starts with the loss of the superconscious vision and institutes—as the only way to fight against doubt—dogmas imposed by decrees, which are themselves overcome by doubt sooner or later. New spiritual visions, new eras of the spirit and of its struggle against the unknown, the philosophical and scientific eras will replace the mythical vision.

Having already started long before the decadence of the mythical era, they will successively predominate without completely destroying the mythical vision and even the remnants of the magical vision.

The medieval culture of the West is basically different from the ancient mythical cultures. In their decline, the latter gave birth to the deepening of philosophical thought, as a means to make up for the later waning of faith. But medieval culture starts with this decline; from the outset it is founded on the dogmatization of the Christian myth struggling against philosophy, while the latter remains speculative, since it lacks the understanding of symbolic language. Theology and philosophy, in spite of their struggle, interact with each other, and it is precisely such a mixture which characterizes dogmatization.

Philosophy deals with the same vital problems as religion: metaphysics and morals. Thus the philosophical solutions of the ancient times (Plato and Aristotle) were used by the fathers of the church in order to speculatively dogmatize the mythical symbols, centered around the filiation symbol taken for a reality. Later on, scholastic philosophy took its inspiration from those ancient solutions while transforming them with the sole purpose of justifying the dogmas. One cannot, however, help but admire certain great figures of the Patristic and Scholastic schools and respect their zeal in struggling against the consequences of the initial error with respect to the "incarnation" symbol, a zeal which animated them with the tragic courage to go all the way in the error—which for them was unavoidable—and to defend it with speculative reasoning, against the imperious demands of reason itself. This initial situation, contradictory and therefore unreasonable—in order to repress doubt—led to devaluate human reason, to treat it with contempt and to oppose it with the so-called superior principle of divine revelation, namely the texts literally understood and declared indisputable.

The flaw of this reasoning going against reason becomes transparent if one realizes that it comes from a confusion between the symbolic and logical planes: myth defines the divinity through images of its activity; philosophy defines it through its attributes. In either case, the image-definition of God can be wrongly accepted as a reality: either concretely according to actions and intentions, or theoretically by attributing pure qualities as is the case with philosophy. It is tempting to believe that philosophy leads to the definition of the concrete image of theology. In fact, the two forms of expression remain on the same plane of misunderstanding of symbolization. However, the philosophical terminology is often closer to the truth. The attributes credited to the divinity are themselves anthropomorphic imaginations. But they are conceptualized images, God himself being understood as an abstract concept without taking into account that this concept cannot be put into any class, and thus cannot be defined or imagined. Hence philosophy is content with making of God a general concept embracing all the existing phenomena—the One, the Being, the Substance, the All, etc.—thus making of "God" a kind of preexisting entity, which is precisely metaphysical speculation. There is a great temptation to claim that only God exists and that the existing world is only illusion. Now nothing preexists existence, and this is precisely the mystery of existence. Only existence exists. It is not an illusion. It is the manifest appearance of mystery. Mystery is not just mystery. It reveals itself, manifests itself, it appears. All the attributes of existence, all its modalities and modifications, are revelations of mystery; and thus one is entitled to credit them to God, the symbol of mystery, provided, however, that they are withdrawn at the same itme, since all projection is anthropomorphic.

Through its twofold meaning, the facade of symbolization projects attributes onto God—he exists, he has intentions with regard to man—while withdrawing them through the underlying significance: the unfathomable mystery. Philosophy is speculative because when it is theistic it strives to prove that God exists and when it is atheistic it proves his non-existence while forgetting mystery. The fact is that this is a game and counter-game between imagination and reflection. Man can create an attribute image through the modalities of existence and thus personalize mystery. But reflection should always then dissolve the superdimensional projections in order not to become duped by them. (Mystery is neither absolute Spirit nor absolute Matter, neither spirit nor matter; it is the limit of the competence of the human spirit.) Mystery is neither infinite nor finite, which is why it cannot be defined. It is neither existent nor nonexistent: it exists, but only for the human mind as the unfathomable mystery of existence. It is neither eternal nor temporal since it is not the apparent fact of an endless flow from the past toward the future; eternity can only be imagined through the unimaginable image of an eternal presence. Mystery is neither immanent nor transcendent to spatio-temporal existence; *it is transcendent to reflection and immanent to emotion.* And the same is true for all the attributions which are both true and false. The human mind, compelled to swing between imagination and reflection, should admit that the mystery exists but that its mode of existence is unimaginable and unthinkable. And yet even this reflection is an anthropomorphic imagination of the mystery called God. Only the symbolic metaphysics of the myths is not speculative, since it is a superconscious imagination and not an unreasonable reasoning.

Theology is merely a logical reflection, a rationalization which is imaginatively distorted. This is why it has to lean on the metaphysical speculations of philosophy in the hope of finding there conclusive proofs for the personal existence of God.

Only the ceaseless self-control of the spirit, eliminating again and again any attribution and conclusion, is capable of leading to emotion in the face of the mysterious depth of existence and life, which includes human life and the life of the individual.

Dogma pretended to explain to human reason (at least to the reasoning of the believers) the mystery of the God symbol. All it did was to pit reason ever more strongly against beliefs. The *credo quia absurdum* became more and more a necessity for dogmatic belief since, having led to absurdity, the only way to vanquish doubt was to make a supreme virtue out of belief in absurdity. (The phrase *"credo quia absurdum"* was not coined by an enemy of the church but by a prelate. According to another version it was coined by a Father of the church.)

Philosophy—unable in the long run to persist in believing against reason—ended up by separating itself completely from religion. But being cut from its mythical roots, reduced to speculative and individual efforts forever contradicting one another it did not take long for metaphysical and moral philosophy to turn into a constant war of opinions. The cause of these divergences—which, however, are often only of a terminological importance—resides in the tendency, inherited from scholastics, to mistake metaphysical attribution for a reality. If this error is avoided, it becomes clear that the great philosophical systems marking the centuries all expressed the same truth: the Father-essence, which in itself is neither body nor spirit but "essence" that is mysteriously out of space and time, out of appearance. In other words: the evident and unfathomable mystery of life. Unable to free itself from an error which is more terminological than fundamental, philosophy starts to doubt its own capacity to grasp the vital truth, the metaphysical essence and the moral meaning of life that the mythical era had already been able to formulate symbolically. Speculative endeavor will show a growing tendency to withdraw in itself, to be content with a criticism of its own means, with a *Criticism of Knowledge*.

Thanks to this auto-criticism of the mind, the error of metaphysical speculations becomes the central problem: what right has human reason to speak of a real god? What right has it to credit him with human attributes?

The problem is formulated for the first time by the cogito of Descartes, "I think therefore I am." The intention of the cogito is to establish the following: "I do not know whether God exists, and therefore I do not know whether he created me. I know only one thing: I think. And since I think, I am, I exist."

The cogito of the great thinker started a renewal of human thought and a current of ideas the discussions of which continue to our time. The cogito implies the finding that human thought—itself an existing phenomenon—should study only existing phenomena and exclude any metaphysical speculation, as Descartes explains in detail in his *Discours de la Méthode*, which remains today the foundation of philosophy in the form of existentialism and phenomenology.

Though it is true that human thought can explain only existing phenomena, the error—already contained in Descartes' *Discours*—was to have forgotten the question imperiously demanded by the cogito: "How is it that I exist? How is it that anything exists?" Forgetting this essential question gave to theological metaphysics the opportunity to affirm that the Criticism of Knowledge started by Descartes, since it dealt only with existing phenomena, proved in the most decisive way that "the reasoning reason" (a phrase coined by theology) of the philosophers is incapable of understanding the depths of theology and its dogmas and thus that reasoning criticism wherever it comes from is worthless.

Criticism is indeed devoid of any efficacy as long as it does not manage to show that the error of theology is to rationalize the mythical "Divinity" symbol. This cuts short all the discussions between the reasoning reason of philosophy and the non-reasoning reason of theology: the only solution to the endless quarrel being to admit the existence of mystery.

In this respect it will be informative to briefly sum up the continuation of Cartesian thought insofar as it deals with the problem of Divinity.

The absence of the notion of mystery and the exclusive reference to logical thought recognized by the cogito as sole criterion of truth leads to *English Empiricism* and finally to the skepticism of Hume. Not only metaphysical thought attempting to scrutinize the supernatural but also logical thought accepted by Descartes as the only source of certainty would be only a trap. Thus, for instance, night follows day; but the day is not the cause of night. The cause is the disappearance of the sun. But then what is the cause of the stellar motions? Before Newton, the only possible answer was the reference to God, eliminated by the cogito. The problem is thus again to know whether God is a real and intentional person or a symbol of mystery. Since he could no longer refer to a real god and not yet to symbolism, Hume quite rightly doubted the very principle of logical thought: causality. The criticism of knowledge that Descartes had ushered in ran the risk of going around in circles.

German Criticism undertakes to study the matter from a new angle. The magistral solution proposed by Kant in his *Critique of Pure Reason* is well known. In order to reestablish the rule of causality, Kant introduces the concept of mystery. He calls it the "In-Itself of things," the unexplainable aspect of existing phenomena, the first cause, as it were; whose effect would be the manifest world, in its turn necessarily subject to the mysteriously preexistent link of cause and effect. Thus Kant for the first time in the history of philosophy introduces the distinction between what can be explained and what cannot be. But since for Kant the unexplainable is not the unfathomable mystery but the "thing in itself," first cause existing outside of the temporal, he does in fact reintroduce a real god, since for theology God has always been "the first cause," *causa sui*, i.e., the causal explanation of the unnameable mystery. The truth is that *Kant does not analyze pure reason, ethical superconscience*, but only logical thought, thus remaining faithful to the cogito while destroying it unknowingly, this being a magistral proof that human reason goes astray when it does not admit the existence of mystery. The unavoidable drift of reason, due to the wrongly posed question, becomes evident in the second part of *Critique of Pure Reason*. There Kant approaches the moral problem. Now morals have—as all existent phenomena—an immanent aspect and a mysterious aspect, the latter being inaccessible to reason and even to "pure reason" (what could be the meaning of that phrase, if not reason purified from any search for impure satisfactions such as sexual and material desires even in their natural form; which is finally the Kantian solution to the ethical problem?). As far as the immanent aspect of morals is concerned, it is the psychically immanent conflict between ethical superconscience and subconscious temptations. The notion of a psychical extra-conscious being unknown in his time, Kant finds himself compelled to reintroduce a real god as the principle of morals. The mystery which is symbolically named "God" is neither a thing nor a being. But since for Kant the mysterious In-Itself of the existing things remains a "Thing in Itself," he is unavoidably led to make it a "Being in Itself": the real god. For Kant, the existence of a real god is *"a postulate of pure reason,"* since, for him, no morals could be without the real existence of God. It is the *categorical imperative* of Kant, the morals of duty, i.e., complete moralism. For Kant, moral sense is not immanent to human nature. Quite the opposite, for him the merit of man is all the greater when he strives to submit against his will to the categorical imperative.

From then on, German Criticism—Fichte, Schelling—endeavors to eliminate the real god who had been reintroduced by Kant. The Criticism of Knowledge reaches its pinnacle in the *Phenomenology of the Spirit* of Hegel. The spirit is no longer a transcendent entity (the absolute Spirit of Scholastics which had become for Kant the unexplainable In-Itself finally explained as moral principle). The spirit, for Hegel, is an immanent phenomenon, leading by way of evolution to man's conscious thought and to the conscious immanence of moral sense. The "In Itself" of Kant is eliminated, but by the same token the notion of mystery is also eliminated. It is replaced by the ideal of the evolution of the psyche, a radically new thought in the history of philosophy. However, having been founded too intuitively, the idea of psychic evolution is finally overcome by the advent of materialistic evolutionism. The cogito philosophy splits, after encountering materialism, into the various schools of Phenomenology and Existentialism, the latter being deeply influenced by the advent of the psychology of the extra-conscious in the form of Freudism.

Yet the crucial problem of the limits of the competence of human thought has been posed, and philosophy cannot afford to ignore it. The critical attacks against the reality of "God" do not cease. But criticism itself falls into the grievous error of believing that metaphysics can only concern the reality of God. Instead of reducing the affirmations of metaphysics to their true symbolic value, criticism mistakes them for improvable opinions and denies them totally, denying at the same time the very possibility of symbolical metaphysics. The circle of error is closed; but it closes only to lead back to symbolic truth. For this circle started with the dogmatization of the symbols, with the speculative explanation of the unexplainable; a speculation through which belief in a real god is opposed to faith in the mystery of life: religion opposed to religiosity. What philosophy denies after having become criticism of knowledge is the possibility of really knowing God as a being supposedly real and living in a spatial beyond outside of the real space and the real world. But critical philosophy, by thus opposing dogmatic metaphysics, also denies the existence of mystery which has not spatial dimension but an emotional one and is thereby immanent to the psyche. It is true that the psyche is a natural and really existing phenomenon. But how could it not also be true that all natural phenomena have a mysterious aspect, immanent to all of nature and which should quite naturally become emotion in the thinking species in the face of the reality of the unthinkable and unexplainable mystery? It is thus not enough to say: "I think, therefore I am." The finding is right in itself, but it very naturally calls for the metaphysical question: "How is it that I think and that I exist?" The criticism of knowledge, by refusing to take into account the necessity of this unanswerable question, becomes itself dogmatic. Having gone through a complete circle in its research, it leads back to the crossroad where mythical truth was abandoned. It reopens the way to the only possible metaphysics: the symbolic metaphysics of the mythical dream.

Access to a true criticism of knowledge can be found only through a clear distinction between the logical plane (conscious) and the symbolic plane (superconscious). This means that the solution cannot be speculative and philosophical. It has to be scientific. Knowledge is a function of the psyche and its methodical analysis is possible only within the framework of the analysis of all the conscious and extra-conscious psychic functions. Like metaphysics and morals, the criticism of knowledge finds itself included in the problems of an introspective psychology when the latter does not shun its most natural and evident task: the analysis of the psychic processes. For indeed what problem endowed with a vital importance could be excluded from such a science when it is proceeding towards finding its proper method?

4. RELIGION AND SCIENCE

Science—a new stage in the evolution of thought—marks, after the end of mythical culture and its symbolical pre-science, the most serious endeavor to enlighten the modalities of existence as yet unknown in order to grasp their immanent meaning: the law.

The emergence and development of the sciences is a decisive reaction, a retort to dogmatic obscurantism, but it runs the risk of ending up in materialistic dogma. Physics, which is imitated in the most servile way by the sciences of life, has to deal only with the outer world and the motions of matter. External observation is its choice method. But if physics is thus an exact science, the sciences of life become inexact in imitating it. Being the science of the motions of matter, physics is content with struggling only against what is unknown in the external environment which has become universally enlarged. The scientific effort seeking to explain the harmony of the material universe, projects onto the exteriority, the organizing intentionality and calls it "Force." The notion of force in physics is metaphysical. Mathematical formulae do not explain "force"; quite the contrary, the harmonious organization which is mathematically expressible compels one to conclude that there is a mysterious organizing force. The mythical image (God) personifies the mysterious intention; physics makes it an abstract concept (force). But imagination as well as abstraction, image as well as concept, are only anthropomorphizations of the manifest mystery.

Physics, in order to become a science, thus started—quite unknowingly—by projecting psychic intentionality in the external world just as animism had done in a primitive way. Science, in order to embrace in its search for laws, the world, and life, might be compelled to go through the same evolutionary circle that led mythical culture from the animation of the environment to the introspective observation of psychic intentions ending in a preconscious formulation of the laws of life.

Proud of its experimental method, science rejects mythical dream and revelation to the extent of not even accepting them as objects of study. But in order to insure a direction for its experiments and to discover a meaning in its results, does it not use a form of revelation: methodically guided intuition? Science insists on expressing its results not in symbolic images but in exact formulae. But projection, personification, and symbolization exist also in the science of our time, the exact science, physics. Only projective personification (the impersonal force of physics conceived—whether one accepts it or not—as an analogy with the motivating force in man) and symbolization (mathematical expression) are not magically or symbolically primitive; they are spiritualized and objectivized.

Two facts have been of primary importance for mythical pre-science and its evolution: on the one hand, the stellar and solar motion, the mythical "theory" of sun and light, as it were; and on the other hand, the symbolization of essence (inner sun) and of the human spirit (inner light) by the stellar sun and its light.

Now with regard to the first fact, in all the past history of science, sun and light kept this primary importance. Not only did science—in its first form of astronomy—emerge from mythical life as soon as the primitive attention was directed to cosmic phenomena, but also all the most decisive gains of science and even the elaboration of its method, are due to the more and more attentive and penetrating observation of the solar system and of light. Physics—whose methodical principles have created and guided scientific research in all the other fields—began to be an exact science thanks to the observation of cosmic phenomena (Copernicus). Through the intuitive explanation of these phenomena the scientific image of the universe was created (Newton), and again, following a more intensified study of light, that image had to be modified. Physics, resorting to revealing intuition as much as to exact observation, created the unifying conceptions of the universe (theory of relativity) and of the atom (quantum theory), conceptions whose consequences for all science, demanding a revision of its methodological basis (the principle of causality) may well go beyond what is foreseeable and seem to bring research on the outer world closer to research on the inner world and its means of knowledge.

All sciences are creations of the human mind, and their value as truth depends on the mind's objectivity. Science thus leads to the very same problem, which is central to life and its comprehensive function, toward which philosophy was obliged to direct itself: the critical study of the human spirit, guiding function of all research and which is undeniably a function of inner life.

Moreover—as far as the second primordial fact of mythical life is concerned—only science enables us to perceive the full depth of the central symbol of myths: the "Sun-Divinity." For only science finds that the sun, source of all physical energy and its transformations, is also the apparent cause of life and its activities, the environmental condition for animalization and animation, therefore the source of psychic energy and its transformations. It is therefore entirely justified to symbolically replace—as the myth does—the mystery of animation, "the Essence," with the apparent principle of animation, the sun, symbol of the spirit. Essence being the inner sun, its radiance, the human spirit is the inner light.

Only by directing our attention toward this manifest radiance of the essence, toward the human spirit (superconscience) and by studying the conditions of its evolutionary emergence will we be able to express in symbols that will be more appropriate to our time what this "radiant" essence, this inner sun is: the God of the mythical era.

Pure science or physics, searching for truth—the law—remains a manifestation of the spirit, a result of evolutionary spiritualization. On the other hand, applied science or technology, seeking only to utilize the laws, looks only for utilitarian goals and is a manifestation of the intellect. Banalization[10] occurs when the intellect which should be a servant of the spirit wants to rule in its stead. Then life is not a spiritual mystery anymore, it is only an intellectual problem. Man falls out of the meaningful direction of life; he becomes senseless. In this state of rebellion against the spirit, man does not admire the creation, he only idolizes his own works. Technical application, justified if a means to overcome environmental obstacles, becomes an exalted and obsessive goal, a vital danger.

The more the conditions of human life, thanks to the research on the laws of the external world, seem to become propitious, the greater is the threat that life, losing its meaning and orientation, will become mired in a confusion of desires and motives. The wrong use of victory over the environmental unknown, technical exaltation, exalts—with the growing means of fulfillment—the natural need of the desires. It

---

10. See note on page 54.

multiplies the desires, and in order to obtain satisfaction at the expense of others, it provides weapons that are more and more frightening (which is one of the most constant themes of myths and even the central theme of the Old Testament). The desires being inextricably exalted, transformed by way of wrong valuation into constant motives of aggression, bring the whole world into bloody disasters which end up by exalting vital anxiety (instead of sublimating it) to the extent of transforming it into fear which again becomes permanent. But this is no longer the fear of primitive man, fear that was rooted in a magical impulse and full of promise, i.e., the call for evolution. This fear which permanently underlies life is the punishment for a guilty and vain life, the tired and degenerate fear that believes life is meaningless, hopeless; tendentious fear, sentimental fear, full of self-pity and brimming with accusations against life: intellectualized fear which becomes a doctrine about life leading—because of its inability to give a meaning to life and define a scale of values—to the despairing tendency which is too common in our time. Now this state of perversion is a frequent theme of the pre-science of the myths, for instance the Tower of Babel: men, trusting only in their intellect, make so bold as to try and reach "mythical heaven," or joy, with the help of a technical construction. The senseless enterprise rapidly mars their friendships. They no longer understand one another; each one of them, living only in accordance with his exalted desires, "speaks his own language." The meaning of life is symbolized by God, who only has to touch with one finger the splendid building for it to collapse (a symbol of the decadence of cultures.) The same is true of the myth of Sodom and Gomorrah. The most eloquent symbolization is that of the Flood, sent by the divinity as a means of both punishment and purification.

Just as the mythical era knew the danger of profanation, the scientific era is exposed to the same danger, and even more so since it has attained a higher evolutionary level on the plane of technical ingenuity. It shows what the human spirit is capable of when methodically guided. On the other hand, does not the misuse of the technical inventions due to the exact sciences prove in a terrifying way the harm that can be done by the sciences of life which are inexact, since they gave up the essential problem—the inner motivating functioning which was the theme of mythical pre-science? Just as the pre-mythical era had to lose the naivete of looking for motives in the objects of the environment, so as to acquire a new depth able to symbolize the intrapsychic motivations, so the guilty dissension of the scientific era should overcome its naivete—the belief that the psyche is an object which can only be observed from the outside—in order to become able to study the distorted and distorting spirit: vain error and its guilty consequence. This can only be accomplished through introspective self-criticism—the only criterion for scientific objectivity allowing the foundation of *a true criti-*

cism of knowledge, based on the elimination of all metaphysical speculation as a result of the acceptance of the mystery. From this it follows
that *we need to study the two modal manifestations of mystery: the world which
excites the psyche and the psyche which is excitable by the world.* Psyche and
world are connected by the desires which, retained and deprived of immediate discharge, become motives, the intrapsychic cause of activity.

A theory of knowledge is impossible without an introspective study of
the intrapsychic functioning. This requirement was already contained
in the cogito. For if thought, excluding all speculation, is the only criterion of truth, one has to admit that thought is only a part of the psychic
functioning and that one should study all its manifestations—be they
conscious or extra-conscious—as well as their interaction. How then
could it be possible to establish objectively a self-criticism of knowledge
without a diagnosis of the principle of inobjectivity, namely, vanity, its
biogenetical roots, the harm it does, and the means to free oneself
from it?

The psychology of inner motivations seeks the laws ruling the inner
world and linking intention to environmental extensions, and it can become possible only insofar as man will be able to ovecome fear in its
most harrowing form: the fear of self, the fear of his heights—his un-
achieved or aborted potentialities, and the fear he experiences when
faced with the abyss of his faults and his subconsciously hidden errors.

Scientific life should therefore take the same step that mythical life
had to take. In a first phase of the scientific era, it was economically
necessary to deal only with the exterior environment in order to find
the laws ruling and enlightening it (laws that had been primitively symbolized by the multiplicity of solar deities). In a more evolved phase of
scientific life, research should turn also to the inner world in order to
study the source of all lawfulness, the primordial law: the ethical requirement to struggle against vain blindness. Life itself, because of its
growing complexity and hence its exalted suffering (brought forcibly to
our attention by its psychopathic aspect), will compel science to take
this step, the only one which will help to find a remedy to the growing
despair, to the feeling of having lost the meaning of life, the essence,
the essential.

Mythical evolution consisted in the ever more distinct separation of
the mysterious unknown on the one hand and manifest life on the other hand: of the "divine" and the earthly, of essence and appearance[11].
The scientific era can but carry on this evolution on a higher plane. For
science, the mystery of life will not become explainable either. All it
can do with regard to mystery will be to distinguish it ever more clearly
from the appearance. Since the explaining spirit will thus become free
from the wrongly posed metaphysical problem (absolute Spirit or abso-

---

11. See note page 23.

lute Matter), its capacity of understanding will necessarily become concentrated on its natural task, which is the study of the manifest appearance in all its modal and modifiable forms: not only the world, but the psyche, extension and intention, quantity and quality, which—far from being mutually exclusive—can unite harmoniously in a methodical endeavor of understanding.

It follows that to refuse mystery is to be insufficiently scientific. It is to live in confusion between appearance and mystery. It is, on the one hand, to leave in the appearance a mysterious principle which, no matter what one does, will always manifest itself and prevent a coherent explanation; and it is, on the other hand, to mistake mystery for some kind of appearance (a real god), cause of all superstition. Mystery does not become entirely clear until it is completely separated from the appearance. For mystery is precisely the mystery of appearance, which would perdure even if the entire appearance were to be explained by science.

In spite of the parallelism between the scientific and mythical eras, there is a difference which has already been indicated and must be stressed. Mythical life, directing the attention toward the inner life, leads in its final phase to the effort of sublimation, individually achieved by the unique hero of the Christian myth. For scientific life, a final phase is inconceivable. Its endeavor is not individual sublimation but collective spiritualization, no longer comparable to a circle closing on itself but to a spiral leading to infinity. The hero of the scientific myth is not the symbolically "deified" individual but all of mankind and its evolutionary effort of spiritualization and sublimation uniting the generations, leading them to the truth, to the lawful meaning (mythically speaking: leading them to the "Father"), to the essence, whose constant "creation" is its ever clearer manifestation in the appearance, in the evolution of the entire appearance toward an ever more conscious manifestation of its animating spirit. It is possible that the scientific effort, understood in this way, the decisive effort to overcome the unknown and its fear, an effort embracing the world and all of life, will present during its barely started evolution new aspects which are not foreseeable for our still too primitive clairvoyance.

Only through a complete separation, a scientific distinction, between appearance and mystery will psychology, the science of the inner world, be able to define its *method* and its *object*. Only as a result of this total separation will the other aspect of the relationship between appearance and essence, i.e., their interpenetration, be clearly established. The inner world, the "object" of psychology, is part of the appearance. The psyche has its modes of temporal existence which must be completely explainable. But the inner world, the psyche, is essentially distinct from the outer world, from the other part of appearance, which is its counter-image. The inner world, the psyche, is not extensive but intensive. Its intensity is due to inner tensions, to motivating intentions. The most important of the motivating intentions is the mysteriously animating inpulse. It is a psychic phenomenon in its motivating effects, but it is mysterious as far as its origins are concerned, and according to the method of mythical pre-science it is represented by an entity symbolically called the "soul."

Science denies the existence of God and the soul. In this it errs. Symbolically, "God" and the "Soul" do exist and have always existed as images having indisputably exerted the most determining influence on human history. Symbols are historically existant realities, and their underlying meanings—dealing with the conflicts of motives—are psychologically existant realities. From this it follows—as has been stated—that the methodological principle of the sciences of life should be the clear distinction between the mystery called "God" and its manifest effect: the world existing under two aspects, matter and spirit, material objects and preconscious spirit which is organizing and finally explaining. This methodological distinction is equally indispensable for the "soul" mystery and its manifest effect: the animating impulse endowed with an evolutionary force leading—on the human plane—to psychic life made up of "psychic objects": the desires, and of the spirit which rightly or wrongly valuates the desires.

The "soul" symbol is also a historical reality, and its underlying significance—the "animating impulse" is the essential phenomenon of life. After creating the psychological pre-science of the myths, the superconscious impulse did not cease to exist; symbolization talks about the "life and death of the soul" and the underlying significance is life and death of the animating impulse.

The vital impulse can die and be reborn during life.

How could psychology, the science of psychic functioning, evade (and for what motive would it evade?) its essential task: the detailed study of the intrapsychic causes of the life and death of the animating impulse?

By evading this task, psychology does not only err, it does harm.

And this is the core of the present chapter whose theme is the relationship between religion and science.

The essential cause of the disarray—of the fear—of our present time is the conflict between religions and sciences.

In symbolic pre-science, science and religiosity were harmoniously united. The present conflict between religions and sciences, the essential cause of all accidental conflicts, whether they be individual or social, will find its reconciliation only in the understanding of the underlying truth of symbolic language. But the study of symbolization could not discover the essential truth; only the introspective study of the intrapsychic conflicts—theme of the mythologies—will be able to provide the key to symbolic language. In this respect, the real cause of the confusion is not religious dogma in the first place, but above all the fundamental dogma of the sciences of life—their anathema against introspection, the abdication of the sciences, and their phobia about the study of intrapsychic phenomena.

The detailed analysis of the "divinity" and "soul" symbols will be undertaken in later chapters because of their complexity. For the time being, we must prepare the ground and set the limits of psychological research by freeing it both from materialistic psychology for which psychic life is only an epiphenomenon of somatic evolution and from esoteric psychology for which the human spirit is not a part of the psychic functioning, but the manifestation in man of an absolute spirit, which opens a new approach to metaphysical speculations.

Since we cannot enter here into a polemic which would no longer deal with the central theme—symbolic language and the "Divinity" symbol—we can only set the position of an introspective psychology for which all ideologies, just as all beliefs, are underlaid with more or less valid motives. In such a situation, it might well be that the only criterion of scientific validity in psychology rests on the demand imposed by life itself that psychic science be capable of grasping the hidden meaning of *the psychological pre-science* of symbolic language, which, being a production of the psychic superconscience, cannot be deciphered without research for the laws ruling the inner psychic functioning of each individual and therefore the superconscious of the researcher himself. Unless the psychologists who object to such a demand of rigorous method can prove—instead of affirming it—that the mythologies on which all human cultures are founded are only senseless fabulations.

In this alternative is summed up the problem we face: the relationship between religion and science. The essential fact of the present time is that religions are not able to take charge of the meaningful orientation, neither through their dogmas nor through their practices and rituals. This being the case, the only hope is that science will undertake the search for the solution. It will not be able to do so without taking into account *the inner deliberation* and its conflict of motives, the theme of symbolic pre-science. Can it be that there is a psychology—or more generally speaking a thinking being, a man—who would dare deny that one deliberates in one's innermost self before acting? And if the inner deliberation is an existant phenomenon, how could it not be the primary task of psychology to study this phenomenon, the essential cause of our volitions, of our acts, and of our social interactions, of our joys and our pains? How can we study them if not introspectively? What is deliberation itself if not a ceaseless self-introspection, a self-observation of our desires and their demand for satisfaction, a search for means of satisfaction, an elaboration of the motives for present and future actions, motives which are nothing else but suspended actions, promises of future satisfactions, though they can be vitally meaningful or senseless? This intentional functioning, these internal tensions between satisfaction and dissatisfaction, these motivating intentions would have no definable meaning *if they were not incarnate in the soma to the extent that they determine not only somatic activity, but also the healthy or unhealthy functioning (harmonious or disharmonious functioning) of all the somatic organs. Inner deliberation is the vital link between soma and psyche.* From it depend on the human plane the destiny and fate of the individual who, from a biogenetical viewpoint, is a psycho-somatic organism in a state of evolution or involution depending on the vital value or nonvalue of his inner deliberation. Deliberating introspection is a constant choice which is the most characteristic feature of the thinking species. Psyche and soma are inseparable. There is no psyche without a soma, and no soma (animated matter) without a psyche. Their parallelism is not a stabilization and *still less a pre-stabilization*, but an evolution which is as manifest in the modalities of its finalistic intentionality as it is mysterious in its origins.

These fundamental findings eliminate from the sciences of life any metaphysical speculation (absolute Spirit or absolute Matter) and replace it with the necessity of studying the evolutionary biogenesis of both the psyche and the soma[12] since biogenesis is precisely the progressive incarnation of the spirit (psychic function) in the soma-matter (meaning of the myth of the incarnation). The psycho-somatic evolution constitutes a continuum which is as mysterious as it is manifest. This enables us without any risk of speculation to go downwards from the present stage (the explaining and valuating spirit of man) to the origins of life or upwards from the origins to the future stages. These complementary ways enable a progressive approach to the achievement of the purpose of deliberation: the essential liberation from error in its theoretical and practical forms. From a biogenetical viewpoint, the evolutionary continuum goes from the primitive reflex reaction to the complicated reflexes which constitute the various forms of animal instinctivity and from there to human reflection, which is exposed to error because it is half-conscious, but which is guided by the survival of instinctive and preconscious unerringness in the evolved form of the ethical superconscience. Even if we knew all the details of the deliberating functioning of the psyche, we would still have to establish its biogenetical basis, which necessarily compels us to go back all the way to the origins of temporal existence of which life is only a late manifestation. This, in its turn, compels us to ask the metaphysical question regarding the mysterious origin of manifest appearance, the question without an answer, but that the human mind is obliged to ask and which should lead science to emotion in the face of the mysterious depth of existence.

The relationship between a genuine science of life and a genuine re-

___
12. P. Diel, *La Peur et l'Angoisse,* Central Phenomenon of Evolution, 2nd edition, Petite Bibliotheque Payot.

ligiosity rests on the fact that the common questioning with respect to the origins found an answer in the superconscious dream of mythical imagination that is condensed in the metaphysical images of "God and soul." The metaphysical images can only be anthropomorphic, even though they are symbolically true. Their truth, psychologically understood, lies in the fact that since the religious images of the myths were created by the superconscious process of the psyche, they are an integral part of the motivating functioning of the psyche.

The science of life has to try and understand the biogenesis of the superconscience and, thereby, the biogenesis of the superconscious productions which religious imaginations, the mythologies, are. Their sublimely motivating force lies in the fact that they stress with the help of their symbolic and metaphysical oneirism not only the mystery of appearance but the mystery of disappearance: the mystery of life and death. Science, however, understanding the anthropomorphism of the images is compelled to warn that the *metaphysical images of the mystery of death do not contain in any way the affirmation or explanation of a life after death.* All their sublimating force resides in the fact that they may help to arouse sacred fear in the face of the ephemeral character of temporal existence. The fear is sublimated into love of life when man achieves joyful harmonization of his desires. For one can love only what brings joy. This is the evolutionary meaning immanent to life; and this is the superconscious ethical value which is immanent to the psychic life of man.

Through emotion in the face of mystery and the understanding of the law of harmony, the meaningful relationship between genuine religiosity and the science of life is achieved; they are in accordance, the accordance between mythical pre-science and the science of the inner psychic functioning.

Part 2
GOD AND MAN

CHAPTER 3

Metaphysical Symbolization

The themes of metaphysics are the three mythical symbols concerning mystery: God, Soul, Freedom.

The problem of freedom appearing here for the first time is of extreme importance in seeking a solution to the ethical problem: how to act in order to live in a meaningful way.

The biogenetically immanent meaning is the harmony of desires. But biogenesis has—like all that exists—a mysterious aspect, and therefore the ethical principle actually stems from the biogenesis of the human psyche and mythically stems from the symbol of the mystery called "God." In creating the "God" image, the myth symbolically defines the meaning of life. But in the final analysis, this metaphysical definition is only a means of deducing the practical and moral meaning of life: the relationship between the God symbol and man. Because of this deduction the metaphysical symbol of "God the Creator" is complemented by the ethical symbolism: "God, judge of man, distributor of rewards and punishments."

The second part of this book will be devoted to the analysis of the psychological significance of this new symbolism. However, it would be impossible to decipher this ethical symbolism without a preliminary detailed analysis of the three metaphysical symbols: "God the Creator" linked to the symbols of "Soul" and "Freedom," in which—because of the indispensable endeavor of liberation—the underlying immanence of the ethical signifiance appears very clearly.

Because of the inseparable bond between symbolic metaphysics and real and practical morals, it goes without saying that the previous analyses have already drawn—at least in general outline—the moral meaning which is immanent to life.

It is in fact contained in the "incarnation" symbol, belonging to the myth of the trinity. It too deals with God the Creator, his incarnation in the soul (the Word), and the immanence of the ethical problem and its liberating force called Christ.

A warning is in order here to draw attention to the definition of "metaphysical psychology."

The phrase does not mean in any way that the psychology of motivations—the tool for deciphering—intends to lose itself in metaphysical speculations. Quite the opposite, metaphysical psychology—the psychology which analyzes the metaphysical images of the myths—intends to eliminate as radically as possible any metaphysical speculation while bringing out the immanence of the underlying significance: emotion in the face of mystery and its sublimely motivating force, the essential root of the ethical problem. In this respect it is not amiss to recall that the superconscious process which creates the metaphysical symbols is identical to the ethical superconscience.

The following analyses will therefore deal with God and his creation, the Soul and its incarnation, and, lastly, the symbolic responsibility of man toward God the Judge.

We must therefore show in detail which formualtions the psycholoy of motivations uses to replace the symbolization through which the myths express the ethical motivation indissolubly linked to the metaphysical images in the three aspects of God, Soul, and Freedom.

A. ANALYSIS OF THE "ONLY GOD" SYMBOL

1. ONENESS

With the symbol of the "only God," mythical symbolization reaches its pinnacle.

Since monotheism is an evolved form of polytheism, all the preceding analyses concerning the relationship of man and the divinity—or the divinities—remain valid for the relationship between the only God and man. According to the biblical myth, God created man in his image. But God being a symbol, it is man who created the image of the only God according to his superconscious and anthropomorphic imagination, just as he created the images of the multiple deities; and it is also man who created the various images of the relationship with the divinity which remain—in their underlying significance—identical from animism to monotheism.

The image which is an exclusive feature of monotheism and the gospels is the incarnation of the Word in a unique man. But since the meaning of this, the most evolved image of the relationship between man of his own superconscious vision of the ideal achievement, is the effort of self-sublimation carried by the hero of the Christian myth to a degree of exemplarity remaining valid for all times, past and future, every man should—within the limits of his own vital impulse—"incarnate the word," through his own sublimating effort. Since this essential relationship depends on the intensity of emotion in the face of mystery it differs profoundly from the ritual relationship achieved through prayers and rituals which can be an expression of emotion but can also be superstitions devoid of any effect of incarnation. The more intense the emotion, the more superfluous prayers and rituals will be. Since it was necessary to speak from the outset about the relationship between man and the divinity symbol, we had to introduce straightaway the significance which opposes superstition and which is nowhere as clearly defined as in the "incarnation" symbol of the New Testament. This having been done, the translation of the most evolved form of the divinity symbol must be completed by a detailed analysis of the "only God" symbol. One cannot fully understand the word "only" if it is perceived merely as a means of expressing opposition to multiple deities.

The expression "only" has two meanings.

One is "the One" from whom issues all apparent multiplicity; the other is "the One" who is beyond any real comparison with appearance and its multiplicity: the Incomparable, the Unnameable, the Undefinable, of whom one can talk only through symbolic comparison.

Thus understood, "oneness" is a symbolic expression used to talk about the mysterious essence, the mystery of life. However, the word "mystery" is by far the more precise. The "One" as opposed to the multiple seems to contain a beginning of definition, which is precisely what must be avoided. This vague semblance of a possible definition of absolute mystery incited philosophy to search for a clearer definition, which led it to pose superfluous and senseless questions ending in metaphysical speculations. One cannot explain, and yet one would like to understand how this limitless and distinctionless "One" can contain the distinct multiplicity which appearance is and how this multiplicity was able to come forth, to emanate from this "One," etc. Mystery loses its clear evidence and becomes the topic of pseudo-profound discussion, a sign that living faith is declining. Thus misunderstood, the "Only God" image is no longer a mythical and symbolic concept: it is downgraded to a theoretical concept of theological philosphy.

The very fact of talking about the oneness of God lends to the essence a feature of the appearance. A oneness can only be represented as limited in space and time. In order not to perturb sublime fear, the adoration of mystery, one should not impose on it any limitation, any definition, not even that it is one. By wanting thus to limit the undefinable mystery, imagination is tempted to lend it a precise form, and what form could be more fitting than that of a man living in body and spirit?

2. GOD PROVIDENCE AND GOD PURE SPIRIT

The symbolization of the mystery of life and death by the image of a dvinity living in the body and in the likeness of man hails from the cradle of mankind, when the father-ancestor was worshipped as living bodily in a world beyond.

This tendency is moreover strengthened by the individual history of every man. A child up to the age of five or seven is a purely imaginative being, eager for fabulations, just like the primitive men who were close to the childhood of mankind. Undoubtedly it would be a mistake not to tell children the myth of the Good God and His Son. But, of course, not the dogma but the genuine myth in order to lead the child little by little, while he is maturing, toward emotion in the face of mystery. This is—we have to admit it—hardly possible nowadays.

Dogmatism offers as a meaning for life the exaltative love for a God the Father mistaken for a real person loving his children, men, and whom his obedient children should love more than themselves. From this rather childish sentimentality comes sentimental altruism: the moralizing imposition to love others more than oneself. This is love-duty, the principal motivation of all the erroneous relationship between man and the God symbol; this present research would be incomplete if it did not approach this particularly important theme, since it is the daily motive in the relationships between the ego and the alter, including this "alter" who is the personal god.

Love is above all a natural and psychic phenomenon, submitted to the analysis of motives and it remains a rightly or wrongly motivated intrapsychic phenomenon even if the object of love is God. Love—like all the psychic phenomena endowed with a positively motivating force—is linked to the metaphysical symbolization of "God" (mystery) and "Soul" (animating impulse). Such bio-psychically based combative and dynamic love is in no way moralizing or banalizing. It is a natural evolutionary phenomenon with a sublimating force.

Since this is the case, love is mythically linked to religiosity, to emotion in the face of the mysterious depth of existence and of its lawfulness. The mythical symbolism "to love God" means to love oneself, not only the apparent self, but the self as a manifestation of mystery, and to love others as a manifestation of mystery. To love one another because we are united in mystery all the way to the perverse motivations of the subconscious, but also united by the superconscious imperative to fight them.

The image of an only God living in the body belongs to symbolic metaphysics and corresponds to the popular belief in a providential God.

In total contradiction to this metaphysical image, which—like all myths—is the illogical facade of an underlying psychological meaning, there is an imagination for which God would be *pure spirit*,

In order to ward off the doubt too easily attached to the beliefs in a god living in the body, theological philosophy has always attempted to transform the naive image into a theoretical and abstract understanding no longer based on the bodily image of the Good God but drawn from the spiritual aspect of man. God would be, in this understanding, the human spirit idealized to the point of excess, a pure and incorporeal spirit. It is true that the myth does use the "God the Spirit" symbol in the meaning of the second person of the trinitarian symbol. But such a meaning has nothing to do with the transcendent existence of a real

God, pure absolute spirit; quite the opposite, the underlying meaning of the symbol is the immanence of the mysterious evolutionary intentionality underlying all nature. The theoretical abstraction of religious philosophy making of God an absolute Spirit is a complicated idea devoid of any symbolic value and of less worth than the naive image of a bodily god. The body exists in the appearance and can serve as a point of comparison. Nobody would believe in an absolute body. An absolute spirit is neither thinkable nor imaginable.

It is but an idol, hypostatized in order to make it suggestive. It is nothing more than an excuse for intellectual doubt, a pretense to believe, a theorem leading to futile discussion, a stillborn product of speculation, an abstraction with no object from which it is abstracted: an apparition which does not appear, an effigy hanging in the air, a target offered to the critical arrows of atheism, the latter being itself prey to metaphysical error through its tendency to eliminate mystery.

The confusion of this dead abstraction with the mysterious essence is no less common than the confusion with the bodily image. People often even prefer the abstraction, precisely because, being impossible to imagine, it seems to offer a sufficiently subtle image of an only God to definitely eliminate mystery with the help of a definition accepted as adequate.

The ancestral and childish image—the providential Good God—remains touching and naive though it prevents one from experiencing emotion in the face of mystery, especially in our time, when the idea of providence is nothing but sentimentality, tending to reawaken—even if in a fleeting way—at the death of a loved one, especially one's own child, in order to overcome sadness. The belief in a providential divinity living in the body in the world beyond is ancestrally anchored in the magical layer and linked to the consoling imagination of meeting with deceased person in the beyond.

Undoutedly there have been and still are believers whose naive belief in a providential help, inculcated from childhood, prevails during their whole life over the belief in dogmas accepted, even to the extent of a cumbersome participation in the rituals, like any other conventional custom based on the suggestive force they exert on the masses. But without any exception, these bliefs rooted in childhood run the risk of preventing the development of the reflective functions.[1]

It is no deviation from the present problem—i.e., the motives for belief and doubt in God as well as the consequences in everyone's practical life—to stress the inner and environmental causes of a generalized disorientation concerning, whether one likes it or not, the meaning of life. This fact is in the final analysis—and very largely so—due to the existence of preestablished beliefs, each one self-contradictory and con-

---

1. *Les Principles de l'Education et de la Reéducation,* ed. Delachaux et Niéstle, 2d ed.

tradicting others, transmitted from one generation to the next from childhood on through education.

The mythical image serves two purposes: it corresponds to the unavoidable, unanswerable metaphysical question, and it offers a means or moral stimulation. The moral importance of the symbol is based on human nature and its suggestibility to images. The "only God" symbol enables man to raise to the highest degree the suggestive force, thanks to the concentration of attention on a sole image, or rather on two diametrically opposed images. The immanent principle of Good is presented in its attractive splendor (God and heaven); the principle of Evil in all its hideousness (Satan and hell). When the emotionally suggestive force declines, it becomes tempting to impose the image as a reality in order to exalt its function as a moral stimulus. All religious institutions make use of this strategem. But the image of the principle of Good, once shorn of its symbolic significance—the mystery—becomes in the long run a convention devoid of any suggestive force, which brings as a consequence that its counterimage of evil in itself no longer serves its suggestive purpose, no longer inspires aversion, so that finally the real seduction of Evil is the winner. Only sublimated fear in the face of mystery insures the force of moral suggestion to the metaphysical images. *To elucidate in detail—the purpose of this book—the significance of the metaphysical symbol "only God" is thus the only remedy for moral disorientation.*

3. THE PSEUDOPROOFS OF GOD'S EXISTENCE

In order to erase any doubt about the real existence of God, theological philosophy attempted to supply apparently logical proofs.

We have to take them into account even though they are all marked with the same error regarding the scope of the logical conclusion.

The possibility of logically conclusive links exists only for concepts which are cliches of existing objects, formed with the help of abstraction. From the outset, it is clear that a God who needs to be proved is no longer an evident mystery; the proof—instead of placing God outside of any discussion—makes him a problematic phenomenon. To want to prove the existence of God through a logical conclusion is to be ignorant of the two meanings of the word "God." It is to make of God-mystery an object, existing like all other objects; and it is to make of the God image a logical concept, an abstraction. *Any proof of the existence of God necessarily becomes a vicious circle. It has to admit the existence of the "object" the existence of which it purports to prove.* Logical calculation cannot prove the existence of any object. The existence of objects comes before it; they have to be given to perception. Logic can prove only the perceived objects have or do not have common qualities, or it can, from the presence of an object changed in its qualities, conclude the present or past existence of a modifying cause. To confuse the quantitative presence of such an such an object with the "essence" which is mysteriously common to all objects, with the mystery of existence, is to confuse logic and metaphysics. It is to believe that there can be a logical metaphysics or a metaphysical logic. This is precisely the error defining theological speculation when it looks for support and proof in the speculations of metaphysical philosophy, instead of being content with its own pseudoproofs based on miracles declared to be divine revelation.

Reason can play its critical and self-critical role only providing that it defines logical concepts and symbolic images. Now the search for definitions of the symbolic terms is the general theme of this work (numerous definitions will also be found in *Symbolism in Greek Mythology*). We now have to define the term "existence" in order to see what value can be credited to the metaphysical pseudoproofs of the personal existence of God.

The word "to exist" indicated the quality common to all the objects located in space-time. This is precisely why the term, in its logical significance, cannot be used for a "god" object who is supposed to exist in a space-time outside of the actually existing space-time. The pseudo philosophical discussions on the metaphysical pseudoproblem are countless: is space-time limited or not? what, in case of limitation, exists outside of space-time? They are as worthless as the discussions of scholastic theology about the sex of angels. The fact is that the term "existence" is the quality that remains if one eliminates all the other modal and modifiable qualities. It is the mysterious quality due to which, all the existing objects have a manifest as well as a mysterious aspect. This is precisely where the mystery of existence lies, inaccessible to logical proof, solely accessible to emotion.

The most secret cause of the error of searching a logical proof for the metaphysical mystery, the deepest cause of the confusion between logics and metaphysics, is hidden in the fact that language uses the word "exist," the most abstract of terms, indiscriminately for all spatial objects and also for indicating the most concrete feeling: the feeling of his own existence animating every man. In this latter meaning, directly opposed to the conceptual and abstract significance concerning exteriorly perceived objects, the term "to exist" deals with the affectively, subjectively experienced intrapsychic life, the universe of the inner feelings going from vain egocentricity all the way to emotion in the face of mystery. Thus if one says, "God exists," there is a great danger that ther term "to exist" might lead to confusion, since one does not make a distinction between the two possible significances: to exist in me, as a feeling, and to exist outside of me as a perceptible object. The only true significance of the term "to exist" when used for the "God" symbol is that it exists in me in the concrete form of emotion in the face of mystery. The other signifiance, that of "outside of me," belongs to dogma. Since God cannot exist in the common environment of all objects, there is no choice but to place him in a space outside of the existing space. One reaches the concept of a personal and intentional God—like man—who would exist in the form of an absolute Man or absolute Spirit living in the beyond. This can be accepted as a symbol, but is inconceivable as a metaphysical concept and object of discussion.

If it is a mistake to confuse symbols with realities, it is no less a mistake to confuse abstract concepts with reality. One ends up by mistaking symbols of concepts. To think is to define. Everything can be defined. Not only objects and their causal relationships, but also feelings and their motivational relationships, including *emotion* in the face of mystery, and hence also symbols and their underlying significance.

The only thing that cannot be defined is the mystery called "God."

4. THE PSYCHOLOGICAL IMAGE OF "THE EXISTENCE OF GOD"

The metaphysical "object" being outside of reality, unperceivable by its very definition, is thus inaccessible to the intellect and its logical procedure. It can try to prove it, it can try to deny it. This is of no importance. The intellect deals only with objects that are concretely given to it. For the intellect—a conscious functions—God the mystery does not exist; it "exists" only for the superconscious spirit.

In the last analysis, the lack of distinction between intellect and spirit, between the logical conscious and the symbolic superconscious, and the lack of psychological understanding are the factors which explain the error of metaphysical philosophy. It attempts to define intellectually and logically the profound emotion which is the characteristic of philosophy insofar as it tries to attain an intuitive vision of the meaning of life. Most of the pseudoproofs of philosophy can take on a valid aspect. It is enough not to see them as an intellectual intention to prove the personal existence of God, but as an intuitive intention to prove the personal existence of God, but as an intuitive intention to take into account *the evidence of the motivating force of the God image*: an attempt to clarify the mythical vision. What is positive in these pseudoproofs is not the logical procedure, but the superconscious vision of the intuitive spirit, though the latter is wavering and perturbed by an insufficient analysis of the psychic processes and their functioning. The role of the logical function of the intellect is utilitarian adjustment to the environment; the role of the spirit is adjustment to the meaning of life.

In order to make the relationship between mystery, spirit, and intellect tangible, one may use a metaphor which, even though it does not have the depth of the symbolic image, uses the fundamental comparison—established by the myths—between mystery and the sun. The doctrine of light will provide the elements of comparison.

If one attempts to look at the sun, the dazzled eye does not see anything. Yet the existence of the sun is made evident by its fecundating and luminous radiance. One can with the help of an optical lens capture its light and obtain at the focus an image of the sun, an image which is an energetic center capable of transforming the objects exposed to its radiant energy. But who would mistake the focus for the sun itself? In the same way, with the help of the spirit—comparable in this case to the lens—one can capture an image of mystery and this image can transform the psyche. If one replaces the optical lens (the spirit) with a plane and flat glass (the intellect), one obtains neither focus nor image, neither energetic manifestation nor transforming power over the exposed objects (the psyche). By trusting its experience, the intellect might be tempted to deny the existence of the sun, were it not sufficient to turn toward the star in order to perceive its evident presence. Mystery, on the contrary, is not a perceptible object. Since its radiance can be captured only by the spirit, the intellect does not obtain an image and cannot be aware in any way of the mystery. It is right rather to deny it than to prove it. Whether it denies it or proves it, the spirit will only trust its own experience. Without having perceived the object, it obtains the image, the focus, and feels its power. It gives the name "God" to the image and does not mistake it for the mysterious source of all reality and all image. However, no matter how mysterious the source, it is evident to the spirit not only through the image it obtains from it, but through its own feeling, its own reality, the mystery of its own existence.

The intellect can be convinced only by a perceptible object. It forgets that besides the dazzling sun another object is given which proves the existence of the sun without having to observe it: the light which fills space. The intellect tends to forget this object and its evident existence because it does not have a determinable form while determining the form of all other perceptible objects, while being the condition of all perceptibility.

Now one can say: the same relationship existing between the sun and the light making the world of objects perceptible, this same relation exists between mystery and the lawfulness of the perceptible world. Lawfulness, perceptible only to the spirit, is the spiritual light emanating from the sun-mystery. The intellect, just as it is unable to obtain the active focus, the image of the sun-mystery (sublimation), is unable to realize the elucidating force of emotion and of the notion of mystery which saves the spirit from any speculative straying and refers it back to the study of the laws ruling intrapsychic life (spiritualization).

Thus, supposing that a man could be only intellect, he could end up by believing superstitiously in a real god; but he could never obtain faith, the vision of God-mystery or of his actively motivating image. On the other hand, if man is endowed with a spirit and he does not obtain the lawful image, it means that his spirit is offectively perturbed (just like a defective optical lens which cannot create a focus). But it is not necessary to call upon the intellect and make it prove the existence of God. One should try and cure the blindness of the human spirit, and the only possibility of enlightment is the elucidation of the (symbolic) image and of the motivating force it inspires. One must elucidate not logically but psychologically the symbolic creation of superconsciousness, the "God-Mystery" image, to finally grasp its radiance: the sublimely motivating force it exerts on the psyche. Just as the mystery need not be proved, the mythical image itself needs no proof: the "God" image and its motivating power is an indisputable historical fact. What must be proved and can be proved is exclusively the true relation between the two meanings of God: God-mystery and God-image. This only possible proof is nothing but the deciphering of the hidden meaning of the "God" symbol.

Having shown how erroneous it is to believe in a god who would exist in the body or as a pure spirit, having refuted the attempt to logically prove the existence of such a god, we must now clarify the vision of mystery, elucidate the image, replace the symbolic image of the myths with less enigmatic images accessible to conscious understanding, not with the help of pseudological proofs but with that of psychologically true formulations which are not explanations of mystery but explanations of the significance of the mythical images or refutations of their speculative interpretations.

According to the myth as well as to psychology, there does not exist on the one hand appearance and on the other hand mystery (the term "exist" has to be understood in its conceptual meaning). Nothing is given but appearance. It is the mystery, or better yet: the fact that appearance exists is mystery. But the appearance evolves, it becomes spiritualized, it grasps and feels, better and better, the mystery itself is. Yet, if the appearance is mystery, mystery is not the appearance. Mystery goes beyond its revelation which is the appearance, and this metaphysical aspect of mystery is symbolized by the myth and called "God." Appearance is the existing reality, and mystery, going beyond all existing reality, acquires a separate "existence," though it is not that of an entity, it is not conceptual, it is purely mysterious. This existence is of a completely new order and does not concern anything but the metaphysical "object"; it is not an irreality, it is not in contradiction with reality. On the contrary, it is the condition for reality (the mysterious principle of all existing reality). It is surreality which can be spoken of only symbolically, with the help of images borrowed from existing reality. But the relationship between existing reality and symbol is reversed in the end. The symbol, the surreality, is the ultimate truth of reality. Reality is only an appearance, an apparent image, a manifest symbol of surreality, of mystery called "God." God is the true significance of the real image, of the manifest which apparent reality is.

B. THE "SOUL" SYMBOL

1. SOUL AND PSYCHE

Just as God is the personified symbol of the mystery of creation, the soul is the personified symbol of the mystery of animation, which is manifest in the form of an animating impulse. The impulse is nothing but the motivating intentionality which is superconsciously guided: the essential desire for harmonization aiming at the essential satisfaction of joy. Opposing essential self-satisfaction—essential and superconsciously immanent desire, animating impulse—is vain egocentrism and its false promise of satisfaction (subconsciously immanent).

Having been thus clearly defined, the animating impulse with its combativity is in no way a supernatural manifestation. It is a natural phenomenon because it is immanent to human nature, immanent to all nature in the form of the mysterious evolutionary intentionality of nature. The notions of evolutionary impulse and of the mysterious finalistic intentionality of nature are not obscure or occult in the least. Quite the contrary, occultism consists in explaining with the help of metaphysical concepts (absolute Spirit or absolute Matter) the existing phenomena: spirit and matter, psyche and world, and their interactions. In psychological terms, the interaction concerns motivating intention and spatial extension, the two being linked by the desires and their search for satisfaction.

These findings, which sum up our method, define quite clearly the relationship between soul and psyche. The term "psyche" is a word covering psychic functions as a whole; the soul is the mythical symbol of the mystery of animation; the animating impulse is the essential phenomenon of psychic life. The impulse lives or dies during life. The life of the impulse is its victory in the struggle against vanity; the death of the impulse is its defeat, its progressive yielding to the unceasing assault of the vanities.

Excessively good intentions cannot reanimate the combative impulse because they are only vanities. The impulse is a motivating force of great intensity, but the motivating force of vanity is no less intense. The successive and progressive victories of the impulse are manifested daily through minute indications: the dissolution of small offended or triumphant vanities, of rancors, accusations, and sentimental complaints— trivial in themselves but tending to become amplified in endless ruminations invading the psyche through imaginative exaltation and ending up by becoming "incarnate," by manifesting themselves in somatic activities, they too, often imponderable: gestures, mimicry, voice intonations which betray the secret ruminations and the latter, through accumulation, become actively manifest in mutual calumnies, intrigues and lastly in explosions of violence. To draw the introspective attention to the intrapsychic spectacle of the ceaseless struggle between vital impulse and vanity is not a waste of time or energy. Quite the opposite is true: time and energies are wasted through lack of self-control, letting the vain ruminations become easily incarnate and thus destroying the vital impulse. The impulse becomes incarnate little by little insofar as it can, with the help of the healthy valuating spirit, fight a daily battle against the false psychopathic motivations as soon as they appear insidiously in the intrapsychic life.

The term "incarnate" has a precise meaning if it is referred to its linguistic root: man lives in spirit and flesh. The soma-flesh is alive as long as it is animated by the spirit: by the healthily motivating intentionality (animating impulse). If the animating intention dies, the soma is nothing but inert matter. The spirit must be incarnate (etymology: carnis = flesh), it must intentionalize the matter in a healthy way so that the psychosomatic organism may live in a healthy and harmonious manner. On the other hand, vanity destroys the psyche by destroying the animating impulse and its intention of harmonization. Man continues, however, to live in the flesh, since he remains animated by perverse intentions. But since his soul is "dead" (dead to the meaning of life), his life is meaningless: he lives only for the satisfaction of the carnal desires, which the myth calls symbolically "death of the soul" (the original sin of human nature). According to the myth, even the "dead in the soul" can be reborn during life. Psychologically speaking, the death of the vital impulse is never total. The vital impulse is dynamic and its dynamics are such that the sublime can be transformed into perversion and perversion into the sublime. The total and irreversible accumulation of energy in the subconscious would imply a complete stagnation of the vital impulse, a stagnation whose consequence would be not only "death of the soul" but also death of the somatic life. The possibility of essential rebirth, were it only at the last moment of life (a proof that the sublimating impulse perdures), is represented by the good thief crucified next to Jesus. The reversals of perversion into the sublime can occur at a decisive moment—especially when faced by a disaster— or by the sudden reversal of perverse valuations into sublime valuation, after a long preparation due to the persistence of the impulse in the form of growing feelings of guiltiness: the apostle Paul and his "dazzling" vision of Christ": the sudden understanding, which had been repressed for a long time, of the life in truth of the first Christians whom he was persecuting and harassing. But essential conversion can also occur—depending on the vital impulse—through a daily effort of perfecting, of elimination of budding rancors. Perfection does not exist. The life of the vital impulse is its active dynamics (joy, the feeling of one's impulse in action) while guilty anxiety (essential guiltiness) is the feeling of stagnation of the impulse.

What is true for the banalism called "death of the vital impulse" also remains true—through an analogy of contrast—for the most intense state in the life of the vital impulse, called sanctity. It cannot be the stagnant condition of total concentration of energy in the superconscience so that nothing would be left to be improved. Such a stagnation would only be a proof of vanity and death of the vital impulse. The life of the vital impulse, especially in a state of the highest intensity, is made

up of ceaselessly renewed victories and, thus, of the growing incarnation of the spirit; for if the sublimating force of the impulse is unlimited the obsessive force of vanity is no less so. Incarnation is constant
dynamics, never fulfilled. It is inscribed in human nature that victories
over vanity run the risk of becoming vanity over victory. The greater
the victory, the greater and the more insidious is the risk of falling into
the temptation of vain stagnation; but the greater also will be the
strength of soul able to resist the dangerous assault of vanity, always
ready to reconstitute itself. However, the all-powerfulness of vanity is
founded only in the suggestive force of imaginative exaltation. This is
why—and it is the ultimate meaning of all mythologies including the
Christian myth—blinding vanity remains subject to the control of the
superconscious truth and its elucidating force. Thus the myth of the
temptation of Jesus in the synoptic gospels is not a mere incident in the
life of Jesus: in it the meaning of life is condensed in the repetition of
the vain promises of the tempter and the repeated victories attained as
a result of the lucidity of the valuating spirit. To quote Luke 4:13:
"Having exhausted all these ways of tempting him, the devil left him,
to return at the appointed time." It is clear that, since the devil does
not really exist, the story of the temptation is the symbol of the inner
deliberation of the man Jesus.

Through the incarnation in psychic life of the victorious combativity
of the animating impulse, psychic life becomes, according to the myth,
the apparent manifestation of the mystery of intentionality. This is only
another way of saying that the mysterious evolutionary intentionality
dispersed throughout all nature is manifested at its highest degree of
intensity in the symbolically sanctified man. His psyche, having become
a manifestation of the mystery symbolized by "God" is symbolically
"deified." United to the mystery by an active love of life, purified from
the exaltation of the carnal desires and their affective clouding, the
hero of the experienced myth no longer needs to create for himself an
image of mystery, since the meaning of the myth is precisely this: he
makes of himself the living image. The mystery is clarified and the image is made real: mystery and image are united and become experienced reality. The symbolically deified man is not compelled—unlike
all other men—to imagine the essential achievement through a naive
and inadequate mythical representation. He knows the mystery because he lives it, and he lives the mystery precisely because his "Soul-
essence" which has become manifest is the essence of "the Father-
Essence."

But this union in essence due to the achievement of the immanent
meaning of life reveals only the symbolic aspect of moral legislator in
the god-mystery. The "Creator" aspect remains mysterious, it remains
mystery. However, the purified man rests with such a degree of trust
and love in the essential, in his intimately experienced knowledge of

the legislator-mystery, that the aspect which remains mysterious, the mystery of creation never to be explained, no longer frightens or disturbs him. He can say that he knows the Father, that he is one with him, because all his activity is motivated by emotion in the face of mystery.

The myth expresses this state of mind through the symbols: incarnation, sanctification, deification. Their common underlying significance is the psychic fact that the soul-mystery has become actively manifest, has become a real life experience. But only the achiever personally lives this incarnate vision of the soul-mystery. His vision is no more the mythical vision that the others can create for themselves. The mythical vision accessible to others—no matter how true it may be—remains pure image, pure symbolically personifying imagination. On the other hand, the actively experienced vision is no longer a symbolic personification, but a real personalization. He can say that he is really God and Son of God. Yet these are only symbols, and very ancient ones at that.

The Buddha, hero of the Hindu myth, expresses the other aspect of this symbolic truth. He affirms that he is more than all the deities. The deities and the demons have become his servants. Since the sublime qualities of the human soul are symbolically represented by the deities, the man who achieves the incarnation of the sublime qualities makes them his servants: he uses them, they are at his service, they have become the motives of his actions. However, to have the free use of his sublime forces he must, through the combativity of his animating impulse, overcome again and again the subconscious temptations. In this way the "demons" also are at his service, because all his animating intentionality is ceaselessly transformed into superconsciously motivating energy. The Hindu myth expresses this in sculptural representations of the Buddha in his characteristic posture, sitting immersed in a healthy valuating introspection.

The Hindu and Christian myths are identical in their deep significance, for there is only one sole essential truth whose value is immutable and "eternal." In this respect the Christian myth is more clearly significant, because it talks explicitly about "life in eternal truth" and opposes it to the symbolism of "death of the soul." Not only the fate of the victorious hero, but also the essential destiny of all men is included in the central symbolism of the Christian myth, "life and death of the soul." The essential death, "the death of the soul," is the absolute opposite of essential life: death is the inability to perfect oneself, to achieve the satisfaction of the essential desire which is superconsciously immanent to all men but which "dies" to the extent that the motivating energy stolen away from the superconscience becomes more and more concentrated in the falsely motivating intentions of the subconscious (the demons).

Thus understood, life and death of the soul are not momentary and miraculous events. They symbolize the essential history of a whole life which has or has not achieved the incarnation of the Soul-Essence in the psyche.

2. ESSENCE AND APPEARANCE[2]

The world and psychic life are the temporal appearance of the mystery of animation. The temporal manifestation of the soul is the psyche, made up of all the desires (and their transformations through the psychic processes). The psyche and its intentionality cannot appear without there appearing—at the same time—its limitation and complement, the world: all the objects of the multiple desires. To the multiple desires corresponds the perception of the multiple and exciting objects. The mutual interpenetration of extension and intention of the world and the psyche, of the excitant and the excited, makes up temporal life. The psyche is the manifest image of the Soul-Essence, and the world is the counter-image of the psyche. Both are rooted in the principle of animation.

This finding includes two significances: psyche and world are on the one hand, the appearance of the Soul-Essence, its manifest image; and on the other hand, they both appear to the Soul-Essence, since without the mysterious animation neither world nor psyche could exist. Which means that the Soul-Essence is the only essentially living and vivifying fact: the essence of life, the meaning of life. The temporal appearances of the essence, on the other hand, make up the reality of life: world and psyche. They are not illusion, but—because they are founded in mystery—they are lawful appearances, realities. Since world and psyche emerge from this common foundation, the psyche is able to grasp the object of its desires—the world—and the latter offers to the psyche the objects of satisfaction. This affective relationship is complemented by a cognitive one. Since the common foundation, the Soul-Essence, is the principle of lawfulness, the spirit, a psychic function, becomes capable of understanding the lawfulness of its counter-image, capable of grasping the truth about the world, though the spirit should endeavor also to grasp the truth about the psyche and is inner functioning.

These findings are self-evident and the human soul, when dreaming about itself, has always known them superconsciously. It expressed them symbolically through the mythical dream. Conscious thought, however, mistakes soul for psyche. The two words are used as if they had an identical meaning. Conscious thought, the intellect, can no longer solve the fundamental problem: how can the subject grasp—understand objectively—the object, the objectal world. The intellect conceives the psyche (subject) and the world (object) as two radically distinct phenomena, without any essential link, and cannot reunite them

---

2. See note on page 23.

anymore. In order to avoid confusion, it is important not to confuse the psychological terms "to excite" and "to perceive" with the metaphysical and symbolical term "to appear"; the world excites the psyche and the psyche perceives the world. But world and psyche appear to the Soul-Essence. Since this is the case, what matters essentially is to reestablish in temporal life the union between the two complementary appearances. Union in its temporal form is harmony. The demand for harmonization concerns the multiformity of the existing modalities and their modifications, harmony being unity within multiplicity. But the multiplicity of the manifest phenomena, including the psychic phenomena, is originally founded in an initial duality (spirit-matter), a duality which becomes—on the plane of life—intention-extension, psyche-world. The immanent meaning of life is the evolutionary transformation of the initial discord (spirit-matter) into a harmonious accord. The link between psyche and world being the desires and their need for satisfaction which makes of them the motives of action, the immanent meaning of human life is the harmonization of the intentionality of the motives, harmonization which is imposed by the mysteriously animating impulse.

The Soul-Essence being the mysterious common root of the two real and complementary appearances—world and psyche—the myth talks about a "soul of the world," the organizing intentionality of all nature, just as it talks about a psyche mysteriously animated by intentions of harmonious self-organization (ethical superconscious). These two images are true when understood as symbolic expressions and according to their real and deep significance.

The symbols "soul of the world" and "psyche-soul" convey the idea of the evident fact of a mysterious animating impulse, a mysterious intentionality manifest in the evolutionary impulse that unites pre-life and life up to the plane of human life. The psyche-soul, individualized on the human plane (dispersed into a multitude of psyches which differ from one another according to the various degrees of intensity of their superconsciously animating imnpulse), is a special case of the mysterious evolutionary intentionality of nature uniting all the forms of existence in one single evolutionary impulse which is both mysterious and manifest. All that which exists is part of the complementary aspects of temporal existence: immutable mystery and manifest appearance fated to disappear.

This enables us to express the relation "psyche-world" through another aspect of the metaphysical image: Soul-Essence.

Every psyche surrounds itself with its own world, its personal universe. The soma belongs to the spatial world, and the psyche (thoughts, feelings, and volitions as a whole) animates it. But it can do so only due to the fact of its own mysterious animation, which is also that of the world. The soma-psyche unit is the individual. The soul is neither inside nor outside of him. It is not a spatio-temporal appearance. What is in the individual is only the feeling of animation: the more or less intense emotion of the mystery of his own existence and of the existence of the universe. The universe perceived and experienced by each individual is the expression of his Soul-Essence. The apparent self, the man alive in body and spirit, is only the animated tool which enables to grasp its counter-reality, the world, to act in the universe, to perceive it, to feel and to think it. Men cannot fathom the experienced universe which is proper to each one of them, they cannot be united in soul, in essence, in harmony except insofar as they feel, think, and act essentially. They can unite essentially only through truth (by spiritualization) and goodness (by sublimation). All the individualized souls being—within the context of this image—mysteriously united in the Father-Essence symbol, the appearance proper to each soul, its individually perceived universe, is in agreement with that proper to the other souls, and all the individual universes seem to be one sole universe common to all. However, men are not completely united in essence; they live at the most only partially and sporadically in truth and goodness. Everyone is endowed with a different degree of intensity of the animating impulse, and therefore the apparent world, perceptively common to all men, remains different for each one of them, excites each one of them in a different way, inspires each one with a different vital feeling, another degree of fear or sublimation, going from ultimate joy to infernal torment.

Being the mysterious foundation of the material spatiality of the soma and of the psychic universe experienced by each individual, the Soul-Essence is not part of the temporality of psychosomatic life. The symbolic name of its "mode" of existence is "eternity," and the most suitable image of eternity is not an infinite extension of apparent time, time going infinitely forward from past to future. The only image that is fit for eternity is "immutable presence." Again, this is an unimaginable image expressing the mystery and its unchangeable evidence.

After the death of the body and the psyche, after the eclipse of the individual universe, the soul does not leave the body, because it was not inside it; it does not go on living through time, because it never started to live in time. But it does not disappear, because it never appeared; what appeared and what disappeared is only its manifest expression: the psychosomatic organization, its sensations and actions, its feelings and thoughts, all the memories of its extensive life through space and time. Even space and time were only appearance. The actual existence of that individual appearance had a beginning, a duration, and an end. The soul does not start to exist and does not cease to exist. Its "eternal presence" perdures, but it is an unfathomable mystery.

Thus the soul-mystery is at the same time the mystery of life and the mystery of death.

The mythologies express both the mystery of existence and the mystery of death through a great variety of metaphysical images.

These images are devoid of any tangible reality save for the sublimating motivational influence they have exerted since the beginnings of mankind on the combativity of the impulse.

The mythical era is characterized by two main forms of belief in immortality. The Christian myth imagines immortality as a definitive union of God and the Soul (eternal reward) or as an eternal separation (life in hell, eternal punishment). The injustice of the inordinate reward and punishment disappears if one understands that eternity is not a temporal flow perpetuated into infinity. The metaphysical image thus recovers its true significance: unfathomable mystery. The other form of metaphysical image, represented by the Hindu myth, is rooted in the belief of a ceaseless reappearance of the Soul. Expelled again and again from rest in mystery, the impure Soul is condemned to create its psychic appearance, in order to purify itself through its repeated apparitions so as to finally reach the "eternal union," the Nirvana.

The two images have a great mythical beauty as long as they are not mistaken for realities.

The human spirit, itself a temporal manifestation, cannot in any way come to the conclusion of a life after death, it can only create anthropomorphic images of it. Even the ethical superconscience—however clairvoyant the symbolic pre-science is with respect to the conflicts of psychic life—cannot abort the reality of the metaphysical image of an eternal reward or an eternal punishment, since superconscience knows nothing about what is after life. In the same way, the superconscience does not present the metaphysical symbol "God the Creator" as a reality.

These images still have a perfectly determinable significance. They are based on the evidence that the mystery of existence does not begin with the birth of the individual and does not cease with the death of the individual. Mystery is intemporal, and the image of intemporality is eternity as opposed to fleeting life.

3. THE "IMMORTAL SOUL" SYMBOL AND THE SYMBOL OF "DEATH OF THE SOUL"

What is before and after temporal life is not absolute nothingness but a nothingness relative to the human capacity of understanding, and this is exactly what the word "mystery" expresses. The entire life of man, all his psychic experience—his thoughts, feelings, volitions, all his motivating intentionality—is only an episode of a mysteriously temporal "existence." The essential part of his apparent life is the mysterious animation, the animating impulse. The victories and defeats of the essential impulse remain linked to the Essence of life, to the mystery symbolically called "God." This religiously deep emotion implied in the metaphysical symbols makes of them a call to accept the fleetingness of apparent life, a salutory remedy against metaphysical anxiety, fear in the face of death. The sublimely motivating force of acceptance (which is a perfect contrast to plaintive resignation) will, however, become much more intense when it refers directly to emotion in the face of mystery without using the intermediary of the ancestral metaphysical imagination of an afterlife.

The most dangerous is to mistake the metaphysical image of justice after death for a reality. Sublimating acceptance runs the risk of being downgraded to the level of an infantile need for consolation. This error totally reverses the moral meaning hidden in the texts, a meaning which refers to the life and death of the animating impulse and not to bodily death and life in the beyond. This meaning, which is common to all the mythologies is: better to die in the body than "to die in the soul," than to undergo during life the death of the animating impulse.

The immoral principle is the exaltation of earthly desires and the oblivion of the superconscious spirit. What earthly desire could be more exalted and senseless than that of indefinitely stretching apparent life? The individual clings to appearance and does not want to abandon it: death is considered as an accident devoid of any mysterious meaning. Beyond the grave, man, too easily duped by the most senseless desire, hopes to safeguard what was only the principle of his apparent life: i.e., individuation.

Since the principle of individuation, the psyche (all the psychic functions linked to the soma) is not immortal, and since there is no tangible reality corresponding to the metaphysical symbols of "God" and "the soul," immortality does not exist in any way. This finding is not based on any kind of speculation. On the contrary, it eliminates all speculation, since it stems from the necessity of acknowledging the existence of a symbolic language whose terminology is common to all mythologies, to dreams and to the biblical texts. Discussions about the reality of God and the Soul deal with the most essential problem of existence in general and the meaning of human life in particular. These discussions, which have often been set against dogma could not successfully oppose the false theological justification which pretended that human reason is incapable of understanding the revelations God made to the prophets of the Old Testament. This is a vicious circle type of proof, since it presupposes the existence of God in the form of a supernatural man who would speak to mortals from mouth to ear, a very old pagan symbol, it goes without saying.

Confronted with this ancient error, we have to acknowledge that human reason is perfectly capable of understanding that God is a symbol and also of understanding the symbolic meaning of the revelations.

This acknowledgment is all the more necessary in that it sums up all the preceding analyses. It would not be superfluous to sum up briefly the results obtained thus far in order to strengthen them by a confrontation with the authentic texts to which theology refers: the epistles of the apostle Paul.

The apostle talks exclusively—which has to be proved—about the conflicts of the inner psychic functioning, thus eliminating the confusion between Psyche and Soul which led to the belief in the immortality of the Psyche. Now this confusion is frequent not only in theology but in daily parlance. In order to eliminate it as radically as possible, it was deemed better to introduce the unusual term of "Soul-Essence," which justifies the introduction of the term "Father-Essence" instead of the symbol of God the Father (an expression which is itself too loaded with confusion). Neither the creator (or the "Father-Essence") nor the Soul (or "Soul-Essence" and its personal immortality exists in reality. On the contrary, what does indeed exist is the mystery of the existence of the world, on the one hand, and the mystery of the animating impulse, a psychic phenomenon, on the other. This is why the texts deal with two forms of resurrection: the resurrection of the Soul after the death of the body, pure metaphysical fiction; and the ethical resurrection during life from the banal fall, from Adam's fall, called "death of the soul": death of the animating impulse. Here the term "resurrection" has obviously no other meaning than its linguistic significance: straightening up.

This fundamentally important distinction is clearly established in the Pauline epistles. The dogmatic error is rooted not only in the misunderstanding of the myth of the trinity but also—and perhaps even more so—in the false interpretation of the epistles of the apostle Paul. When confronting the theological interpretation with the text of the epistles, the point will be to demonstrate that the error consists in thinking about bodily death each time the author refers to the death of the animating impulse and in thinking about "eternal life after death" each time he refers to ethical resurrection, the recovery of the impulse during life.

According to the apostle, man dies during his life *through sin* (by sinning). He rises again during his life by ceasing to sin: by *dying for sin* or *to sin*. The sin for which one must die during life in order to rise again—or be reborn during life to eternal truth—is the sin of Adam through which appeared "the death of the soul," the banalizing temptation, according to the myth of Genesis.

The fact is that the Pauline epistles are an incomprehensible gibberish if one reads them without a knowledge of the symbolism underlying all the biblical texts from the myth of Genesis to the myth of Christ. Dogmatism, unable to understand symbols, could only interpret them according to the letter. "The letter kills," says the apostle, "only the spirit brings life." The life-giving spirit can only be the truth underlying the symbolic facade which, understood textually, is only a dead letter.

Here are some quotations which will give food for thought to those who wish to understand.

Romans 7:21–24: *"In fact, this seems to be the rule, that every single time I want to do good it is something evil that comes to hand. In my inmost self I dearly love God's Law, but I can see that my body follows a different law that battles against the law which my reason dictates. This is what makes me a prisoner of that law of sin which lives inside my body."*

This is awareness of the original sin, i.e., of the weakness innate in human nature (which in psychological terms is the conflict of motivations, the conflict between the law of the superconscience and the law of the subconscious), and hence of the necessity of elucidating introspection, of the inner eye, the theme of all mythologies. Can one deny that the apostle, having the courage of confessing his own weakness, proves his introspection lucidly, and having yet the greater courage of confessing his weakness to others, intends to propose to them introspective elucidation as the way to salvation? In his epistles, the apostle only speaks about salvation, and all his quotations refer to the message of salvation of "Christ" to whom he is witnessing.

8:6 (RSV): *"To set the mind on the flesh is death but to set the mind on the spirit is life and peace."*

Is it not evident that in this passage death is not bodily death but "to set the mind on the flesh," i.e., exaltation of earthly desires, and that the life Paul refers to is not "life after death" but the force of spiritualization (to love, "to set the mind on" the spirit, or, better, spiritualizing emotion)?

8:13–14: *"If you live in that way (in the flesh), you are doomed to die; but if by the Spirit you put an end to the misdeeds of the body, you will live. Everyone moved by the Spirit is a son of God."*

This is the very ancient symbol of filiation, which leads to think that for Paul also, Jesus is *symbolically* son of God and that his life was exemplary and salutory because—actual man—he was able to kill, thanks to his living spirit, the motives determining the perverse actions of the body.

10:9: *"If your lips confess that Jesus is Lord and if you believe in your heart that God raised him from the dead, then you will be saved."*

It is not enough to confess with the lips; one must bear God in one's heart, be able to be moved in the face of mystery and its manifestation, in order to resurrect from banalization of the vital impulse and conventionalization of the spirit. Since Jesus carried God in his heart, God in him, his own vital impulse, brought him back to life.

But would Jesus, according to the apostle, need to resurrect if the temptation to fall—if the threat of death of the soul—did not also exist in him? Does not the apostle say: "God raised him *from THE DEAD*"? This plural form is highly significant. It clearly denotes that we are not dealing with the death of the body and its resurrection after the death of Jesus, but with the death of the soul of the multitude of men among whom Jesus alone—though he was "son of Man"—was able to overcome the temptation of Adam. This is why the apostle, writing to those he converted, refers to the example of the unique man. And in order to better explain the eternal truth, the message of salvation, he tells them:

6:13: *"Offer yourselves to God and consider yourselves dead men brought back to life."*

It is impossible to express oneself more clearly in symbolic language, which at the same time both unveils and veils the essential truth concerning the life and death of the animating impulse. God is the symbol of the superconscious truth and to give oneself to God is the active implementation of the superconscious truth. The superconsciously immanent truth is the essential desire, and man cannot do himself a greater good than to satisfy his essential desire, the condition for salvation. The greatest error lies in reversing this truth and in believing that salvation is a gratuitous gift made by a real god to men "dead in the soul," so as to spare them the effort of saving themselves. Writing to his disciples, the apostle says: "Offer yourselves to God" according to the strength of your own vital impulse and you will participate in salvation. And to encourage them, he does not hesitate to relate his own difficulties (7:19): ". . . instead of doing the good things I want to do, I carry out the sinful things I do not want." Talking about his own difficulties but also about his own effort to overcome them, he is entitled to tell the others, (10:9 already quoted): "If you believe in your heart that God raised him from the dead" (raised Jesus, which means that man can rise from the dead): if you understand in the depth of your own emotivity, in your innermost motivity, the meaning and value of the salutory example, you will be saved. You will trust only in yourself, and your faith in the genuine strength of human nature will save you. This is the message of joy of the Pauline epistles, the Gospels, and all the mythologies.

Most surprising is that this understanding of the message is also to be found in the epistle of 1 Peter 2:24 (RSV:): *"that we might die to sin and live to righteousness"* (immanent justice), and in the epistle of James, 1:14: *"Everyone who is tempted is attracted and seduced by his own wrong desire. Then the desire conceives and gives birth to sin and when sin is fully grown, it too has a child, and the child is death."*

Should we then conclude that primitive Christianity knew and understood the meaning of the example and message of Jesus, and that the truth was lost due to the dogmatization of the texts?

Nothing, absolutely nothing is more important for the understanding of the texts than the clear distinction between the two forms of resurrection: the ethical uprising and the union of the Soul-Essence with the Father-Essence. The confusion is inevitable if the difference between ethical symbolism founded in reality and metaphysical symbolism founded in pure fiction is not understood. Whether moral or meta-physical, resurrection is manifested after a death: moral, it follows the "death of the soul" (its perverse state); metaphysical, it follows the death of the body. In the biblical texts, the two meanings of death are not always differentiated: the symbol "resurrection from death" bears at times the moral meaning, and at times the metaphysical one, since the two aspects express the mystery of life.

Theology, too exclusively set in the belief in the metaphysical image of the immortality of the Soul-Essence and its reunion with the Father-Essence, could still have avoided the harmful error by paying attention to the fact that the texts do not only talk about the *immortality* of the Soul-Essence, but also about the *death of the soul*. It would thus have been possible to avoid the misunderstanding of the texts from the myth of Adam's sin, the fall of the soul, to the myth of salvation, wrongly tak-en for a promise of eternal life for the immortal soul.

C. FREEDOM

1. FREEDOM AND MOTIVATING DETERMINATION

The problem of freedom links the metaphysical symbols (God and soul) to the moral reality: to the effort of liberation. That which is called on the mythical plane "incarnation," "resurrection," or, as we shall see, "redemption," is called on the moral plane "liberation." The essential (moral) task is to liberate the soul (the animating impulse) from the grip of the subconscious (vanity). But the subject can only act directly on the psyche linked to the world by the desires. Now the de-sires (material, sexual, and spiritual) being too numerous and contra-dictory to be discharged in the present moment, accumulate in the psy-che and constitute *motives for future actions*, exposed to the permanent choice of the INNER DELIBERATION, an intrapsychic phenomenon, which exists beyond any dispute. Its vitally important task is the elabo-ration of voluntary decisions. The purpose of deliberation is—as the name itself indicates—LIBERATION.

The essential fate of man is determined on the intrapsychic level of his inner deliberation. Everyone should—for his own essential good—purify his psyche from affective trouble by liberating the desires—and hence the motives—from imaginative exaltation, principle of evil, and this can only be accomplished with the help of the animating impulse. In doing this, the soul is gradually liberated. For perfect liberation—freedom[3]—is the union of soul and psyche: the soul having become psychic manifestation, the apparent psyche itself.

---

3. The French *liberté* stresses the link between man's *deliberation*, the function of which is to *liberate* him dynamically from inner conflict, and freedom, the ideal goal of deliberation.

The solution to the problem of freedom is included in the analysis of the psychic processes culminating in the finding of a lawful relationship between essence and appearance, between soul and psyche.

If, by his very nature, man understood himself (if there was no beclouding process or subconscious), all men would only want to achieve the essence. In so doing, they would become free. For to be free is synonymous with being able to do what one wants; not what one desires accidentally and through error about one's nature and real need, but what one really wants in the depths of one's being. To be free is to be able to achieve the essential desire of harmonization ruling over the deliberation, whose motivating intention is the union between the animating impulse and the mystery of animation.

It follows that even if the human being understood, not only superconsciously but consciously, the law of his nature and wanted to abide by it, he would not be able to do so, since the achievement of the essential desire—freedom, the mastery of all the excitations, which is the condition for joy—is a remote and only guiding ideal. However, a clear vision of the guiding aim can become the surest lead in the struggle for liberation. The evolutionary elaboration of the knowledge of the laws of human nature—though insufficient in itself to liberate the individual—can have the practical importance of a stimulation for the sublime effort, can provide the most spiritualized motivating determination, the most decisive weapon in this essential struggle imposed on everyone according to the strength of his vital impules. Every individual is an attempt by nature to achieve the struggle for liberation and to bring life closer to its remotest goal: freedom. The individual can become more or less free. He is not free. Freedom is the ideal goal; it is not a real fact.

According to this definition, freedom is the contrary of "free-will" (indeterminate choice).

The ideal and directive goal being imposed on man by his own essential desire—the desire to liberate the soul—this subjection, the fundamental law, excludes any indeterminism, any unmotivated freedom. It includes the lawful determination of every psychic effort. Sublime effort as well as stagnation is determined by the strength or weakness of the essential desire, in other words, of the animating impulse. The impulse can die, it can also become weaker or stronger with variable degrees of intensity, which implies the essential responsibility of the individual.

The ideal meaning of life, freedom, is the control of the motives, in a self-determination so strong that all the energy, concentrated in the essential desire, become freely available to the individual. The real meaning of life is the capacity for lucid deliberation, i.e., the free fluctuation of energy between the essential desire and the multiple—but not exalted—desires, according to the demands of the changing situations. To go against this meaning is to interrupt the free fluctuation in two ambivalent ways: through convulsion of pseudo-spiritual energy (moralizing inhibition) or through the laxity without scruples of exalted materials and sexual desires (banal exhibition). Because of the motivating self-determination, both the effort of liberation and stagnation involve the individual's responsibility. The individual is responsible for the determined form of life he is. This form, distinct against the background of life and its meaning, is his self. All his responsibility lies in the fact that he is what he is. And what he is will show in his capacity or incapacity to control his inner motivations, which are the essentially determinating factors of his activities.

It is vain to believe that one must invent the concept of free-will in order to understand responsibility. The concept, on the contrary, prevents any real understanding because it eliminates all psychic lawfulness. According to the concept of free-will, man—without any determination—would be free to achieve or inhibit his accidental desires. The multiple desires and their biological greed would not be individually determined any more than the tendency to spiritual inhibition (the restraint of reason). It should be clear that from such a complete indeterminism does not follow freedom but only the least free, the blindest of determinations: the determination by whim. The responsibility that this concept proposes is not the task of man toward himself, toward his own nature, toward life and its mystery, but an obligation toward a spectator-judge: a real god.

But, beside these speculations, what is it that can sublimely control the multiple desires if not a desire capable of becoming stronger than all multiple desires and each and every one of them? And this can only be the essential desire for harmonization, i.e., for freedom. And how could it spiritually inhibit the exaltation of the multiple desires if it were not in a constant energetic exchange with them, i.e., if the accidental scattering and the essential concentration of energy were not determined by the biological requirement of the desires, their need for satisfaction, which on the human plane finds its highest intensity through the superconsciously motivating force of the law of harmonization?

What we call "will" is originally nothing but the blind tension of the desires toward a meaningful or senseless goal, their rightly or wrongly motivating force. The liberated will, on the contrary, is the mastery of the desires, the essential capacity of replacing the senseless goals with meaningful goals which are healthily valuated (spiritualization) and of controlling their affective tension through the capacity of patient retention (sublimation). These manifestations of the liberated will remain, however, determined by a constant choice: the *inner deliberation* which, preceding activity, elaborates the voluntary decisions on the intrapsychic level. *There is only one possible case in which it can be said that the decision was not imposed but freely wanted, and this is achieved insofar as the decision was determined by sublimating energy, by the essential desire, in other words, by the impulse of harmonization. Liberated will is the essential determination, the self-determination to harmony and the joy it brings.*

The feeling of indeterminate freedom—the feeling of arbitrary free-will—is a deception, the erroneous product of a theoretical abstraction with regard to the only psychic reality which is the inner motivating deliberation.

The theoretical abstraction (oblivion of the deliberation that led to the decision) comes after the event when the inner split (the conflict of motivations) has found its temporary appeasement by means of the decision of the motivating deliberation. It is clear that after the decision, the conflict is not felt nor experienced, and it becomes easy to imagine that one has freely and arbitrarily made the decision.

The error about will and freedom, the error about the deliberating and motivating functioning of the psyche—belief in free-will—proceeds, here as always, from the most primitive tendency of the human spirit to transform its superstitions into dogmas, to hypostatize its imaginative fictions. Free-will is an imagination raised to the level of dogma in order to establish the responsibility of man toward the celestial Judge.

The truth is that the deliberating process is imposed on man by his own nature, it is a proceeding in which man is the defendant (in case of a violation of the law of harmony) while being at the same time his own superconscious judge and his own attorney (most of the time through attempts at false self-justification).

Neither God nor free-will exist. The deep significance of the deliberating self-determination is the fundamental law of human nature: man's responsibility for himself, facing the mystery of his animation.

Nothing is more enlightening for the deep understanding of the essential problem of human life—freedom and the conditions for its achievement—than to research its biogenetical roots.

The deliberation is a permanent introspection, the feature which essentially disinguishes man from animals.

An animated being—as its name implies—the animal is part of the mystery of animation.

All the problems falsely posed by theological spiritualism and by the materialism of the sciences of life vanish in face of the simplicity and the evidence of such a finding.

Where would the animating impulse of man come from, had it not been evolutionarily prefigured?

The mystery of animation is manifested in the superior animals in the form of instinctivity, of preconscious spirit, an inconceivable and yet manifest pre-science, capable of harmoniously adjusting the various animal species to the conditions of existence offered by the environment. Animating instinctivity in its evolved form becomes the ethical superconscience in man, the animal who has become half-conscious and exposed to choice and possible errors.

The superconscious spirit of man is no less mysterious than the preconscious spirit of the animal, but is is more clairvoyant still. The differential features are in fact quite numerous. The superconscious instinctivity is no longer common to all the members of the thinking species: it is individualized in degrees of intensity and is the personal animating impulse of each human being. Besides this, the superconscious instinct of man is no longer constitutive as is the animal instinct ruling undisturbed over its activity. The ethical superconscience is only consultative since it is fought by the disharmonizing subconscious. Hence the most essential and important distinctive feature: the human superconscience does not only have to undertake harmonization with the environment but also the harmonization of the intrapsychic processes. The human psyche is divided into more or less conscious processes and is assailed by a multitude of material and sexual desires that are prone to subconscious influence which complicates and disorients conscious choice. This means that the psyche must continuously elaborate the motivating choice through an inner deliberation in which all the processes participate, which explains the conflictual state of the human psyche. The individually animating impulse guides the motivating deliberation. In other words, the essential desire for harmonization is superconsciously immanent.

The psychic processes do not have a spatial existence. They are more or less lucid functions which are interrelated, since they fluctuate between lucidity and blindness. The subconscious is nothing else than the superconscious in a state of partial blindness due to vain egocentricism. Total blindness of the superconscience is mythically represented by the symbol "death of the animating impulse."

The mythical pre-science of the superconscious instinct—because it is the evolutionary product of the instinctive pre-science of animals— was able to formulate the conflicts of the thinking species' deliberation through the myth of Man's genesis: God is the symbol of the superconscience, Adam is the symbol of the conscious and its wavering choice; the subconscious is represented by Satan, in the form of the tempter-serpent, the symbol of vanity.

2. THE MOTIVATING DELIBERATION

The erroneous belief in indeterminate freedom is mainly due to the fact that the intrapsychic phenomenon—deliberation—is prevented from becoming conscious by the anathema against introspection.

Since the subconscious temptations take part in the introspective deliberation, introspection becomes easily morbid. *The opposite of freedom is not determination, but subconscious obsession* (terminology used in psychiatry for a particular neurosis, used here for all psychopathic distortions). All subconscious manifestations contain an obsessive element: the imaginative exaltation of desires which being repressed (nervosity[4]) or obsessively achieved (banalization[5]) do not cease to exert their power of fascination, which has become uncontrollable.

Since this is the case and since man is biogenetically compelled to deliberate before acting, he should try to obtain individually the control of the inner deliberation which is lawfully common to all but has different shades, and is differently patterned in every indivdual.

As long as the essential desire is alive, it will manifest itself after action in the form of essential satisfaction (joy) or essential dissatisfaction (guilty anxiety). But man is able to foresee the consequence of his mistaken action, the torment of guilt and to use this foresight in order to make right value judgments which will form the sensible self-determinations of his future activity. Man can, thanks to this foreseen guiltiness, determine himself and act according to his essential desire so as to avoid the vague torment essentially and lawfully following his mistaken action. (It is important not to confuse the guilty anxiety of the superconscience with false guiltiness in the face of social conventions.)

Thus, the essential desire (its guilty constraint and joyful satisfaction) rules over the entire deliberation, even the subconscious part of it. But the essential desire itself is not indeterminate. The individual cannot arbitrarily choose his essential desire, his vital impulse: it is imposed on him by nature, and its essence remains identical in all men. The only difference is the degree of its strength: the capacity ot avoid guilty error, to form right value judgments. The latter, since they are formed by man, express his will and his degree of freedom. As a result of right value judgments, the essential desire can take shape and become aware of itself. Through right value judgments, man is able to determine himself essentially. He can adopt (consciously) the essential determination (which is superconscious). This determination of man by himself is the essential determination that has become voluntary, the liberated will of man.

This is real freedom, the only freedom that exists. It is—mythically speaking—the emergence of the soul into appearance. It is the penetration of the psyche by essence, the incarnation of the word (the evolutionary impulse).

At the highest degree of incarnation of the superconscious spirit, deliberation achieves its goal of liberation: perfect freedom, not in an absolute sense, but in the meaning of perfecting, achieving.

It is necessary to know the peak of liberation to understand that it is a natural phenomenon connected, on the level of inner deliberation, to all the other states of mind, to all the degrees of intensity of liberation,

---

4. Diel distinguishes three levels of mental disorder: "nervosité," "névrose," and "psychose," which have been translated as "nervosity," "neurosis," and "psychosis."

5. See note on page 54.

and to all the degrees of perversion. From sanctity to "death of the vital impulse," from psychic health and psychoses, the process of deliberation forms an uninterrupted continuum of all the positive and negative states of mind. *Motivating deliberation constitutes the scale of values,* values and non-values are graded according to their degree of satisfaction and dissatisfaction. The understanding of this essential phenomenon is disturbed by the false promises of satisfaction of vanity, which mistakes non-values for values and values for non-values, truth for error and error for truth, right for wrong and wrong for right, thus ignoring the ethical law in its practically experienced form: immanent justice.

It is inscribed in human nature that every man can—at least in principle—on the level of his inner deliberation achieve a liberation in conformity with his own effort and with the reactivation of his vital impulse—certainly not through good intentions, but through the review of the motivating valuations which determine his actions. If he does not do so, he will be determined by his valuations, which are too often subject to conventions which determine the moralizing convulsion of the vital impulse or its banal laxity leading to search for freedom in licentiousness. Even the moralizer is invaded in his secret imaginations by the desire for banal breakout. He cannot achieve it because his vital impulse—since it is not dead—inhibits him. The more convulsed and exalted is his impulse, the more the inhibition runs the risk of becoming pathological and stifling his most natural desires. On the other hand, the banalized person cannot satisfy his natural desires. His obsession with breaking out misconstrued as freedom of mind, leads him to seek for satisfactions that are more and more against nature, to gradually destroy the vital impulse which, in spite of all, remains active to some degree and fills him with vague guiltiness, half disgust and half obsessive envy; though banalism is not only the search for pleasures but also ambition for success at any cost. The combinations of nervosity and banalism are countless. Their common feature is that they are determined by imaginative exaltation mistaken for unconditional and unlimited freedom.

Man does not really know how to act because he knows nothing of his essential desire ruling over spiritual inhibition (the restraint of reason). He thinks that he can act with impunity against the essential desire, and this leads him to exalt it senselessly or to look for freedom in perverse uninhibition, in the breakout of multiple desires and in licentiousness.

But this perverse possibility of the inner life is only a semblance of freedom. It is in fact totally determined by false collective justifications and by perverse motives which are individually obsessive and excluded from conscious control.

Genuine freedom is the conscious control of the motives. It cannot be achieved without liberation from public opinion.

The effort of liberation, therefore, demands a penetrating awareness of the subconsciously hidden determination. This effort is unbearable if one does not have the pertinent awareness of the existence of a fundamental wrong motivation, based not only on false individual justifications, but far more insidiously on the existence of false collective justifications: prevailing ideologies, each being armed with a complete arsenal of justifications. Freedom of the spirit is achieved to the extent that man dares to raise to the level of his own consciousness the harmfulness of endless discussions—of their triumphs and vexations—real hot beds for mental illnesses where each party perceives the wrong motivations of the other while being unaware of the conventionalism of his own wrongly motivated spirit.

The essential truth is that wrong motivation resides in the innermost self of all men and that the only way to get rid of it—within the limits of possibility—is to fight it in one's own innermost self. Man is entirely free not to accept this. But this freedom is itself determined, vainly motivated, because the epitome of vanity would be to believe oneself free from all wrong motivation.

The double error (theoretical and practical) about freedom is itself due to the most deeply hidden subconscious motive: vanity and its anxiety in the face of truth.

Because, and only because, freedom—even at its highest degree of achievement—remains determined, even blind determination can achieve liberation. Because of this possibility, man, no matter what he does, remains responsible before life and its immutable law, the very essence of life.

Determination which wants to free itself—the principle of all lawfulness in life—does not only decide responsibility toward the *ideal of sublimation*, which is inaccessible and solely directive (perfect freedom). It also decides the *ideal of spiritualization* through a tireless and progressive search for the lawful truth ruling over the intrapsychic processes. Since everything, freedom, and superconscience included, remains determined, the human spirit must be able to discover the lawful determinants.

As long as psychology does not focus its research on the superconscious and subconscious determinations of human reactions—right and wrong motivation, the study of inner deliberation—the problem of freedom cannot be solved. It remains as speculative to pretend that human actions are not determined as it is to say that they are determined. The problem of freedom, understood as the problem of right and wrong, superconscious and subconscious motivation, is the central problem of psychology. Even more so, this problem *is* psychology. Insofar as its solution is found, psychology will know the human psyche, the object of its research. However, even detailed knowledge of the motivating functions of the psyche would remain insufficient without a complementary study of the biogenesis of the deliberating function and its purpose: freedom. But as soon as psychology starts to study all these problems, it is faced with the fact that they all have a metaphysical aspect: the mystery of existence and of animation, a metaphysical mystery whose symbolic personification in mythologies has exerted an immense motivating influence on the history of thought. For reasons of scientific prudence, the study of motivations must revise the speculative solutions of metaphysics. Psychology could certainly give an account of the laws governing life, i.e., of the terrifying punishment set off by subconscious distortion, as well as of the joy rewarding superconscious formation, even without going back to the mythical and mysterious source of these laws, without concerning itself with the metaphysical images. But it would then remain *on one plane*, it would not cover all the aspects of life, it would lack its essential dimension, that is: depth and height.

The essential phenomenon of human life—deliberation and its goal of liberation—is not understood in all its scope and depth as long as one ignores the connection between inner deliberation and the ultimate image of the divinity: the "God-the-Judge" symbol and its significance which can only be the immanence of justice.

If God and the soul are symbols, God-the-judge is also a symbol. If all the mythical symbols are images with a hidden meaning representing the inner conflicts of the human soul, the symbol of a divine justice—shared by all mythologies—must necessarily represent the essential responsibility of man: the responsibility for his own fate depending—though he does not know it—on the inner deliberation through which everyone elaborates vitally right or wrong solutions for all the problems of life.

According to all mythologies, God does not judge man according to his acts, which are often hypocritical, but according to his hidden motives.

The immanence of justice—superconsciously evident—is hidden by the manifestations of subconscious life which constitute immanent injustice. *Justice is immanent to life; injustice is immanent to man.* The symbol of "God-the-Judge meting out rewards and punishments" belongs to both the metaphysical and the ethical spheres.

According to all mythologies man is judged after his death, which is a metaphysical image concerning the mystery of death.

However, the judgment after the death of the body, no matter how fictional it is, concerns ethical behavior during this fleeting life: the life or death of the animating impulse. More yet, according to all mythologies, the divinity oversees and judges man throughout his life and down to his least activities.

The "God-the-Judge" symbol leads from symbolism endowed with a purely metaphysical meaning and concerning the mastery of life and death to a sumbolization whose significance is purely ethical: it concerns the mystery of life: *the ethical law* which is superconsciously immanent to the human psyche.

CHAPTER 4

Ethical Symbolization

The metaphysical symbols of God, Soul, Freedom concern the mystery of creation, the mystery of animation and the mystery of freedom: the mysterious possibility that man has to determine himself either to the life of the animating impulse or to "the death of the impulse."

The mystery of Freedom thus contains the mystery of the human superconscience, which is at the same time the source of the metaphysical symbols and of the ethical symbolization condensed in the image of "God-the-Judge."

A. THE "GOD-THE-JUDGE" SYMBOL

1. THE SYMBOL OF "TRANSCENDENT JUSTICE" AND THE REALITY OF IMMANENT JUSTICE

Immanent justice is the eternal truth of the myths.

The deepest significance of all the mythologies of all the peoples and of all the metaphysical and ethical symbolization is the fact that the judgment which is symbolically called "eternal" is immanent to the deliberating psyche and its goal of liberation.

Reward and punishment take place in temporal life even though this temporal justice is perceivable only *at the level of inner deliberation*, i.e., through self-analysis and introspective self-control which are perfectly capable of probing the extra-conscious depths of the psyche, since the conscious and the extra-conscious are not spatially separated, but functionally connected.

The temptation to ignore the immanence of justice is all the greater that one opposes to it the evident injustice of human interactions and that one seeks a consolation for this manifest and supposedly incurable injustice in the belief in a justice after death.

Did not humans try to establish a pseudoproof of the personal existence of God by using the excuse—this is a vicious circle—that a personal God must necessarily exist in order to compensate the injustices of temporal life through the justice of a life after death!

The metaphysical image of a transcendent justice would have no foundation without the reality of immanent justice: without the fact that reward and punishment are achieved in life on both the individual and the social planes.

The manifest injustices of social life are the most frequent cause for complaints. Every individual tends to complain about the injustice of all the others, to accuse them of being unjust while believing himself to be the only just man. Whatever the accidental and historical causes of social injustice, it is vain to look there for the main argument against the immanence of justice. Essentially, injustice will rule over the interactions and the social institutions as long as false justification rules over the secret motivating intentions of individuals. Social injustices are, essentially, the consequence of the interactions of individuals who are wrongly motivated.

Man is free to do what he wants; he is even free to falsely justify himself, and to exclude himself through complaints and false accusations from the essential fault shared by all. Who does not do so? But if he wants to live in essential satisfaction, in joy—and who would not want to do so?—he cannot do as he pleases. He must accept the conditions for joy: the harmony of desires and motives which cannot be achieved without intrapsychic struggle against the disharmonizing temptations of the subconscious.

Justice is immanent because it is based on the law of harmony, and its immanent reward: joy; the law of disharmony and the pathological anxiety it entails is only its negative aspect, immanent punishment.

The punishments that are immanent to the psychic functioning are the psychopathologies: nervosity and banalization. Nervosity and its excessively good and moralizing intentions are ambivalently connected to the excessively aggressive and hateful bad intentions of banalism.

The countless psychopathological variations have as their essential cause (whatever the external causations be) the pathetic and pathogenic complaint about the injustice of the world and life: consequence of the self-disculpation of every one of us and the mutual inculpation of all.

Justice is immanent because the lawfully immanent punishment for the disharmonies of the inner deliberating functioning is psychopathic anxiety in principle, anxiety in the face of truth about oneself: guilty vanity and its tendency to false justification of each error and each fault. The essential cause of psychopathologies is the repression of every feeling of guiltiness, a tendency which—unbeknownst to everyone and with various degrees of intensity—is subconsciously hidden in the inner self of every man. It is the principal motive for the pathetic and pathogenic complaint about the injustice of the world and life, for the excess of false self-justification is balanced by an excess of inculpation of all the others who are deemed unjust. The complaint is too easily justifiable, since all men are wrongly motivated so that offended vanities obsessively seek vain triumphs over others, whether it be in the im-

potent ruminations of the nervous type or by an explosion of unscrupulous revenge, the characteristic feature of banalization.

The common fault—though it is ambivalently contrasted—leads to a
common punishment. Each individual shares in the fault and the punishment in the exact measure of his excessive complaint or his triumph,
proofs of his vain justification. Punishment is not added to the fault:
fault and punishment are one and the same thing. Since they are indivis-
ible, each one of us carries fault and punishment within himself. Fault
and punishment are not half mine and half thine or half mine and half
everyone else's. Everyone is in principle entirely and absolutely responsible for the evil of the world to the extent that he carries in himself the
principle of evil, i.e., false motivation. Immanent justice lies in the fact
that the intensity of the punishment diminishes in the exact measure the
individual—thanks to his combative impulse—manages to free himself
even in his inner deliberation from the temptation of false justification,
which is the means by which man represses his fault to the extent of believing himself to be the only just person in an unjust world.

Whoever would pretend to be exempt from vanity would thereby
prove the excess of his false justification.

Collective false justification is the principle of psychopathology:
namely, phobia in the face of introspection. Its immanent punishment
is ignorance of the essential problem of human life.

The immanence of punitive justice becomes fully manifest if one
takes into account the fact that the pathological ambivalences (the exaltation-inhibition peculiar to all the perverse motivations) extend to all
material, sexual, and spiritual desires and gradually render them powerless. This is due to the fact that ambivalence, by pulling in two opposite directions (amoralizing, excitation-moralizing inhibition), brings
energy to a dead lock (which the myth expresses in the "death of the
soul" symbol: the death of the animating impulse). All the ambivalences come from the contradictory valuation of the perverse spirit
which thus creates the two ambivalent forms of psychic illness: nervo-
sity-banalization. *This is why linguistic wisdom has one name for all the psychopathologies: "illnesses of the mind."*[1] The generally misunderstood intention of linguistic wisdom is undoubtedly to include in the illnesses of
the mind the ambivalent counter-pole of inhibitive nervosity: triumphant banalization, the scourge of social life, the principal cause of the
rule of injustice in the world. Mythical wisdom expresses this in the
"Prince of the World" symbol, represented by Satan, the symbol of the
subconscious intentions that are either too good or too bad. The excessively bad intentions of banalism are the principle of evil because even
more than moralism—at least during eras of decadence—they are hypostatized into an ideal, and this to the extent that complaints about

---

1. In French, "maladies de l'esprit." See note on page 2.

the injustice of life are subconsciously motivated by the regret of not being able to take part in the triumph of those that are banalized. Mythical wisdom stigmatizes inhibiting moralism with the symbol of "being possessed by the Devil," expressing that moralizing mortification is a psychic illness which is less serious than "death of the soul" or banalization. Immanent justice, the expression of essential responsibility, reaches its peak in the fact that even from "death of the soul" man can be reborn to a life in conformity with the "eternal truth": the law of harmony, principle of joy. Joy is the opposite of the death of the vital impulse: the impulse in activity without exaltation or inhibition, which is the very definiton of psychic health as opposed to psychopathological distortion.

Everyone's essential responsibility is based on the fact that the conditions of psychic health and illness—being superconsciously and subconsciously immanent—can be raised to the level of conciousness and subjected to healing control. The harmonizing superconscience is more-than-conscious, the disharmonizing subconscious is less-than-conscious. Since the whole psyche is a functional unit which is either pathologically split asunder or healthily reunited, depending on the degrees of lucidity, it must be possible in principle for conscious reflection to acquire a degree of introspective lucidity enabling it to penetrate better the more-than-conscious as well as the less-than-conscious intentions. All the more so that contradictory intentions are functionally connected by a feeling of guiltiness. Guilty anxiety emanates from the ethical superconscience, indicating the more or less sensible intentions of the conscious, the danger of a gradual loss of harmonious joy. Conscious understanding, instead of hearing the salutory warning, can remain deaf to the call of the superconscious. The introspective eye can blind itself intentionally and thus make itself less-than-conscious, rather than seize the opportunity of strengthening its lucidity by listening to the superconscious call.

This description of the deliberating functioning is enlightening but still insufficient to show the real magnitude of man's individual responsibility.

Justice is immanent because ethical values are immanent.

Ethical values, if taken literally according to dogmatized symbolization, would be alien to man's nature, imposed on man by the divinity.

If the deities—including the only God—are symbols, the transcendent imposition of values is also a symbol.

For theology, the supreme value is the unconditional belief in the personal existence of God-the-Judge and his constant surveillance of the behavior of every man. Obeying God-the-Judge and fearing his judgment are thus an absolute value, a supreme virtue, and the least failure runs the risk of being judged as an absolute non-value, which can be redeemed only through the imploration of a supernatural grace. The excess of such imaginations necessarily results in an opposite imaginative exaltation: doubt in the value of any judgment whatsoever;

belief in the total absence of values or non-values: total irresponsibility, supposedly unconditioned freedom.

In fact, values and non-values are biogenetically immanent. They are immanent because the harmonizing superconscience and the disharmonizing subconscious are products of biogenesis (myth of Adam). The demand for self-harmonization under the penalty of guilty dissatisfaction, just like the temptation of disharmonization based on vain oversatisfaction, is a special case of the law of harmony which is valid for all that exists: pre-life and life. At the evolutionary level of animalization, harmony becomes a condition of satisfactory survival. The search for satisfaction is already, at the animal level, proper to the drives of nutrition and reproduction which are values because they are indispensable for survival. In man, the drives are divided into a multiplicity of desires which are often contradictory, each seeking its own satisfaction. From this comes the fact that values and non-values are manifested in man by rightly or wrongly valuating choice, by vitally right or wrong value judgments. The authentic satisfaction of the valuating spirit is the truth, truth with respect to the promises of satisfaction of materiality and sexuality often imaginatively exalted or inhibited. But over and above all truth of the spirit with the spirit to itself for the spirit is only too easily prey to lying self-overvaluation—vanity—the false promise of satisfaction in principle.

Everything concerning the meaning or lack of meaning in life is superconsciously or subconsciously immanent: the valuating spirit, the right or wrong value judgments, the salutory warning of the ethical superconscience, the feeling of guiltiness, all is immanent to the psyche and can therefore be introspectively raised to the level of consciousness and subjected to self-control. All that which is immanent to the psyche has a motivating force which sublimates or perverts and is part of the inner deliberation, bringing it closer to or leading it further away from its goal of liberation. Because of the vain obsession of the subconscious, man is not free, but he can become free by introspective self-determination to the endeavor of liberation, to the awakening of his vital impulse. Only the valuations of the ethical superconscience are able to fight and dissolve the subconscious temptations of vain self-overvaluation and of the egocentric greed of the desires, the causes of complaints about the injustice of life. The destiny of man depends on the justness of his own value judgments. The judge of man is his own superconscience. This is the essential truth: the imperturbable rule of the law of harmony, mythically called "eternal truth" and represented by the "God-the-Judge" symbol.

2. GRACE AND MERIT

The immanence of justice excludes the possibility of a grace without merit. In other words, there is no such thing as supernatural and miraculous grace.

If God is a symbol, grace is also a symbol.

According to the texts, Jesus works miracles: he cures the lame, the blind and the deaf; he even brings the dead back to life.

Textual interpretation of this sees there miraculous cures brought about by the supernatural power of "the Son of God." Theology even sees there the proof that Jesus is really Son of God and God in person. It supposes that Jesus, each time he talks about his works (his words and example) refers to his miracles as proofs of his divine nature.

Here is what Jesus says about belief in miracles (John 2:23–25): "During his stay in Jerusalem for the Passover many believed in his name when they saw the signs that he gave, but Jesus knew them all and did not trust himself to them; he never needed evidence about any man; he could tell what a man had in him" (the motives and superstitions that make people believe in miracles). This quotation radically excludes the belief in supernatural miracles.

The so-called miracles are symbols of psychic cures implying the merit of the person receiving the miracle. Through word and example, Jesus heals "the lame of soul," men whose inner eye "was blind" or whose understanding "was deaf." He even awakens the "dead of soul." Added to these "miracles," due to the strength of his word or example capable of reanimating the vital impulse, are cures of psychosomatic illnesses, often caused—as is well known—by pathological suggestibility and which can regress by countersuggestions. (In the sanctuary of Asclepius there were as many testimonies of cures as there are in Lourdes. A proof based on miracles would be irrevocable if—and this is an impossible case—a leg, an arm, even only a cut-off small finger started to grow again.)

As to theological grace, it would be a gratuitous gift granted exclusively to the implorations of believers and to their participation in rituals which have been used—as history shows—in all religious sects from animism up until today and which were addressed to countless deities who, in fact, never existed.

On the other hand, seen in relation to mystery, seen metaphysically and symbolically, every man is included in grace. Everything is grace: the gift of existence and qualities, i.e., the mystery of animation and the individual intensity of the impulse. Seen from the viewpoint of appearance, all is merit or demerit: the use one makes of one's existence, namely the development or destruction of one's innate qualities, the degree of achievement or destruction of one's vital impulse.

The individual intensity of the vital impulse—the characteristic feature of the human species—is in no way in contradiction with immanent justice. A more intense impulse calls for a greater endeavor of achievement, a higher concentration on the essential, and implies a more intense guiltiness in case of dispersion. The fact is that no one knows the intensity of his vital impulse before having developed it. But its development is never complete as long as one lives. It is only at the moment of death that essential merit or demerit become definitive and definable. Often during life, the accidental upheavals seen as disastrous become or are capable of becoming decisive factors in the awakening of the vital impulse and its development. Confronted with disasters, man collapses or is animated by an arousal of essential courage never before known, capable of jolting him—for his greater good—out of the apathy and monotony of his habits, which is one of the aspects of immanent justice. For the vital impulse could not awaken in the face of disasters if it had not already—in the small daily problems of life—exerted its force of acceptance, which is the diametrical opposite of complaining resignation. In this respect, excessive privilege can be as harmful as excessive frustration. The vital impulse is generally blocked by banal success hunting, lulled by triumph over external success or warped through bitterness over social failure, exalted or inhibited because it is deflected from the essential task (harmonious growth of the character) toward all kinds of exalted tasks (pseudoreligious, pseudoartistic, political, etc.). A frequent cause is the confusion between the authentic impulse, which is quite rare, and the diversity of talents—be they real or purely imaginary—which are often accompanied by wrong motives of excessive ambition because of the bonuses of excessive self-satisfaction that society conventionally grants them. No matter how beautiful a talent carried by a vital impulse is, the inauthenticity caused by over-competitiveness is harmful to both individuals and society. Life could possibly do without talents, but it cannot do without vital impulse without losing its meaningful direction. This theme is of extreme importance, because the exalted tasks of all kinds are the principal causes of psychopathologies, being at the same time signs and immanent punishments for the destruction of the vital impulse. "Exalted task" means overtension of the energy toward a secondary aim which, going beyond the strength of the vital impulse, remains impossible to achieve or, even if the capabilities are present, does not bring the expected satisfactions. To the very extent that any goal is marred by the vanity of superiority or excessive ambition, all the procession of resentments will follow: triumphs and vexations, rancors and excessive complaints about the injustice of men, of life, and even of God.

For at the very heart of vanity lies a complaint about the injustice of divine grace: the accusation and vexation of not being the first among all men. Why would others deserve to have superior gifts and talents and above all to be animated by a more intense impulse? This is the exalted task in all its excess: jealous vanity. To be sure, it is barely conscious. It is repressed. This is why it manifests itself with all its obsessive and wrongly motivating force. It comes up from the depths of the subconscious, unidentifiable because it is dispersed into countless wrong motivations and false justifications. It is the exalted task in principle, the principle of pathogenesis, carrying its own punishment. Mythically speaking, it is "the Prince of the World," Satan the tempter.

Demerit is imaginative dispersion through past and future; merit is spiritual concentration on the present: presence of mind. The former is the principle of slavery to perverse motivations (which can become blind and obsessive); the latter is the principle of liberation, which becomes freedom when presence of mind is acquired, when past and future vanish after having lost their obsessive and disquietening attraction. This is just another way of expressing the reconcentration of multiple desires in the essential desire. Such a reconcentration is the supreme reward of merit, the "locus" of joy; it is "the narrow gate" leading to the symbolic locus of reward, called in the Christian myth "the kingdom of Heaven" (that man bears in himself). It has other mythical names: Nirvana and Tao. The fact that the manifestation of the soul through the psyche is not completed as long as man lives, explains the mythical truth that man—even if his entire life were a succession of crimes—can attain in the last minute of his life, the state of mind symbolized by the term "grace." The condition is not repentance for fear of being excluded from a Heaven mistaken for a reality, but that, confronted with the mystery of death, he becomes aware of the errors of his past life and that this new understanding is so sincere that it would determine all the actions of that man if, snatched back from death, he were able again to disperse the new awakened essential desire into multiple and exalted desires. In other words, the condition for such a "resurrection," rare indeed but possible in principle, is that repentance not be due to fear of death but to the vision of mystery aroused by the threat of death.

3. ESSENTIAL RESPONSIBILITY AND SOCIAL RESPONSIBILITY

It is important to make a distinction between essential and social responsibility.

Essential responsibility is the authentic relationship of a person with his/her self. It is the responsibility of an individual for himself, for his essential desire; it is the relationship between the essential ego and the apparent self. Deviation is indicated by essential guiltiness, measure of the offense against the essential desire, measure of all the essential harm man inflicts on himself.

On the other hand, social responsibility is the wrong that wrongly motivated individuals inflict on one another and the offense against the laws of society which attempt to restrain this mutual wrong, the consequence of the essential injustice ruling over the souls of individuals who make up society. It is the explosion of the inner malaise leading to the common malaise. Because of essential injustice, because of the wrong motivations of each and every individual in society, the very laws through which society wants to protect itself against this explosion of individual injustice are often only a hypostatized and collective manifestation of the prevailing injustice. If, therefore, due to the essential injustice of individuals, society cannot survive without protecting itself by "rules of the game," by juridical laws, it cannot survive either without endeavoring to improve these laws. It becomes evident that in the face of the historical necessity of social struggle, meaningful or senseless orientation depends on the essential justice or injustice of the individuals, i.e., on the superconscious and free or subconscious and obsessive motivations that animate them, and thus in the last analysis on the essential and wholly internal struggle of individual liberation.

Even though social laws are only a convention, the punishment by these laws and the imputability of the individual remain founded on the fundamental lawfulness of life, on the motivating determination of the psychic functioning. the "raison d'etre" of the social laws is the creation of psychic determinants meant to inhibit trespasses through the threat of accidental dissatisfactions. But in fact, this is nothing more than an intimidation, which is more or less socially effective, a conventional subjection, a self-righteous posture, as long as the underlying wrong valuations remain repressed instead of being dissolved. The only fully liberating valuation—since it is not dependent on external threats—is genuine self-valuation: the understanding that all is determined by the need for self-satisfaction and that perversion and the sublime are only distinguishable by the fact that the former is inconsistent egoism considering only the good of the accidental self, while the latter is self-consistent egoism adding to the search for accidental satisfactions which are vitally indispensable, the desire to achieve one's own essential good: the harmony of motives. This desire is liberating because it does not leave room for any subjection, any hypocrisy, any regret. The benefits of sublime egoism—of the sublimation of vain egocentricity—are in reality far more essential yet: the sublimating force of consistent egoism and its harmonizing intention (which is nothing but the essential desire) extend to the least details of daily life and above all to the parade of disharmonizing resentments. Through the successive elimination of the perverse egotism of resentments and their constraining ambivalence (guilty vanity and complaining accusation), there is a reawakening of warmth of soul, a harmonious union of self-love and love of others: objective love, diametrically opposed to altruistic sentimentality (the perverse counterpole of vain egocentricity). The objectivization of love implies love of truth about oneself and others: the lucidity of the valuating spirit. The highest degree in the immanence of justice is attained by the fact that even the effort of self-liberation remains biogenetically determined by the essential desire, by the vital impulse and its need for harmonious self-satisfaction while being—by this very fact—linked to the mystery of animation.

Outside of the deep religiosity which is emotion in the face of mystery, the effort of self-liberation is only a good intention and even an excessively good and vain intention. To feel mystery is to feel one's own responsibility. For it would be clearly absurd to impute a responsibility to mystery.

The diversity of the animating impulses is the free expression of the apparent mystery embodied in every individual.

The diversity of the individual impulses belongs to the mystery of animation. Whatever the degree of intensity of the animating impulse, its development and its destruction indicate the essential value or non-value of the individual.

According therefore to the symbolization in the mythologies of all peoples, only this life as a whole and when it is completed will be "judged" according to its responsibility in the face of mystery. In accordance with the metaphysical image of justice after death, the mysteriously animating intentionality—which entered into appearance and disappeared mysteriously, leaving the body inanimate—is personified symbolically by "the immortal soul." It returns to the eternal presence from which it emanated—in the symbolic imagination of the myths. Freed from the psyche and its determination, and again become eternal presence, the soul will be "judged" by the eternal presence whose symbol is the divinity who—as a symbol of an eternal judgment—is the judge-divinity. The judgment itself is therefore mystery and symbol. But it is possible to have an image of this mystery because the psychic intentionality was the manifest expression of the soul, and, using an image one can say that the soul will be judged according to the merit or demerit of the psyche.

It cannot be repeated too often that all the images of transcendent justice and the prolongation of individual life in an infinite time, reward and punishment after death, all these are only formulations and prolongations of the collective dream through which the primitive soul, moved by the mystery of death, projected the memory of the father-ancestor into another world. That ancestral metaphysical image was justified by its motivating value rooted in the suggestibility of primitive peoples, thanks to which the idealized example of the deified ancestor exerted a decisively motivating influence on their behavior during life. The hope of being reunited after death with a father-ancestor, deified and immortalized, had as sole valid meaning, the emotional influence that the image of a transcendent justice exerted on the actual life of primitive peoples. This is therefore a problem which has an individual as well as a social scope.

The belief in a compensating justice after death, calling for the belief in a real god, is so deeply rooted in the human psyche that it can be said without any fear of exaggeration that few men—even among atheists—do not (at least at certain moments in their life) believe in a real god and his capricious, and thus unjust, intervention, were it only in the form of providence. The only way to free oneself from this obsessive relic of superstition is through the sublimated fear in the face of the mystery of life, through the awareness of true responsibility, through the salutory understanding that one is alone, mysteriously alone, before life and its law.

B. IMMANENT JUSTICE AND IMMANENT INJUSTICE

1. IMMANENT JUSTICE AND SANCTIFICATION

Sanctification is a myth insofar as it is linked by the "Only Son of God" symbolism to the central theme of all mythologies: the "Divinity" symbol.

In this symbolic aspect, sanctification has been previously analyzed.

We have to go back to the analysis of sanctification because, as a real phenomenon, it is the highest degree, the exemplification of the immanence of justice.

In order for the symbolic projection into the beyond to take the form of a justice after death, it was necessary that emotion in the face of the mystery of temporal existence include the superconscious presentiment of a justice immanent to life.

Immanent justice implies reward and punishment during life. It can therefore be a beatitude gratuitously and uniformly granted to all. Now this fact of individual difference is precisely the central motive of all the unjust complaints about the injustice of life. To base immanent justice on uniformity of happiness is to demand either that all participate uniformly in a common absolute happiness; or that happiness and unhappiness be meted out without any differentiation of individual merit; or again that all receive after death a uniform compensation for common unhappiness, which would imply a radical elimination of merit and demerit, on both the plane of individual life and that of societies. This would not have to be stressed if complaints or triumphs on the inequality of happiness (too exclusively seen as the equal distribution of material goods) were not precisely the most secretly hidden motives of all the vexed or triumphant vanities which are the essential cause of prevailing injustice.

The Old Testament talks about the temporal fate of the people who are symbolically "chosen," symbolically called to a covenant during life with the "Eternal god" (with the eternal truth which is the immanence of justice). The immanent punishment of the "breach of the covenant" is "the death of cultures": the collapse into banalization. The punishment is not added to the consequences of banalization. Its consequence is immanent because it is the collapse of the guiding values, the overvaluation of material and sexual pleasures, a depravity which destroys not only ethical courage but also physical courage, making individuals and nations incapable of defending themselves against the invading enemy looking for the riches accumulated in the large cities. This is the truth of immanent justice exemplified throughout history and in the Old Testament by the fate of the Babylonians (the Tower of Babel) and the Egyptians (the seven plagues), by the destruction of Sodom and Gomorrah, and especially by the fate of Israel. The immanence of essential justice is manifested through historical events by temporal "punishments" which through the destiny of the depraved and punished peoples touch each individual. Moses exhorts the Hebrews to abandon their "dance around the golden calf," the symbol of banalization, and in the same vein the prophets warn the people, reminding them of the promises and threats, the rewards and punishments that the justice of the Eternal God (symbol of eternal truth) will mete out to mortals, not after death, but during life. "God will deliver the people into the hands of the enemy." The enemy is accidentally a too easily victorious invader; essentially it is the hereditary fault, the serpent in paradise: "vanity," "Satan," who is at the same time inducing banalization and enforcing the punishment. The "gift of prophecy" is the symbol of a deep faith to which "the mystery is revealed," which knows the "designs of God," who is the symbol of immanent justice manifested through the temporal: the laws of harmony and disharmony, implying reward and punishment that are foreseeable since they are the consequences of superconsciously and subconsciously immanent laws. (Justice immanent, not only to the life of peoples but also the individual, already finds a clear expression in the Psalms of the Old Testament.)

The New Testament completes the essential truth of the Old Testament concerning almost exclusively the fate of the peoples. The individual and his essential destiny during life is its central theme and acquires in the gospels all its mythical and historical importance.

The Hebrews living in decadence fell under the Roman yoke. The ancient prophecies were fulfilled. The Roman power would have invaded Palestine even if the people had not fallen into decadence. But in that case, the outer defeat would only have been an accident. Intact in its inner strength, in its essentially motivating strength, the people would have found in the very disaster—or rather because of the disaster—a renewal of their vital impulse as had been the case during the slavery in Egypt. (Symbolically speaking, God would have given up the people into the hands of the Romans but not into the hands of Satan the banalizer.) In this respect, it must be clearly understood that the immanence of justice does not exclude a cruelty which is immanent to temporal existence where all is limited in duration, and where limitation depends on accidents. During the youth of a nation, the cultural institutions can be destroyed by an invader. But culture does not depend on the institutions, and it often happened in history that accidentally vanquished nations did essentially vanquish the victors, bringing to their culture a renewal of vital impulse and youthfulness. Cruelty resides in the temporal, justice in the essential. And this to the extent that the disasters of the temporal—which are frequent causes of collapse—can become essential cause for straightening up. It all depends on moral strength, on the strength of the vital impulse.

These are very ancient truths: eternal truths. They are easy to express and difficult to live. To make the living easier, the best way is to bring these truths back to their essential source: the inner motives.

The Old and New Testaments constitute an unbreakable unity.

From the fall of Adam to the death of Jesus and from the death of Jesus to the Parousia, they talk about the essential history of all peoples and all men, the essential history of mankind subject to the ethical law of immanent justice.

The essential depth is due to the fact that the tale of the real history of the Hebrews is intermingled with symbolic episodes and complemented all through the two Testaments with the symbolic story of the "covenant," called "salvation" in the New Testament, in which the covenant no longer concerns a "deaf and blind" people, prisoners of a dead and dogmatized belief, but the individual capable of hearing the call for the renewal of the covenant, the message of joy: *in the midst of the decadence of the peoples and the death of the cultures, individuals can be reborn to eternal truth* (to the covenant with the Eternal God). In the midst of the people of Israel, who are in a state of breach of the covenant, arises a new prophet "messenger of God," a real man as were the ancient prophets, inspired as they were by the "Eternal God," the Messiah of the New Testament; Jesus who is symbolically called the "Christ."

The people, misunderstanding the ancient prophecies announcing the advent of the messiah according to the spirit, expect a messiah according to the flesh, a demagogue who would lead them in a victorious struggle against the Romans. But the kingdom of Christ is "not of this world" (of this perverted world in a state of constant struggle for power). Disappointed, the enslaved people deny the new prophet and abandon him to his fate, in his struggle against the Pharisees. His life and his death on the cross witness to the most ancient truth, the essential and eternal truth: better to die than to give in to the powers that be and compromise with the false justifiers and their false demagogical promises. He dies in the joy of his combative impulse. His life and his death are the verification and supreme proof of the most ancient truth, which is the immanence of justice.

The Gospels, in their deepest meaning, are the illustration of immanent justice at its highest degree of manifestation. The meaning of the message of joy is that the essential is not what happens to man, but what man makes of it at the level of his valuating and motivating deliberation: the degree of liberation he is capable of achieving. He can just as well collapse in the face of the most insignificant accidents or—as the Christian myth shows—he can die in the joy of his achievement even though being subject to extreme torture.

Even if Jesus—as certain historians affirm—had never lived and his life had thus been symbolic, as were those of so many mythical heroes, it still remains true that mythical symbolism reaches its peak in the biblical texts, which condense the common meaning of all mythologies in the laws of essential justice: harmony and its joy, represented by the only God, and disharmony and its nefarious consequences, represented by Satan the tempter.

Whether sanctification is a really experienced event or a pure symbol, one must still understand its significant scope. *Sanctity and the peak of its joy are not achievable for most mortals*; what does, however, remain achievable is the emotional understanding based on extrapolation from our own joys and our own anxieties (in the same way a partially given graph can be determined in its entirety, provided that one knows the law of its development).

By way of analogy, sanctity can be understood as a complete reversal of the habitual view of life. In the face of the evidence of mystery, the apparent event loses its affective and sensorially compact evidence, its predominant importance. The mystery of life is unveiled through the most routine daily occurrences. The appearance having become transparent, accidental sufferings and pleasures lose their predominant importance. Joy—the opposite of fear (in all its primitive and pathological forms)—becomes a certitude. In this certitude of the essential, all the possible accidents of temporal life are accepted from the outset and are assembled in a harmonious vision including life and death. Energy, freed from anxiety, attains its highest degree of concentration in the animating impulse and its sublimating combativity, which is the very definition of imperturbable joy, symbolically called "sanctity," "Heaven in us," "incarnation of the soul in psychic life." In this state of plenitude of soul and spirit, nothing is supernatural, all is natural. Sanctity is the sublime contemplation of temporal life which is naturally exposed to disturbance and suffering, though the latter—and this is immanent justice—can be overcome in principle without any supernatural grace, but solely through the force of the combative impulse. Its highest manifestation is the acceptance of biological suffering which cannot be changed (aging and death) and of the accidental sufferings which cannot be reasonably changed and which we meet repeatedly in everyday life due to the vicissitudes of the environment and to wrongly motivated human interactions.

We must therefore distinguish from the principle, from sanctity, the effort of sanctification which is repeated every day and never perfect. Going beyond the strength of acceptance of the majority of people, sanctification remains analogically linked to psychic health, of which it is the highest manifestation.

Sanctification is not an immutable and superhuman state of mind. It is a dynamic achievement: the victory of man's sublime nature over the weaknesses of human nature. As such it is the crowning of mythical symbolization, whose constant theme is the heroic and intrapsychic struggle against the attack of constraining and unhealthy resentments.

The dynamics of sanctification is included in the deliberation: it is the highest degree of liberation.

Since this is the case, the dynamics of sanctification did not manifest itself only in the man Jesus. Other men have lived it. Countless men have attempted to achieve it without success, since their way was not the "Tao" (the right way)—the review of motives—but the error of asceticism, which is only an excessively good moralizing intention. In the "Sermons of the Buddha," asceticism is radically rejected, and the right way is clearly described: one must in this life go beyond the appearance—"veil of Maya"—in order to reach the Nirvana. One must give up multiple desires. The Nirvana, the dissolution, the elimination of the exalted and multiple desires, does not symbolize absolute nothingness but a state of perfect concentration, the state of absorption of the multiple desires by the essential desire. Nothing could determine man to want to go beyond the appearance to attain the essence—relative nothingness, the Nirvana, reunion with Brahma (God-the-Father)—if not a desire stronger than all the multiple desires: the essential desire. The Nirvana is relative nothingness, mystery become manifest, the achievement of the incarnation of the Soul-Essence.

The "good news" of the gospel has a parallel in India and China and perhaps in cultures whose history is not sufficiently known. The Tao is identical to the example and teaching of Jesus; and because Lao-Tze actually lived as well as the universal truth. Jesus is "the savior," Buddha is "the saved" because he too overcame the vanity of the world. Symbolism expresses this by showing Buddha surrounded by a shield of najas: the vanquished serpent, the vanquished vanity having become a salutary and protective force. Does not this same significance also appear in the serpent of Asclepius pouring its venom in the salutary cup: symbol that victory over vanity is the principle of psychic health? Does not Jesus express the same truth when he calls himself "Son of God" (incarnation of the superconscious force) and victor over "the prince of the world," victor over Satan the serpent, vain temptation, the principle of evil ruling over the world?

Wherever sanctification was manifested, where immanent justice was unvelied, it marked an epoch. The whole life of the influenced people was split into two eras representing a before and an after, witnessing to the importance of the event. The importance resides in the fact that sanctification is the most striking proof of the rule of essential justice in the temporal. This proof, this verification, is the accomplishment of the meaning of life, a meaning achieved by the sanctified man, and for the others who cannot attain ultimate joy it is an orientation, a remote ideal which remains only directive. How could all these achievements and symbols not express the immanence of justice? For "immanent justice" means: the possibility of victory over evil: all is unjust in the life of individuals and societies as long as vain egocentricity, a subconsciously motivating force, rules over souls; all would become just—the meaning of the message of joy—if the animating impulse were able to understand the essential truth: *reward and punishment are immanent to the psychic functioning*. They are accomplished through extra-conscious means so that immanent justice is not perceived by the inner eye as long as it is vainly blinded.

It would certainly be better not to make any image of life after death—an unfathomable mystery—and to study the real fact instead; the injustice of vain egocentricity bearing its punishment in itself: guilty anxiety, which, unjustly justified, projected onto the world of others and reprojected by each one onto all the others, gives birth to the vicious circle of generalized complaints about the injustice of the world and life. This is the common error and everyone should struggle against it in himself with the help of his vital impulse. This is the prescientific truth common to all mythologies.

Sanctification is both a mythical symbol (Christ) and an experiential reality (Jesus).

On the plane of the man Jesus' real life, the myth of the incarnation of the spirit reveals its meaning. Thanks to his own animating impulse, thanks to his own essential desire and for his own essential good, Jesus sanctifies himself. He determines himself freely, deliberately, to the purification of his own motivating intentionality. He frees himself from the hold of his subconscious intentions, an obsessive hold due to the vain excess of self-satisfaction. He vanquishes vanity, the innate weakness of human nature (the Prince of the World) and thus becomes the salutary example of the immanent possibility of self-liberation, an example which is essentially valid for all men ("I have sanctified myself for you").

Sanctification is the most decisive illustration of immanent justice because it proves that through an exceptional strength of soul—and yet one which, with various degrees of intensity is shared by all, man can overcome accidental sufferings and even the essential suffering of guilty anxiety. He can transform them into joy. Suffering itself is justified: it appears as the indispensable condition for joy, the obstacle to overcome.

To fully demonstrate temporal justice, it is therefore necessary to analyze this psychic phenomenon—sanctification—not only in its principle but in the details of its manifestation.

For theology, sanctification is total obedience to the commandments of a real God, dogmatically interpreted.

In accordance with psychological truth, sanctification belongs to the motivating phenomena that have no surreal significance. "Sanctification" is only a general term for the superconscious reactions, studied until now under different names: harmonization of the multiple desires, satisfaction of the essential desire, combativity of the impulse, appearance of the soul through the psyche, free determination.

It was indispensable to introduce these different expressions because they describe the various aspects of the superconscious reaction which—rightly so—has been called: the fundamental law of life, i.e., the foundation of all psychic lawfulness.

The myth relates this achievement by calling it "incarnation, filiation, deification." This is the metaphysical and symbolic aspect, "grace."

All these symbols have been explained. The translation has still to be expanded by studying this unique life in its real aspect, that of merit. If justice is inherent in life, it is clear that salvation must be deserved, and it is also clear that salvation can only be the essential satisfaction of life: joy. This significance of the myth of salvation, which, however, remains too global, was already indicated in the preceding analyses. It remains to be seen in what way the myth of salvation, according to its hidden meaning, expresses in detail this significance (merit), which is analogically linked to all the other significances of the "God" symbol, and thus of the "God-the-Son" symbol (the sanctified) and the "God-the-Judge" symbol (immanent justice).

Opposition to the immanence of justice is based above all on material poverty, which is accused of being a patent injustice. However, it is not poverty which is unjust in itself, but its ambivalent decomposition into two extremes: misery and luxury, consequences of the fierce stuggle for the possession of material goods, making man an enemy of man, and nations the enemies of nations as is stressed in the Old Testament. This is prophetical for the history of mankind up to and including our time. Struggles between nations and revolutions within societies have never ceased. They have led to the abolition of slavery and the elimination of some privileges. But the improvements have always degenerated into abuses on the part of the ruling caste which became finally unbearable, and into doctrinal fanaticism on the part of the improvers who do not shun any means to seize power in their turn. It is certainly justified to look for a solution to social injustice, but it is unjustified to believe that the search for this solution could exempt man from solving the essential problem: the abolition of the greed of desires, the essentially motivating cause of all the individual or social injustices.

Affective explosions against abuses are undoubtedly historical necessities, but would not abuse itself also be a historical necessity? Justice and injustice are intrapsychic phenomena before they explode into social interactions. Would it not be the consequence of immanent justice

that nothing will essentially change as long as false justification perdures on all sides as well as its ineluctable consequence: mutual accusation and aggression? At the essential level of secret motivations, nothing matters but the poverty or riches of souls and spirits. If one took
the trouble to think back on the history of mankind, going from generation to generation all the way back to the origins of the thinking
species, one would discover that the greed of desires and the oblivion
of the spirit's call is nothing but the sin of Adam and that mythical wisdom foresaw its nefarious, destructive, and hereditary consequence: its
propagation from generation to generation has been fully verified by
the history of mankind. The hope remains that the other prediction
does not prove to be true—in the near future—by way of immanent
justice, i.e., the apocalypse of the thinking species, victim of the spirit's
blindness which was denounced by the myth of Genesis as the immanent motive of destruction.

Because moral superstition believes in the essential injustice of life
on earth, it is led to believe in a compensatory justice after death, or
inversely, to look for compensation through aggressive revenge that
would immediately abolish all forms of injustice. These two superstitions rooted in the ancestral magical layer are ambivalently linked and
can be transformed one into the other.

Immanent justice in the form of punishment concerns the external
relationships between men (the injustice of the world) precisely because
it concerns in the first place the essential relation of each man with
himself, the relation between his essential self and his apparent self.
The crowning truth of all the mythical images is that the manifestation
of justice—symbolized by the intervention of God—rules in the innermost self of each man in a mysterious manner which cannot be perceived by man as long as he is affectively blinded, as long as his spirit is
absent, his imagination is dispersed, and he is in a state of inner torment due to exalted anxieties and exalted desires.

The historical necessities caused by the exaltation of anxieties and
desires and their obsessive quest for an establishment of justice
through aggression are not the ideal they pretend to be. The ideal is to
overcome historical necessities as far as they are wrongly motivated.
This historical ideal is the eternal truth, the theme of all mythologies
and of their heroic struggles. The ideal is represented at its highest degree by the fate of the hero of the gospels who, a poor creature in the
eyes of the world, without any help from a real god nor from anyone,
misunderstood by all, even by the apostles, and who, living not in
unanimous admiration—unlike Lao-Tze and the Buddha—dares to
confront the error and injustice of the whole world, without refuge or
the least possibility of being spared the fate that he knows and predicts.

It must be mentioned that sanctification is excluded from all achievement in Northern climates because of an accidental factor: the rigor-

ous conditions of life. The Nordic man is too dependent on the environment, and this dependence makes him ingenious and combative. This is at the same time the strength and the weakness of Western culture. Technical ingenuity leads to multiplying the desires, and combativity is finally used to satisfy them at the expense of others. The West has downgraded culture into a material and utilitarian civilization but is all the more in need of an appeasing ideal. Being unable to create it, this ideal was borrowed from another cultural cycle through turning love—a sublimating force—into a flat sentimentality, the perverse counterideal of brutal combativity. The excess of suavity makes the dogmatized ideal unacceptable, and, instead of neutralizing the excess of aggressivity, it ends up by exacerbating it. Banality raised to the rank of ideal provides an excuse to devalutate from the outset any effort of sublimation which is impossible without the combative force of acceptance, rejected because of the confusion with its caricature: resignation, or absence of combativity. The two forms of excess—brutal combativity and unacceptable resignation—are the ambivalent counterpoles of the decay of the force of acceptance. However, the lack of sublimating force in the West is counterbalanced by its force of spiritualization, which has succeeded in creating the scientific spirit. The West can attain sublimation only through spiritualization, the ideal through the idea. Will it dare to approach the essential problem imposed on research: the scientific study of the mythical pre-science whose theme is the combativity of the vital impulse?

Depth psychology does not borrow from religion when it talks about sanctification as an ideal of joy. For psychology, the ideal is not summed up in the "oh my sweet Jesus" formula, but in the most difficult task to be achieved: the mastery of all the excitations, freedom, which is the ultimate goal of deliberation. It defines the ideal by two conditions: *one is the dissolution of the subconscious and obsessive determination*, of wrong motivation (liberation); *the other is the reconcentration of the energy that has thus been fired in the essential desire*, which is the ideal of freedom. Depth psychology recognizes sanctity as an unattainable ideal because it is the vanishing point into the infinite of the efforts of healing and because the essential desire immanent to the ethical supreconscience has—as its pole of attraction in the infinite—the ideal of energetic concentration in the Essence. When, exceptionally, this concentration is charged with all the psychic energies, it generates quite naturally its own essential satisfaction: ultimate joy, fullness of life.

Psychology learns from the history of religions not the concept of the ideal, but the fact that complete liberation did historically occur *in extremely exceptional individuals* and conditions.

Science cannot ignore this psychological phenomenon which has manifested itself in various cultural cycles. It talks of sanctification by lawfully elaborating, by extrapolation—starting from the functioning of the psychic processes—the significance of the "sanctification" symbol: the ideal of harmonizing sublimation. When studying this phenomenon—the extreme limit of the healing possibilities of the psychic functioning—one cannot avoid the use of superlatives: supreme ideal, highest ideal, perfect joy, etc. Now objective research has good reason to avoid superlatives. But how can this be done if the object of research is precisely the loftiest ideal in life? Since the expression cannot be avoided, it is necessary to remember that psychology does not preach the ideal and does not impose it. It finds it and endeavors to define it.

2. THE MYTH OF REDEMPTION

After these warnings, it becomes possible to confront the most daunting of all enigmas.

The "God" symbol covers not only the image of the trinitarian divinity but also the "God-the-Judge" symbol, linked by the dogmatic interpretation of the "Grace" symbol, to the myth of redemption.

The difficulty is not in the research of the hidden meaning of the "Redeemer" symbol, which is just as clear for the psychological translation as other symbolic formulations. The difficulty comes from the fact that exegesis has accumulated around this symbol an interpretative system which is so complex that only a long and very delicate work can succeed in dismantling the artificial dogmatic construction connecting redemption—atonement—exclusively to the death of the God-man, Jesus. According to the myth, on the other hand, Jesus, being a real man, "redeems mankind" from the sin of Adam by his life as a sanctified man whose death on the cross is only an episode. The myth of "atonement" is nothing but the myth of salvation.

Freed from any worldly desire, magnetized by love for mystery, the hero of the Christian myth is subjected to the intrigues of the world, the "sin" of the world, without any perturbance in his love for the world, as manifestation of mystery. He sublimely resists the world and its original sin: the exaltation of desires and hence of anxieties, the wrong motivation of all men and the false reactions that follow. This evil, the guilt of the world (the injustice of the world) and its consequence, suffering, cannot touch him except externally in his corporal organization and can even destroy him. But they cannot touch him decisively in his inner organization, in his harmony, in his joy. His joy is renewed after each assault, and it even resists the threat of death. The hero takes upon himself—as the myth puts it—the sin of the world, i.e., he accepts subjection to its guilty action, the "sin" of others, and while being subjected to outward defeat, he transforms it into inner victory. He overcomes the sin of the world. He abolishes it, he makes it powerless through his sublime resistance. Symbolically speaking, "He offers himself in sacrifice to abolish sin."

However, the hidden and real meaning of this symbolism is not sacrifice in its sentimental sense, self-abnegation for the sake of others, but heroic sacrifice: *the sacrifice of the apparent self in order to save the essential self.* The hero dies because the suffering of death is, as far as he is concerned, of lesser importance than the suffering of betraying the meaning of life. This means that the joy of remaining faithful unto death to the meaning of his life is for him more important than the joy of living. Moreover, the death of the hero would not have the importance of an "atonement" if the meaning of his life had not been that of all life: purification, liberation, the manifestation of the soul through the psyche. *And it is even more difficult to achieve without faltering this joyful sacrifice of the apparent self to the essential self during one's lifetime than to witness to it through death.* Every man who tries to do so finds himself on the way to redemption through the healing—although a relative one—of his psychic state because he follows this to the end. *However, the achievement is not, it has to be stressed again, the accidental ending of his life: it is the essential success during life, the constant purification or, symbolically speaking, sanctification.* This is a natural task for the uniquely strong impulse, but for all other men—this can never be repeated enough—it is a vainly exalted task that will lead them neither to salvation nor to healing, but to the pathological exaltation and to the perverse inhibition of their vital impulse.

Sanctification being a unique achievement, redemption is the hope that it entails for others; the salvation of each one being the fulfillment of this hope within the limits of his own strength.

The myth of redemption cannot be separated from that of the original fall, since redemption is raising up from the common fall. The sin of Adam—in its hidden meaning—stands for the banal exaltation of desires, and the myth of redemption for the harmony of the desires (the victory of the vital impulse over vain obsession: freedom.)

The dogma of redemption also remains linked to the fall, but to the dogma of the fall. Since the symbolism of the fall is mistaken for a reality, the initial error about the fall, by spreading through all dogmatization and developing its consequences can lead only to an inordinate error about the myth of redemption.

In the dogma of redemption are finally concentrated all the errors resulting from the dogma of man's fall. The erroneous explanation of redemption is the knot of the theological complication. In it philosophical speculation is inextricably interwoven with the most primitive animistic elements. And the latter elements are those that exert a charm which is difficult to dissipate, since the magical layer is still present today. It is not a process, but it underlies—an ancestral foundation—the whole psychic functioning. In the absence of a more natural food for spirit and soul, man who is eager to believe is attracted by magic no less than the man who is looking only for a conventional consolation. Moved to the depths of the magical layer—which is but groundless superstition nowadays—he tends to believe that any natural explanation is but a profanation. And yet, here as everywhere, the depth of mystery can only be safeguarded by the elimination of all miraculous elements.

According to dogma, God-the-Father, angry with the descendants of Adam, can only be reconciled by a sacrifice in blood. He himself comes down from Heaven in the form of his Son, to offer himself as a holocaust.

Dogma affirms that through the enduring death unjustly afflicted upon God in person, a superabundant grace is now available to the Church, called upon to share it among the faithful through ceremonies.

Dogma is inspired by the symbolism of Jesus, "Son and the One sent by God" who *"dies for the sin of the world."'* The symbolic meaning of "dying for sin" has already been given. Dogma refers only to the death of Jesus on the cross and introduces, instead of the true meaning, the age-old magical element: the ritual of "atonement by the sacrifice of the lamb." To understand the details of the myth of redemption, one must understand above all the significance of the magical element so as to isolate it and finally eliminate it from the authentic myth.

In animism, shed blood had the magical power of redemption and pardon. In magic rituals, primitive man offered blood to the deified ancestor, to the father, in order to get in contact with him, to obtain his good will, to give him blood to drink so that he would be reanimated and thus capable of protecting him. Without a performance of the sacrifice, the father divinity might become a hostile spirit, a vampire-ghost ready to revenge himself for the sacrilege against him, and claiming the offering, he would persecute and punish the culprits. When the mores evolved and became less ferocious, the blood of the man to be sacrificed to the divinity—and who, in this still primitive significance is "sanctified" (purified by magic rituals)—is replaced by the blood of a lamb, an animal representing a purity worthy of being sacrificed and whose sacrifice means the promise of self-purification. (This evolutionary step is symbolized in the episode of the myth of Abraham in which—at the request of God himself, i.e., due to the progressive sublimation of the mores—the son to be sacrificed is replaced by a ram, having the same significance as a lamb.) In animism, this dealing with the father-divinity—redemption through blood—was an imagination which was developed in a consistent way. Primitive man believed with all his soul in the magic power of the blood sacrifice both for the satisfaction of the father-divinity and for the help granted by the father ancestor, and that belief was so strong that it inspired in primitive man what he wanted to obtain through sacrifice: the strength to be worthy of the ancestors (the Father). Thus it was quite frequent that blood (representing the animating impulse) was not only offered but drunk by the magician priest and by the members of the tribe in order to attain communion with the father-divinity.

The biblical texts no longer belong to the animistic era; they witness to the most evolved mythical period. Yet, they continue to speak of the man-lamb sacrificed to the father-divinity. However, these are no longer magical realities, but images raised to the level of symbols. The man-lamb has become the symbol of innocence and purity of soul. The son to be sacrificed is replaced by the lamb because both signify innocence, redemption from sins that were committed and brought guiltiness.

In the Christian myth, Jesus does not die in order to ensure an undeserved, magical, and supernatural grace for those who sacrificed him. Quite the contrary, he dies because he did not give in to those who crucified him.

In this respect, we have to stress that the "lamb" symbol is not an invention of the Christian myth; an inheritance from animism, it is found in polytheistic myths (for instance: the golden fleece defended by the dragon, a devouring monster symbolizing aggressive banalism). In order to acquire purity, man must struggle, overcome, kill within himself his own tendency to aggressivity mistaken for the ideal of virility. The very ancient symbol of "lamb-sublimity" means that man, through his spiritual struggle—through the genuine virility of his spirit—can purify himself, overcome in himself hateful aggressivity, the only way to overcome anxiety in the face of the world's aggressivity which causes grievances and desire for revenge. For the myth, what matters is only the significance of the "lamb" symbol with respect to sublime motives and heroic courage. The symbol is not based in the least—contrary to what dogma says—on the real and sentimental comparison of the "sweet Jesus" who dies like a lamb without offering resistance. The salutary example of the myth is not the pathetic sight of a god who suffers and offers himself to the pity of sensitive souls, but that of a real man who by confronting suffering, struggles against the perversions of the world. The hero of the myth, a real man, accepts death by his sublime resistance, his refusal to compromise and to subject himself; his death does not miraculously save mankind. Salvation comes only from the sublime motives which animated the crucified man who was apparently vanquished by the world. This apparent passivity is the most intense activity. It shows that the agitation of the world, mutual aggressions, just as covenants and compromises are only passivity: a subjection to the perverse tendencies of human nature. The accidental defeat, the death of the crucified one, is an essential victory. He dies so as to remain faithful to his life, he dies for his own salvation. His joy is accepted suffering, the guilt of the world that he took upon himself and thus transformed into the most intense sublime energy, into a capacity of radiance which is sublimely fecund and salutary.

What matters is not the fatal accident (the shed blood) but the unalterable joy (offered blood). The hero brings salvation which consists in not responding to injustice by injustice. The world will remain unjust as long as false justification rules men; the world will be just when people will no longer push one another to injustice: when—even in the imagination, even in their secret motivations—they will love essential justice more than life; when they will renounce perverse attack (as the hero shows by his own life) and when they will no longer use perverse and hateful defense, even in imagination (as the hero exemplifies it by his death). This is the loftiest ideal that is, the most difficult to achieve, because it is opposed by the "original sin" of human nature—excessive individuation—the tendency to desire only "the earth and its fruits" and thus to heed only vanity and its promises (the serpent), which make one deaf to the call of the spirit: to reason, the greatest force in man (symbolized by God). Vain deafness is the cause of all the ills of the spirit and of all unreasonableness, which is immanent punishment.

To understand this significance of the Christian myth—from the myth of the fall of Adam to the myth of redemption and salvation—is to have faith in life, faith in the justice immanent to life; immanent to its mysterious lawfulness. Because of this link between achievement and mystery, the myth can symbolically call the victorious hero "Son of God and God himself" (understood as "God-the-symbol within us"), and it can symbolically say that "God sent his Son to redeem his other sons," fallible men, to show to men the way to redemption and salvation. *The myth of redemption does not speak of a gratuitous gift made by a real god to unworthy men: it illustrates the highest manifestation of human dignity. It shows the essential reality in the life of man: the intrapsychic conflict between perversion and sublimation, possible victory.*

What is true for the myth is true for the ritual. The latter also is symbolic, and "sacramental" only for this reason. Just like the myth, the symbolic ritual, denoting the participation in salvation by active faith—communion (with the hero)—has nothing in common with the magical significance of redemption by shed blood. Symbolic communion was instituted by the hero himself during his life, before his blood had been shed. *The blood given to drink cannot therefore symbolize redemption by death,* but union by life and its activity: the "offered blood" symbolizes the gift, the bond of warmth of soul. Since this is the case, the symbol of offered blood—signifying the soul—can be replaced by other symbols having the same meaning, for instance: wine. The symbolism of blood-soul-wine—already known by pagan myth—enables the myth to prefigure real participation in salvation. By drinking wine, symbol of blood (soul), one enters symbolically into an exchange of soul with the hero. The symbolic exchange of the Last Supper testifies to the fact that men (the apostles) followed the example of the hero, and it contains the promise that they will continue to act in keeping with his example.

The symbolic significance of this ritual is also the promise of an action which has to last all life long, and not a magically transmitted power. The significance is real merit (i.e., symbolic grace) and not real grace. The term "grace," being only an image, can be used either *as a magic image*, in which case it refers to the sublimely suggestive force of the ritual, or as a *metaphysical symbol*: a pure image according to which not only the whole of life, but also all qualities, all merits, can be represented as a gift, a grace flowing from the essential and mysterious "source." Symbolic communion consists in drinking wine, symbol of the blood and soul and in eating bread, symbol of the body and spirit, symbol of the spiritualized body (purified of desires), of the body in which the spirit became incarnate and which has thus become the symbol of the spirit: the symbol of essential truth, which is food for the human spirit. This symbolic communion prefigures the effort of real liberation, of purification, undertaken during a lifetime and it has meaning only insofar as the symbolically prefigured promise becomes a figure and a reality.

The inexhaustible depth of symbolic language is illustrated by the fact that the "bread-and-wine" symbolism is used in the Christian myth—and in the very same episode where it is used to represent communion—to express its absolute opposite: betrayal. The bread dipped into wine that Jesus offers to Judas symbolizes the bloodied body, the work of the traitor. But since wine is both symbol of blood and of the soul, the offering pointing to the traitor and his work, expresses at the same time that Jesus offers him his soul, grants him forgiveness.

The translation of the symbolism of "Redemption" does away with miracles and replaces them with the psychologically natural significance, evident to the human psyche (as long as it is not blinded by affective prejudices). The explanation of this evidence is complex because it has to struggle against the pseudodepth of the miraculous, magical, and animistic element wrongly introduced into the symbolic myth.

Salvation, that of the hero and of every man, lies in the real effort which must bear on the essential activity of life, i.e., on *inner valuation*: motivation. Given that the discernment of right or wrong motivation and its lawfulness—the reversal of wrong motivation into right motivation—is the task of inner psychology, the salutary achievement of the deified hero is in the last analysis only a special case of psychological lawfulness; it could not be otherwise, since the mythical hero is a real man, a human being and his activity remains therefore necessarily included in the law ruling over the human psyche. Thus does psychology enable us to detach ourselves from all symbolic rituals. It shows the direct way to achievement, it replaces faith in the hero by an understanding of the law. Replacing the special case of the most sublime achievement by the elucidation of the general law in which it is included, psychology even enables us to detach ourselves from the adoration of the symbolically deified hero. However, psychological understanding cannot but admire the ultimate achievement of its own law. It is compelled—in keeping with its own law—to see in the hero of the experienced myth the realization of a unique achievement. What is important is to be detached from all exalted ties, be they sentimental or hostile, so as to be able to admire freely (without superstition) and to act freely (without lapsing into an imitation or a convulsed aversion). This transformation of faith into law can shock only affective thought which is incapable of ridding itself of the erroneous association, "Jesus-real-God," and which wants to remain attached to it at any cost either by blind belief or by sterile doubt.

Belief and doubt are two ways of avoiding the real effort imposed by both real religious faith (faith in mystery, faith in life) and psychological understanding. Blind belief replaces real effort with rituals, while sterile doubt eliminates both dead belief and active faith, and finds it advantageous to prefer—without any feeling of guiltiness—material interest to essential effort. Since blind belief destroys active faith in life, since belief in dogma neglects (or convulses) just activity (the real meaning of salvation), the world—becoming more and more unjust, losing the vision of the essential need—falls more and more into the exaltation of material need; every man is led to find his salvation in it. Between the miraculous and magical exaltation of salvation and the exaltation of material need, there is a lawful relation: the belief in the efficacy of rituals becomes too easily an invitation to take part in them to obtain gratuitous forgiveness, which then leaves people free to deal on a daily basis with the conventional concerns of life.

The complete absence of affective exaltation which is characteristic of the highest degree of sublimation is not a lack of interest in the world and its present state. On the contrary, it is genuine interest whose motives are purified, sublime disinterest for one's own concerns, sublimated interest objectively encompassing the whole world. Since the mass of the people cannot attain the ideal, the effort of individual sublimation which is partially deficient must be accompanied by intellectual effort: the organization of the world through real projects though the latter cannot be fruitful unless they are based on spiritualization, on true ideas, on ideas that do not lose sight of the deep meaning of life. The ultimate ideal will always remain the sublimation of all the individual members of society, since social organization can be fruitful only to the extent that motives are pure, that ideas are not marred by imaginative blindness, and that projects are not tainted with affective exaltation.

There are worthy efforts in all fields of activity. Man is characterized not only by the right or wrong ideal he chooses but also by the right or wrong way he defends it, by his certitude or his fanaticism, by the strength of his spirit or his aggressivity in the pursuit of triumph that shows that the ideal he defends is erroneous.

The evident ideal is to overcome hateful aggressivity. But is also requires not to lose—through a false vision of sublimation—the courage which is at the root of instinctive aggressivity, a relic of animality. The danger inherent in human life does not come from this unconscious substructure, but from its subconscious distortion in its two ambivalent and exaltative forms: intimidating violence and meekness, hypocritical sweetness, which are but forms of vital anxiety, of cowardice. Salvation lies in the courage to face and revaluate the tendency to perversion, the subconscious motivation: it lies in spiritual and sublime combativity.

Since this is not the case, the human spirit should reach a more and more enlightened psychological understanding of the directive goal (already contained in an underlying form in mythical pre-science). The task of the spirit would be to seek the laws of life even if the evolutionary tendency had not been able to raise out of human misery due to perverse aggressivity the example of the achieving man, purified of all hateful aggressivity and all perversion of desires.

The myth of redemption must be explained at more length, since the world misery comes from the divergent opinions regarding the world salvation.

Salvation can only be the attainment of the meaning of life.

The meaning of life—its immanent truth, lawfulness—cannot be a theory which would have to be tested through discussions. The truth of life must pass the test of life: truth about life can only be joy, and salvation can only be that which gives essential satisfaction: joy.

Now nothing, in the last analysis, can give joy, harmony of feelings, except the mastery of excitations which is nothing but the mastery of self: freedom, the strength to bear with even the most irritating excitations, i.e., the unjust actions of others, due to unavowable motives. It is impossible to conceive of greater strength, because strength is measured by the accomplished effort, and a strength greater than that which masters all excitations would no more be measurable or calculable, would have nothing left to accomplish. Essential strength, measured by its achievement, is undoubtedly the highest ideal and the highest manifestation of the immanence of justice: the punishment for the disorder of the world is lack of joy. The world is in disorder because there are not enough mastered and sublimated energies.

The vision of the essential ideal is necessary because it indicates the direction to follow and measures the strength of each one of us with regard to the supreme strength. This is the most effective way to combat vain self-overvaluation. The myth of redemption offers support to this salutary vision because its meaning—which can never be stressed enough—is not an ascetic love of suffering and death, but the unalterable joy which is stronger than suffering and death.

To eliminate the joy—attested by the texts—and to insist only on the suffering and death is to ruin the salutary vision. At the moment when the hero prepares to face death, he tells his disciples who communed with him during life and to whom—summing up this real communion

—he symbolically gives his "blood" and his "flesh": "I have told you this so that my joy may be in you and your joy be complete" (John 15:11). This essential and essentially important joy expressed in the face of the threat of certain death, will overcome in him the last spasms of anxiety in the Garden of Gethsemane and on the cross: "Why have you abandoned me?" Then the fullness of joy will not leave him anymore, in spite of the sadness that comes over him and which is far less due to his own fate than to the awareness of the others' crime. This joy overcomes injustice, it is the proof of immanent justice and the only guarantee of the message of salvation. This essential joy, this salutary proof gives to the whole narration of the death of Jesus a unique beauty, not in a sentimental way but in a tragically touching one. When all is accomplished, at the moment of agony, when in a last gesture only the very depth of the soul can express itself, the inexhaustible fullness finds its most perfect exteriorization, the expression of goodness unchanged by the world and its injustice: "Forgive them; they know not what they do."

The achievement is so impossible to equal that the question naturally arises whether it is not a last proof of credulity to admit that the hero of the myth did really exist; whether he is not—like all the other mythical heroes—a vision of the human soul, superconsciously conceived and veraciously developed. But if one understands the surprising veracity of mythical symbolism, the hypothesis proves to be impossible, and rational critique would be insufficient to shake this conviction. For the Christian myth would be far more astonishing still: it would remain the symbolic expression of the peak of psychological truth and contain at the same time a lie of the imagination. If the myth had not really been experienced, if the victorious hero had not been a man of flesh and blood, the central symbol, the symbolic affirmation "The Spirit became flesh," the symbolism of the "incarnate Word" would no longer make sense. To understand the myth of redemption is to understand the reality of the myth of Jesus, the real example, even though it is only one of directive significance; and it is to understand the energetic and superconsciously motivating reality of the symbolic image of Christ.

The salutary example was not lived in joy in order to be received in sadness: thus it is to be understood in joy. Not to awaken joy, not to be received in joy would be contrary to the message of joy which gave the mythical tale its name of "Good News."

What brings joy is precisely the fact that the achievement is not due to a real god, that the hope of such an achievement is included in the possibilities of human nature.

Many men have had to undergo a more painful death, and undoubtedly there were some who did not show any exterior distress. But either their apparent calm was only the mask of an immense torment, a contemptuous pride and an unlimited and sterile hatred; or they felt that they were supported by the admiration of a group. True, they showed rare courage, and courage is always beautiful. The limited beauty of hateful courage resides in the strength which—contrary to coward-ice—is capable of mastering the external signs of trouble. But beauty is defined by the absence of trouble, by harmony which is incomparably superior to courage which only imitates the external show of calm: harmony is the inner calm which, since trouble is unable to reach it, can only be imperturbable joy sustained by the intensity of the vital impulse in the fullness of its active manifestation. The perturbation due to anxiety in the face of suffering and death is a form of self-pity, in itself quite natural. An inner perturbation, still greater than natural anxiety—to the very extent that aggressive courage is strong enough to overcome self-pity—is the impotent rage against the injustice one has to suffer. Now no man ever had to suffer such an undeserved death. Never was there greater contrast between merit and fate, never was injustice greater. In this fate are included all the possible fates to which men can be subjected, all the outrages which, even though they are lesser ones men can only master to a lesser degree. Justice immanent to life is proved, for this is a demonstration that the greatest injustice possible is powerless to destroy the harmony of feelings when man does not let himself be dragged into the vicious circle of hateful accusation and self-pity.

To feel sentimental pity for the fate of the hero is to be insensitive to the meaning of the message. To pity him can only be—unless the attitude is merely a convention—the effect of a secret self-pity, of an awareness of one's own exceptionally deep compassion, through which—the stress being laid not on the greatness of the joyous victory but on the greatness of suffering—one believes that one feels the magnitude of the injustice better than the others who are deemed to be insensitive. This is to add accusation to sentimentality; it is but vanity. It is finally to believe oneself better than others, a chosen soul, and to vainly condemn as guilty the unjust and insensitive world. The absence of this false reaction is precisely what makes the example salutary. Pity leads directly to wrong motivation; it reverses the significance of the achievement.

The salutary meaning is the absence of wrong motivation. Meaningful participation cannot be an exalted compassion but an inner attitude: the impulse to combat wrong motivation in conformity with the limited strength available, which is liable to wax or wane depending on the meaningful or exalted use one makes of it. Pity is an exaltation: either it replaces real effort with imaginative sentimentality, or else it leads to exalting the real effort, wanting to identify oneself with the hero and his victory. This is to vainly ignore the unique greatness of the accomplishment and to believe that one is capable of imitating it. This is pathologically exalted imitation: false sanctity which must be clearly distinguished from the real achievement.

2. FALSE SANCTITY

The most advanced degree of this false imitation is to seek salvation in suffering and death, to impose on oneself suffering and to desire death, to flee the world: it is false, ascetic sanctity, which belongs to the field of pathology.

The sanctified man does not desire death, though he accepts it. He does not flee the world and its threats or seductions. He feels sufficiently self-confident, safe in his essential desire, to confront without danger seductions as well as threats of the world. This feature is proper to the hero of the Christian myth as well as to the hero of the Hindu myth. They take part in others' lives; they converse with the rich as well as with the poor.

The saint cannot be imitated. Any imitator, in order not to fall prey to the threats and seductions of the world, must flee the world. This flight in itself is the proof of wrong motivation, however secret and unavowed it is: a proof of accusatory sentimentality and guilty vanity. The saint cannot be imitated precisely because he does not follow any example, he simply obeys the greatness of his essential desire. All others are imitators, and the danger of imitation is that it goes beyond the strength of the vital impulse, the limits of the essential desire, that it exalts and convulses, that it take pity on the exalted suffering and that it invests its hope not in immanent justice but in a compensatory justice after death.

To expect justice after death implies a devaluation of life and the world. Instead of seeing life as the realm of achievement which is possible in principle, making of it a vale of tears signifies that the meaning of life is not assumed, that essential joy is not achieved.

The false saint believes in the union of the individual psyche with a real god and he longs for the death of the apparent self because he feels himself incapable of achieving the essential union during his lifetime. This is only a form of despair with respect to life, due—as is any type of discouragement—to self-distrust. Excess of moralism or asceticism is the compressed and symbolic expression of the rage of despair directed toward the apparent self which is incapable of fulfilling its vital task: union with the essence during life. Asceticism is an exalted punishment inflicted on the apparent self, which is essentially deficient, and at the same time it is the expression of the exalted desire to destroy, to kill this despairing self, in order to attain the superstitious union.

However, asceticism is not only characterized by an obsession of exalted self-punishment due to an excess of guiltiness. There are forms of asceticism caused by an excess of vanity.

To give only one of the most aberrant but most significant cases in point: the stylites spend their lives on a pillar (symbol of elevation but also pedestal) to expose themselves, in the most visible way, to the admiration they expect. Such forms of ascetic madness are not frequent in the West, where they would lead to commitment to a mental institution, but rather in India, where they seem to have a certain chance of obtaining the admiration—if not the adoration—of the crowds.

In the West holy madness is rather manifested in mystical delusion complete with hallucinations expressing and alternation between periods of vanity and of guiltiness. The subject longing for perfect purity feels, in the nightmares of his guilty stages, that he is attacked by succubae or incubae who are raping him/her (which shows that repressed sexuality haunts his imagination), while during the stages of vain ecstasy, his hallucination shows him the open Heaven peopled with all the characters of popular belief: God seated on his throne, surrounded by angels and saints.

This leads us to conclude that the saints of the Church who are supposed to live in the presence of a real god have nothing in common with the saint as mythical hero. The saints of the Church were undoubtedly men and women endowed with a religious zeal that earned them the admiration of believers to the extent that they were canonized after their death. This does in no way exclude the fact that some of the saints of the Church were men endowed with a very genuine vital impulse, such as, for instance, the apostles whom the Church elevated to the rank of saints.

It is indispensable at this point, when we want to define the mythical symbol of "sanctity," to mention all the usual significances that are alien to the analysis of symbolism, the central theme of our research.

Insofar as caricatures of sanctity are concerned—the ascetic and delusional psychoses—it would certainly be mistaken to look for their motivating cause exclusively in a misunderstanding of symbolism, though the latter can indeed—as these cases show—lead to this rather infrequent excess of aberration. The aberrations of imaginative exaltation can worsen into hallucinations and delusions of grandeur through the imitation of any historical character whatever his field of celebrity (religion, art, politics, etc.). In this respect, nothing is more useful—more important even—than to understand the progressive aggravation of vain motivations which can make of any leading figure an image, an exalted and exalting imagination, which at the limit can end in a delusional identification which, in mystical madness, is identification with Jesus. It is enough for the believer to begin *wanting* to imitate him for the exalted task to take shape and become the central motive of the nervous states essentially due to feelings of superiority with respect to others, whose vital impulse has less pretensions. To enjoy even more delights in this superiority, imagination has only to go one step further to become an obsession, thus risking aggravating nervosity into neurosis: I *should* do everything to become perfect like him, admired and adored like the one I love and adore above all. It is evident that the task thus more and more vainly exalted, less and less attainable, starts to produce feelings of exalted guiltiness, triumphant or offended vanities, and complaining accusations against the world, which does not appreciate the loftiness of the intentions and which opposes their achievement through the many temptations it offers.

Social failures inevitably ensue, reinforcing the exalted task which is at the same time a consolation and a torment, and worsening neurosis into psychosis. Obsessive vanity can go so far as suggesting the "idée fixe" of being personally called by God to imitate Jesus, to follow his way to sanctity, to undertake the imperious duty of sacrificing oneself to God's will, to flee the world, its lack of understanding, and its temptations and to take refuge in a convent. The motives for such an extreme decision can be many, they are not necessarily pathological ones. The point here is only to try to outline the origin and the consequences of an exalted task of sanctity. All forms of exalted tasks, leading to neuroses or psychoses have this in common, that they ambivalently want and do not want and flee in the face of a pathologically imposed duty, which leads to short-circuiting reactions if not to a more and more unbearable increase of guilty feelings risking to end in the most extreme and harmful reaction: flight into madness. In his distorted deliberation, the patient has the delusional idea not only *that he wants to become a saint but that he is one.* He manages to imagine that he is a saint and demands from others the admiration they have for saints and that he has for himself.

It is evident that of all the vain tasks, none is as exalted and exalting as the desire—brought to the point of a duty and even of a certainty—to be as perfect as a saint in order to deserve the adoration he receives. It must be said that the sentence in Matthew 5:48, "Be perfect just as your heavenly Father is perfect," is for believers endowed with an exaltative tendency, a pathogenic danger. This invitation to unachievable perfection is an interpolation! For it is in total contradiction with the symbolic meaning of the gospels. It has nothing in common with the message of salvation. The literal injunction to believers to be "perfect as the heavenly Father" is necessarily an interpolation, because anybody who would endeavor to fulfill this demand would really run the risk of ending in a frenzy of mystical delusion.

When the interpolation is eliminated the fact remains that vanity is found in all fields of life with all the intermediate degrees between the imaginative exaltation of nervosity and delusional exaltation, whatever the form of the underlying exalted task.

It is therefore natural for all these multiple degrees of vanity also to be found in religious beliefs. But the hidden meaning of the gospels, which is precisely the immanence of the possibility of avoiding the traps of vanity (of "Satan"), is diametrically opposed to these degrees of aberration. Consequently at all times and in all places there must have been men and women, within and without the different churches, who—far from being perfect—emotionally grasped the mystery symbolically represented by the word "God" with varying degrees of intensity and who thus did not make an entity of mystery—a thing or a being—but experienced it as an inner motivating force.

This fact is proved by a historical movement called mysticism.

In this respect, it is useful to point out that the term "mystery" has two adjectival forms: "mysterious" and "mystical." The term "mystical" is too easily misunderstood and taken for a "mystification," out of distrust for any deep investigation encompassing mystery.

Mystical delusion is a mystification. But what is mystical madness if not a need for a deeper understanding which fails to find the way out of conventional error? The fact is that in the mysteries of ancient peoples, the initiates were called "mystics" and that the purpose of these institutions was to reveal the mysterious meaning of mythical images to those whose minds were not contented with popular beliefs.

The opposition of mysticism to the mystification of popular beliefs is a generalized historical phenomenon. This opposition to dogma occurred in all religions: the Bhagavad Gita in India, the Jewish Cabbalah, the mysteries of Egypt and Greece, Neo-Platonism; in the framework of Christianity; Paracelsius, Nostradamus, German mysticism with Eckhardt and Boehme, and, to a degree, Pascal.

This summary is far too succinct. But the point is only to mention here the very ancient historical movement of mysticism in order to avoid that—out of concern for classification—this study of motives and symbols be labeled as "antique" due to the common foundation on mystery. The radical difference in the methods has to be stressed all the more so that Christian theology, in order to defend itself against mysticism born within its own bounds, tries to present itself as a deep investigation going all the way to mystery by claiming that the dogmas are mysteriously profound since they are a divine revelation going beyond any human criticism. Criticism does indeed remain inadequate as long as it has not proved that God himself and his revelations are symbols endowed with a very precise meaning. This demands—is it necessary to repeat—a detailed study of symbolization, the latter being impossible without a preliminary and detailed study of the inner motivating and deliberating functioning which is the theme of symbolization. The psychic functioning is not a mystery but an enigma clamoring for its solution because—and this is of major importance—it implies the only possibility of finding a solution to the problem of ethical values. The absence of such solutions is precisely that which compelled mysticism—seeing the ethical problem as a mystery—to resort to a kind of purely intuitive self-contemplation, and to found ethical initiation (its fundamental concern) on vague pseudosymbolical references.

It remains true, however, that mysticism was a prescientific effort marked by a moving sincerity which prepared the ground for two diametrically opposed ways of research: philosophical investigation (the criticism of knowledge) and mystifying esoterism.

In concluding this historical outline of mysticism, the opportunity occurs to honor one of the greatest figures in the history of philosophy: Giordano Bruno, now forgotten and unrecognized. Having dared, during the Inquisition, to affirm that God is mystery, he was given the choice of reneging or dying at the stake. He had two weeks to reflect upon the matter. He preferred to die at the stake rather than perjure himself.

As to esoterism, in all cultures it was the mark of the decadence of mysticism in two ambivalent forms, theosophical speculation and satanism: the reversal of ethics into excessive banalization. These two forms of ambivalence do not fail to announce themselves and even to flourish in our time.

4. THE PRESENT RELEVANCE OF THE ESSENTIAL PROBLEM

At every stage of the historical process, the state of the world is determined by all the conscious, superconscious, and subconscious reactions of all men; by the sublimations and the spiritualizations that guide them and by the perversions and superstitions that agitate the individuals. But all these motivating forces are themselves motivated by traditions that are common to such a collectivity or another. Motives are called *reasons for acting*, and some of these motivating reasons date from the reasoning of generations long since dead. Transmitted from early childhood onwards, they become predominating motives, principles of action which are all the more difficult to uproot, because man has a deep need to feel anchored by his thought and way of acting in a collectivity, a group, even a small group where he enjoys mutual esteem. Add to this extra-conscious motives endowed with a biogenetically hereditary strength in which vain obsession is only too easily victorious and one can understand how difficult it is for the individual to think for himself in an essentially important and authentic way.

Wrong motivations create not only falsified and unjust actions, but also wrong and unjust ideas, which finally become ideologies guiding societies and endowed with an excess of wrongly motivating power. Since ideologies claim to offer guidance ot disoriented souls, they lead to the fanaticism of quarrels whose hateful explosions make social life more and more unbearable.

Societies are divided between oppressors and oppressed by the pseudospiritual greed inherent in all exalted tasks and by the greed of overvalued or undervalued sexuality and materiality. The ambivalences of the underlying motivations are transformed in the end, according to the law of punitive justice, into the ambivalence of interactions and situations. The prevailing injustices and all the attempts to overcome them by violent means are based on the present state of evolution of the thinking being who refuses to think his life in terms of the motivations that agitate him.

But the injustice of the world does not contradict the justice which is immanent to life. On the contrary, it is its condition, its executive. Any form of justice needs an executive to impose its laws. The law of harmony will not be imposed without the punishment of disharmony. The punishment is not added to it: disharmony is its own punishment. It is painful to experience in our innermost self, and it is painful to experience in its consequences, in the interactive situations. Guilty anxiety, subconsciously linked to the vanities, become collective cupidity when it is projected onto the world. Each individual, to the extent that he bears guilty vanity in himself and projects it in accusations and clamoring complaints, becomes guilty for the prevailing state of the world, because he bears its principle in himself, i.e., vanity (the "Prince of the world"), the essential fault which does not belong half to one and half to the others. Wrong motivation and its false justification by pseudo-sublimity—the Adamic weakness of human nature—is, in principle, though with various degrees of intensity, entirely in each individual. It is precisely the mark of essential justice that each one of us will suffer from the current state of the world only to the extent of the intensity of his own wrong motivation which pushes him to fall into vain self-pity, to be indignant and accuse, to lament or to become aggressive. Would we all be, without knowing it, provoked *provokers*? We see—as the saying goes—"the mote in our neighbor's eye, but not the beam in our own." This blinding beam, is it not vanity which blinds the inner eye, the introspective eye?

5. SATAN, THE COUNTER-GOD

The "God-the-Judge" symbol cannot be fully translated without analysis of the lawfulness of psychic functioning which encompasses all the processes, going from superconscious purification (God-the-Son ascending to Heaven) to subconscious perversion (Satan who drags people down to Hell).

Immanent justice is manifested not only by ideal achievement but also by its opposite, perversion.

In order to complete the analysis of the "God" symbol, one must add the translation of its counter-symbol: "Satan."

In all the preceding pages, scattered elements of the analysis of the Satan symbol are to be found. These must now be collected and completed to give a general view.

Satan symbolizes the psychic function of imaginative exaltation, principle of the evil man inflicts on himself, and whose most dangerous and pernicious form is imaginative exaltation with respect to oneself: vanity.

The danger of imaginative exaltation lies in its seductive force which has an omnipotent strength because it blinds man with respect to the real environment and the obstacles to be overcome in order to obtain real satisfaction and also with respect to the essential reality, namely, truth about the meaning of life.

The seductive force of imaginative exaltation symbolized by Satan takes two forms: *escapist imagination* concerning material, sexual and pseudospiritual desires, and *self-justifying imagination* of this first form of vital fault. This false justification, which has countless shades of meaning, operates according to four typical categories: vanity, repressed guiltiness, hateful accusation, and plaintive sentimentality. In other words, vain self-disculpation through the tendency to repress every fault, aggravated by a vain inculpation of others, the world, and life. The ambivalence between disculpation and inculpation is the law of the disharmonizing functioning of the subconscious.

Escapist imagination provides an inner show in which we are at the same time hero and spectator, anxious at one moment, triumphant at another. On the other hand, justifying imagination is a kind of inner dialogue in which imaginative exaltation, symbolized by Satan, "whispers" its false promises which—because of our (Adamic) seductivity—become irresistible and obsessive motivations.

Destroying the superconscious impulse, the demonic temptations are manifested in two ambivalent forms: hypocritical exaltation toward the spirit and banal exaltation, devoid of scruples, of the material and sexual desires.

Because of their subconsciously obsessive and motivating power, imaginative exaltations—symbolically the invitations of Satan—take part, unbeknown, in everyone's inner deliberation all day long and all life long.

Mythically speaking, Satan drags us into Hell each time we listen to his fallacious promises or when we have actively done his will which is in fact our own subconscious will, implying self-responsibility. Hell is not a place but a psychic functioning: subconscious blinding caused and created by the vanity of the false and repressing self-justifications.

In case of nervosity[2], Satan—subconscious temptation—is manifested at times in excessively good and pseudosublime intentions, and at times in excessively subtle and nefarious banalizing temptations. The pathologically distorted psyche is invaded by the obsessive temptation of escapist daydreams loaded with material and sexual desires, which are all the more imaginatively exalted that they are—in the case of nervosity—inhibited (cut off from any discharge) by the vanity of excessively good intentions which are reinforced since they are reconcentrated in pseudosublime exalted tasks.

---

2. See note on page 144.

From repression to repression accumulated in the subconscious, perverted energy runs the risk of finally exploding in the form of psychopathological symptoms, symbolically expressing either repressed desires or excessively good intentions of purification. The hell of nervosity is repressed guiltiness subconsciously transformed into the torment of sterile remorse: the infernal fire of the biblical Hell and the Inferno of Greek mythology, the Erinyes, symbol of repressed guiltiness.

On the other hand, in case of banalization, the imaginative exaltation symbolized by Satan is not fought by the excessively good intentions which are the perverted remnant of the superconscious impulse. Vain false justification imperiously insures repression, "the hold of Satan," successively destroys the guilty anxieties coming from the superconscious, which leads to the progressive destruction of the ethical superconscience and its animating impulse, to "death of the soul": the unfetterd desires are finally actively expressed without scruple and without shame. The law of subconscious disharmony represented by Satan prevails against the superconscious law of harmony, mythically symbolized by "the will of God." The "will of Satan" is, in case of banalization, the symbol of the active expression of temptations in the form of triumphant vanities. *This is no longer the intrapsychic hell of the nervous type of person, it is "the hell of life on earth,"* created by the cupidity of the perverse interactions of the multitudes of men who are, in varying degrees, "dead in the soul and spirit."

One feature shared by all the ills of the spirit caused by Satan the Counter-Spirit is the vain attempt to reestablish harmony, bearer of joy since it is the condition for accordance with oneself. The nervous type of man tries in vain to reestablish accordance through repeated repressions of the guilty discord. Banalization succeeds in this, but at the cost of the destruction of the harmonizing intention of the essential desire and of its sublimely motivating force. Nothing is left but the struggle for the pleasures of materiality and sexuality and the conventional euphorias of social success, founded on the very loss of the vision of more intense satisfactions, the essential impoverishment of life.

Perversion and the exalted suffering that ensues (guilt and its punishment) are Evil in itself, the principle of evil (mythically called "the prince of evil," Satan). *Evil in itself—dispersed into countless forms of evil—is the distance between the meaning of life and its individual or collective nonachievement. Good in itself is the accordance between the meaning of life and its achievement (harmonization).*

One must especially stress these definitions. The essential error is condensed in a false definition of good and evil, or rather in the absence of a definition. Theological moralism turns the notions of good and evil into a dogmatic sentimentality, which the materialism of the sciences of life opposes on the pretext of objectivty. Wanting to eliminate as radically as possible any intentionality, materialism replaces the notions of good and evil by that of chance, which leaves no room for a distinction between value and non-value. The distinction between good and evil would therefore be of no value. Human thought, based on a clear distinction between right and wrong, true and absurd, would itself be nothing but the result of chance, a worthless theory. Let everyone do as he pleases. It would be perfectly superfluous to stress the evident difference between truth and absurdity, between value and non-value if pseudoscientific false justification, eliminating the essential difference, had not become a slogan, a manifest cause and hidden motive of the disorientation of spirits and of its most spectacular consequence: rampant criminality and licentiousness raised to the rank of idea.

The words "mal" (evil) and "malady" have a common root. Essential evil is malady of the spirit in its two forms: nervosity and banalization.

For the man who is stricken by evil, who is prey to nervous suffering or to banal triumph, evil is not the wrong motivation he harbors in himself but the false reaction that others inflict on him in an exalted way. In truth, under the shock of unhealthy excitations, it is difficult to recognize evil in its objective and lawful aspect, yet this is the only way to overcome the ill. But unhealthy excitations are unbearable just as the ill being is insuperable only to the extent that man bears in himself the lawful principle of evil—wrong motivation—before being stricken by the accidental ills coming from the environment. Healthy excitation easily becomes overexcitation: exaltation. The effort to guard against the lawful hold of evil (the transformation of unhealthy excitations into inner over-excitations) is the essential difficulty of life. But it is precisely this very difficulty that gives to life its unique value. The value of life can only be victory over evil in its subjective aspect, which causes ill being, and the intrapsychic struggle on the level of the inner deliberation fought by the vital impulse for victory is the price, the effort it costs, in order to approach the meaning of life: joy. It is in the nature of evil, its *raison d'etre*, to test the vital impulse, the essential value. Evil therefore carries two possibilities: that of overcoming it by diagnosing it and that of falling prey to it by falsely justifying it. The entire life of the human being on the road to spiritualization takes place between these two poles: exalted evil or sublimated evil. Man is called to choice: it is the very meaning of his life. The mythical symbol of Satan is a synthesis of these two significances: Satan represents on the one hand subconscious lawfulness and, on the other hand, individual fault exalted imagination, the first degree of vain blindness.

Good and evil, harmony and disharmony, reward and punishment, essential satisfaction or dissatisfaction, are the positive and negative manifestations of the law of harmony and its immanent justice. In this respect we can say that evil is the shadow that light casts when encountering an obstacle. The latter is perduring and vainly justified guiltiness. (The serpent-vanity symbol of Satan the tempter).

The lawful function of evil—of suffering that tends to become exalted—is to warn of the essential danger (just as pain is a warning of a somatic danger). This warning, precisely because it is lawful, cannot cease as long as the individual remains exposed to the essential vital danger: vain false justification. If he vainly persists in it and continues to expose himself to the essential danger, if he does not want to heed the warning, vital suffering will only worsen. It will end up by invading the whole of life. The blinding of the vainly stubborn psyche will not fail to darken its surrounding world; the essence of that psyche cannot express itself save through the warning of suffering, which for the nervous type of person, strikes back at him from all parts of the world. Or else man is banalized; he perversely frees himself from all guiltiness, all superconscious warning: he kills "the animating impulse." Mythically speaking, he is subject to the "death of the soul," a punishment man inflicts on himself.

Evil is the result of the rebellion against the essence (essential desire). In essence, there is no evil; evil has no essential existence outside the lawfulness through which it remains incorporated in harmony.

Against the mystery of lawfulness any claim is senseless. The meaning of life is the capacity to live the mystery through the accidents of temporal existence. In order not to inspire sentimentality which turns too easily into accusation, vanity which too easily becomes an exalted feeling of guiltiness, in order not to introduce wrong motivation into the relationship of man to mystery, the symbol "love" must retain its only genuine significance: justice. Just as "the love of God for man" is only a symbol for justice, for the lawfulness of life, the "love of man for God" is only a symbol of the justice of man toward himself, through which he reaches accordance with the lawfulness of life. Love being understood as justice, the frightening solitude of man in the face of mystery is all that remains. But this is precisely true religious sentiment, which, through its own sublimation, was capable of inspiring the mythical images which can be summed up in these two mythical images, both opposed and complementary: God and his love, Satan and Evil.

Mythically speaking, satanic evil is disobedience to God, the symbol of mystery. The hidden significance of these images is summed up in the vital danger of falling prey to conventional temptation, to the seductive lie of the subconscious leading to believe that there is no danger in letting oneself go to all the whims of exalted desires and forgetting the mysterious lawfulness of life: the immanence of justice.

C. VALUES AND NON-VALUES

1. SANCTITY AND PSYCHIC HEALTH

Immanent justice implies not only punishment represented by Satan and Hell (in ourselves) but also its remedy. And not only the biblical remedy (sanctity, salvation, redemption) but also the therapeutical remedy adapted to over limited vital impulses: the ethical principle, the just valuation of the self and others.

The lawfulness of the relations between psychic health (sanity) and sickness (insanity), on the one hand, and psychic health and sanctity, on the other hand, is of major importance in order to understand the parallelism between mythological pre-science and the science of motives: in other words, for the science of life. *From psychopathology (nervosity and banalization) to psychical health, and from psychic health to the extreme and exceptional state of sanctity, the deliberating psyche constitutes a continuum liable to endless functional transformations depending on the right or wrong valuations of the spirit.* Even sanctity (in its mythical sense, which has nothing to do with the saints of the Church) in order to remain a quasi-permanent state, needs to be sustained by the renewal of superconscious valuations (the "Angels of God" in the myth of the Temptation). The maladies of the spirit are only permanent states insofar as they are based on "idées fixes," false valuations which are subconsciously obsessive and block psychic energy while they can be reached and cured with the help of the sublimely motivating force of the superconscious valuations of which the most intensively healing is the force of acceptance. It is in no way opposed to the sensible effort of improving as best as one can those environmental situations which can be changed. But in order to do so in a sensible way, the individual must perforce place himself sensibly in relation to the environment, and he cannot do so without the lucidity of a healthily valuating spirit.

Sanctity is a state of exceptional psychic health, continuously sustained by the harmonizing valuations of the superconscience. It is total acceptance of the accidents that are individually constraining. Being the ultimate achievement of deliberation and of its goal of liberation, sanctity remains analogically linked to the inner deliberation of every man. It is at the same time the guiding ideal and the exact measure of the deviations which are all characterized by a more or less intense degree of nervosity and banalization. However this essential link is not conscious. It is more than conscious: superconscious. The hidden meaning of the psychological pre-science of all mythologies is to establish this motivating link with the help of the symbols "deities and sons of deities." It is the task of psychological science to establish this link not symbolically, but knowingly; it has to explain the myth—as we have done—and translate it into psychological concepts with the help of precise definitions.

Psychic health, which is desirable for all men, is the capacity to change in a sensible way what can be changed and to accept what cannot be changed. He who would, in all circumstances, know how to change or to accept in a sensible way all constraining situations would never lapse into a state of excessive dissatisfaction. The happy medium, good sense (the opposite of common sense, which is only a convention), the sense of moderation due to sensible valuations, protects him against the excess of psychic unbalance.

Psychic illness in the form of nervosity consists in knowing neither how to change nor how to accept in a sensible way. The inability to change situations which are in principle changeable, leads to failures whose accumulation discourages the force of acceptance and splits it ambivalently into accesses of resignation alternating with aggressive irritability, which, kept on the level of exaltative imagination, pours out into ruminations that only reinforce impotent rage. In the form of banalization, psychic illness is an exalted task of ambition at any cost, destroying the force of acceptance and creating vain agitation in all directions which is generally mistaken for meaningful combative activity.

The perverse opposite of the force of acceptance is *indignation*. Even banalization is based on a form of indignation, since its guiding principle is the indignant foresight of the abuse to which one would be subject if one did not defend oneself in advance by an excess of abuse mistaken for virility. True virility is, on the contrary, the healthy and authentically valuating force of the spirit and the sublimating force of acceptance whose sublimity consists precisely in a lucid resistance to perverse temptations of both resignation and aggression at any cost.

Indignation is the common feature of all guilty vanities and all complaining and aggressive accusations.

Just like mythical wisdom, linguistic wisdom denounces the flight from responsibility that is manifested by indignation, resentment in principle. But the latter is also a dynamic process, at the same time cause and effect of all morbid deliberations: by becoming indignant, one becomes progressively unworthy (*"indigne"* in French). Man is worthy (and this is true dignity) of reward (joy) only when he ceases to be indignant. Reward is not an addition: the joy of living is nothing but the absence of indignation. The latter does not disappear by means of excessively good and moralizing intentions but only through the daily and introspective review of one's own temptations to indignation with the help of sensible valuations. This is neither moralism nor amoralism. It is a scientific experiment, methodically based, mythically prefigured by the struggle against the demons (temptations) and the devouring monsters (greeds). It is, mythically speaking, the way to salvation (the good news of the gospels), and it is, psychologically speaking, the way to healing. It is the truth, the just, based on the understanding of immanent justice according to which each man is—seen essentially—through superconscious and subconscious channels, his own executor of his essential rewards and punishments. It is the dignity of the human being: his essential responsibility. This understanding is just, because it leads to goodness which is active love, the opposite of indignation. Like love, goodness is not sentimentality. It implies firmness with respect to oneself and others. It is in this vein that the hero of the Christian myth says: "I did not come to bring peace, but a sword." The sword is the very ancient symbol of the weapon of the spirit: the cutting edge of truth opposed to the fallacious peace of rest in conventions and compromises. The weapon of truth, the cutting sword (the force of definitions) does not attack men but erroneous ideas. On the plane of human life, nothing is definable without reference to the secret motives, be they perverse or sublime. A sublime motive, goodness is a form of acceptance, the acceptance of objective truth about oneself: a wrong motivator among wrong motivators. It is the most reconciling valuation, the opposite of the egocentricity of guilty vanities and complaining and aggressive accusations, the opposite of all the resentments condensed in indignation. Goodness, a sign of just motivations, is the ideal link between men. Perfect goodness is as unattainable as perfect love and perfect joy. Yet it remains the directive ideal.

Goodness is the expression of joy. One can be good only to the extent one has the strength to enjoy life sublimely, including the state of the world as it is. This is asking too much when vanity is strong. But it may be the unique means of participation in the evolution toward a better state, which would be impossible without control of the resentments which, in the face of the attacks of the world, tend to be renewed every day and to perpetuate themselves in ruminations. Their healing dissolution is impossible without resorting to reconciling valuations. By admitting that one is a wrong motivator, introspection becomes humor, since the latter—supreme force of acceptance—consists in including oneself in the common fault so as to transform the resentment of accusation into *an acknowledgement of the superconscious message* of reconciliation, instead of the subconscious message which is the obsession of complaint and revenge. This sublimating transformation, characteristic of goodness, convert—in the absence of perfect joy—the convulsion of resentment into a sense of measure, a state of more or less constant gaiety.

While joy is the cause-effect of the inner harmony of the individual, goodness is the only cause-effect of the harmonious relationships between men. Just as joy indicates the degree of liberation with regard to one's own wrong motivations, goodness results from the degree of liberation with regard to anxiety in the face of the false reactions of others. This liberation has two significances: on the one hand, the liberated individual does not suffer in an exalted way from the false reactions of others; and on the other hand, he does not let himself be induced to respond to false reactions in the environment by his own false reaction. This is quite clearly the only way to break the vicious circle of false reactivity which binds men and is the essential cause of the world's distortion.

2. THE SCALE OF VALUES AND ITS BIOGENETICAL IMMANENCE

Because of the indissoluble link between psychic health and sanctity, the health of the individual and the health of society are in danger when the vision of its ideal pole and the magnetic attraction of this pole are lost, since they are the conditions for health not only in individual life but—by this very fact—also in social life. The positive degrees of the scale of values go up from psychic health to sanctity or—if preferred—go down from sanctity to psychic health.

Since psychic health is the health of the valuating spirit, the negative degrees of the scale of values—the non-values—are constituted by the various degrees of vanity, the principle of false valuation. It is evidently impossible to establish the scale of values without diagnosing the states of banalization as illnesses of the spirit.

Since the positive or negative values are motivating forces, their gradation is due to the most natural phenomenon in life: the desires and their need for satisfaction, including the desires of the spirit whose satisfaction is the truth. The positive values are the promises of genuine satisfaction, vitally valid motives because they are proposed by a healthily valuating spirit. The non-values are promises of false satisfaction, lying temptations falsified by the false promises of satisfaction of vanity. It is enough for vanity to be grafted onto a valid motive, a positive value for the value to be morbidly decomposed—in keeping with the law of ambivalence of the subconscious—and split into two non-values that are contradictorily linked, one being vainly exalted and the other guilty and inhibited.

However unfortunate this dynamics of perversion may be in itself, it is quite fortunately and justly the indispensable condition for the sublimating dynamics allowing the vain false valuations to be turned into a harmonious and healing valuation with the help ofthe combative impulse, which is itself a motivating force immanent to the psyche.

The possibility of these positive or negative transformations exists only on the human level. It comes from the fact that the purpose of vital energy is, from the outset of life itself, the search for satisfactions, which, in man, can stray into vain self-satisfactions and guilty self-dissatisfactions. As such, even the guiding values of the ethical superconscience and their authentic satisfactions are—we can never stress it enough—biogenetically founded. The characteristic feature which is common to all living beings is excitability searching for its adapted reactivity (enabling to live), but excitablity does not come primarily from the environment. Quite the contrary, it originates in the periodic awakening of the appetences of the drives demanding their satisfaction. At the human level, these appetences are diversified into a multiplicity of material and sexual desires which can awaken—even in the absence of real need—at any time whatever by way of imaginative exaltation.

The valuating spirit of man does not create the values. They preexist independently of him. The human spirit should rediscover the guiding values, since man is exposed to a valuating choice between a multiplicity of contradictory desires. Ethical superconscience is nothing but the biogenetically immanent memory of the original unity with its preconscious drives which was instinctively guided and free from any aberration and which has become on the human plane superconscious instinct; the ethical imperative of harmonious reunification of the multiple desires for the sake of their meaningful satisfaction.

The authentic values of the ethical superconscience are the harmonies of thought, feelings, volitions, and, therefore, the harmony of individual actions and of social interactions.

Pinnacle of psychic health, sanctity is the guiding ideal because in it and through it all the harmonies are in their turn harmoniously linked and unified. *Sanctity is the achievement of the superconscience of the species.*

The link between psychic health and sanctity lies in the fact that sanctity is the highest degree of intensity of healthy and authentic self-satisfaction. This is the only reason for making sanctity the guiding value, the directive pole, the ideal of the healthily valuating spirit. It is also the only reason for symbolic language, a superconsciously immanent faculty of expression of the psychic functioning, to represent the guiding ideal which is valid for all men by the personifying symbol of "Divinity" and to represent by the transcendent image of "Divinity-Judge" the origin of values that are in fact biogenetically immanent.

The ideal is imposed on life quite naturally, because it is the only possibility of a natural morality: the love of one's essential self instead of a vain phantom.

Genuine self-love is the acceptance of the necessity to struggle introspectively against vain self-overvaluation linked to an excessive devaluation of others. This acceptance is the contrary of indignation, whose ruminations do not cease to aggravate the resentments, a characteristic of morbid introspection. In the struggle of the essential self and its essential desire to free itself of resentments for love of self, one must include all the problems of introspective deliberation and its conflict between healthy and unhealthy motives, theme of all mythologies. All the problems of the inner deliberation symbolized by the mythical struggle are included in the essential problem of life: love. Vanity is the excess of self-love opposed to all the forms of genuine love: love of truth in general, love of truth for oneself and others, sexual love in its positive form of bond of soul, love between parents and children, love linking the generations, love of life, joy of life. Vain resentments do not capitulate to excessively good and altruistic intentions. Love is not a duty toward others. It is the duty of man toward himself, toward his nature, toward life and the essence that animates it. *Love is the combativity of the animating impulse:* to love oneself enough to achieve one's reality, to love oneself essentially in order to draw as much joy as possible from life. Understood in its essence, in its genuine meaning, love is the most striking achievement of the truth that mythical life was able to formulate. "Love your neighbor as yourself." Nowhere is it said to love others more than oneself, as altruistic sentimentality pretends. The formula is the definition of goodness: to love the essence in others, even when it is perturbed, as one should love the essence in oneself, even if it is perturbed. Only the sanctified man, purified from any perversion, can love himself without restriction; only he can love others without restriction, without being essentially troubled: dragged into hatred by the injustice inflicted on him by the perversion of others.

The effort to come as close as possible to the significance of the "Divinity" symbol with the help of successive definitions of the inner deliberating functioning has, in the end, led to bring to light the psychic immanence of ethical values, mythically condensed in the "Son of God" symbol. But the ethical problem does not have only a theoretical aspect. One must know what to do—or rather what should be done—if by chance someone wanted to be able to love himself. The question then arises: how to do it?

In this respect it is helpful to understand that the biblical formula "to love oneself so as to be able to love one's neighbor" is identical to the formula inscribed on the facade of the temple of Apollo: "Know thyself." To be able to know oneself authentically, one must perceive, and in the end know, the difference between the essential self and the vain phantom. This knowledge is not acquired at a glance. The introspective eye has to be trained little by little.

We engage in introspection all day long without knowing or controlling it. How can we not fall into the trap of spectacular and complacent ruminations, the favorite food of resentments? By ruminating, we waste our time and our energy. It is evidently impossible to engage in lucid introspection all day long. But to gain time and energy and to dissolve the ruminative resentments with the help of reconciling valuations, it is always possible to awaken ourselves from our half-subconscious daydreams, and open-eyed reveries where we feed our energy to the offended vanity in search of its triumph, where we waste the time of our life in rehashing indignant complaints and in the preparation of projects of revenge; where we see ourselves, a pitiable hero, as the imaginary victor over all adversities and adversaries, unless we collapse into morbid anxiety in the face of the least obstacles which are imaginatively exalted. To really love oneself, one must have the ethical courage to see oneself as one is, to acquire little by little a better knowledge of oneself, not by theoretical reflections but by elucidating experience. The repetition of this experience is the only effective way to struggle against the obsession of self-overvaluation and the undervaluation of others. Everything is a value or non-value (in terms of authentic or inauthentic satisfaction), because everything is an objective or affective valuation of the self, of others, of accidental situations, and lastly, of life itself, its meaning or meaninglessness, its value or non-value. All the value judgments—whether they be just or unjust—have an unsuspected motivating power endowed with an immediately felt healing or perverting ability. No discussion can be admissible in the absence of experience. The only experience necessary is to take the trouble—or rather the joy—to dissolve, were it only one resentment, by objectivating countervaluations, for instance, one's offended vanity, to immediately become aware that liberating joy has replaced it. If this is true for only one resentment, it is true for all the resentments that darken psychic life. And if it is true for the psyche of one sole man, it is also true for the psyche of all men. If it is valid for all men, it is also valid for psychologists and for the science of life that psychology should be.

Only from the perseverance of self-analysis will stem the synthesis which is not a speculative theory but a knowledge methodically based on self-experimentation, the only valid method for the study of the inner motivating functioning. This study leads infallibly to emotion in the face of the immanence of the mystery of the ethical law and of the scale of values, implying the immanence of justice and essential responsibility, the theme of the psychological pre-science of all mythologies. This is the point of union between religiosity and the psychology of motivations, the junction between the ideal of moral liberation and the ideal of freedom of spirit: objective clairvoyance, the ideal of all the sciences.

Freedom of the spirit and moral liberation condition each other, complete each other, and reinforce each other. They are one.

There is only one genuine superiority: modest pride, proud because it trusts the combative impulse and its evolutionary power, modest because it knows that vanity will never be definitively conquered.

The only salvation of the thinking species lies in struggling against vanity so as to be able to think life in a just way, which is precisely the ethical imperative. It does not rule only the spirit of individuals but also the spirit of all the sciences and should especially rule the spirit of the sciences of life—psychology, sociology, the study of biogenesis—whose specific task is precisely to think life in a just way so as to provide the individuals with the indispensable help for healing, a help which is all the more indispensable since the miracles of the technical inventions of physics—a proof of what the human spirit is capable of when it is methodically guided—threaten to become, as we all know, a crushing weight for the very existence of life, since the sciences of life are presently incapable of creating the balancing counterpole which could only be the orientation toward the meaning of life. By undertaking their task, instead of wasting their time in phobic anxiety in face of introspection, the sciences of life may one day discover—however remote that day be—not only that the values and non-values are immanent to the extra-conscious functioning and that they must become conscious, but that justice is therefore necessarily immanent because of the simple reason that the laws of harmony and disharmony, the laws of composition and decomposition, rule everything from atom to man, all the temporal phenomena and become, from animalization on, the laws of life and death.

Astonished by the unfathomable mystery of all that is, the sciences of life, moved and capable of contemplative observation (and not only intellectual observation), will see the mystery down to the incredible finesse of organization that they observe with the help of marvelous instruments the precision of physical science has created for them. They will perhaps wonder—among other very natural miracles—about the miracle of the chromosomes and the genes out of which life is born in its apparent aspects. Finally seeing manifest mystery in all its unthinkable depth, the sciences of life will perhaps abandon their materialistic dogma according to which the organization of the chromosomes and the genes, just like the evolutionary life issuing forth from them, would be only the result of chance. For even if—and it is impossible—such were the case, how is it that chance exists? How is it that anything exists? Through finally asking the most natural question, the sciences of life will make the most evident discovery, so evident that it has always prescientifically existed in the mythologies of all peoples.

The meaning and value of life are at the same time both manifestly and mysteriously immanent to temporal existence. The human mind must study all the modes and modifications of existence—not only the extension of spatial objects but also the intention of the psychic motivations—in order to discover the immanence of ethical values. But even in going to the extreme limit of its competence, the human mind will not be able to discover the mysterious source of existence, which is not transcendent to space or time, but to human understanding. It is mythically personified and called "God," symbol of unnameable mystery.

The analysis of the "Divinity" image is nothing but the analysis of the inner psychic functioning that created the "Divinity" symbol.